WRONG, Dennis Hume. Skeptical sociology. Columbia, 1976. 322p index 76-18843. 14.95 ISBN 04231-04014-8. C.I.P.

A collection of essays, most of which have been published previously in such scholarly journals as the *American Journal of Sociology*. Wrong's essay, "The oversocialized conception of man in modern sociology," is included in this collection. Even though these essays range from strict sociological analysis to political and social commentary, Wrong has arranged them in such a way that there is a unified and logical organization. His work in sociology has been extremely influential over the years. Wrong has an extremely lucid and logical writing style and an ability to get at the heart of the problem he is working on. The balance that he has been able to maintain between strictly theoretical work and social commentary reminds us of the late C. Wright Mills, without Mills's sometimes heavy polemic. This book is highly recommended for both the professional scholar and the intelligent and concerned layman — it has something for both. Although this work does not contain a bibliography, the extensive footnotes are helpful. Adequate index.

Skeptical Sociology

Skeptical Sociology

DENNIS H. WRONG

New York   **Columbia University Press**   *1976*

Dennis H. Wrong is professor of sociology at New York University.

Library of Congress Cataloging in Publication Data

Wrong, Dennis Hume, 1923–
Skeptical sociology.

Includes bibliographical references and index.
1. Sociology—History. I. Title.
HM19.W76   301'.09   76-18843
ISBN 0-231-04014-8

Preface and Acknowledgments

MY EDITOR asked me to write a general prologue and short introductions to the three sections into which the book has been divided, so I shall not comment here on the subjects, themes, and occasions of particular essays. Under his stern pressure—always a necessary bridle on an author's overweening vanity—I have largely omitted book reviews and polemics, on the one hand, and reports of research, on the other, although I have been writing the former for a variety of political and intellectual journals for twenty-five years and have published a fair number of the latter in social-science journals over the same period. The essays included are fairly evenly divided between those written for a general intellectual audience and those written for my colleagues in sociology. Seven were originally published in general intellectual journals (namely, *Dissent* and *Commentary*), five appeared in sociological or social-science journals, one is excerpted from a long introduction to an anthology. Four have not previously been published.

I should like to express my gratitude to the following editors who encouraged me to write most of these essays and often made helpful criticisms and suggestions for improvement: Lewis Coser, Martin Greenberg, Irving Howe, Charles Page, and Norman Podhoretz. Karen Mitchell provided valuable editorial assistance in preparing the manuscript for Columbia University Press, as did Edith Tarcov for those essays first published in *Dissent*. Marguerita Contreras, Avrama Gingold, and Geraldine Novasic extended themselves nobly to type the manuscript in the course of a long hot summer. I owe a very special debt to John D. Moore of Columbia University Press for the encouragement he gave from the beginning to the project of collecting my essays into a book and for his shrewd and sound judgments that shaped so much of its final contents.

The following essays are included in whole or in part in the present book and I should like to thank their original publishers for permission to reprint them:

"The Failure of American Sociology," *Commentary* 28 (November 1959), 375–80. Copyright © 1959 by the American Jewish Committee.

"The Oversocialized Conception of Man in Modern Sociology," *American Sociological Review* 26 (April 1961), 183–93.

"Human Nature and the Perspective of Sociology," *Social Research* 30 (Fall 1963), 300–18.

"The Idea of 'Community': A Critique," *Dissent* 13 (May–June 1966), 290–97.

"Identity: Problem and Catchword," *Dissent* 15 (September–October 1968), 427–35.

"The Functional Theory of Stratification: Some Neglected Considerations," *American Sociological Review* 24 (December 1959), 772–82.

"Social Inequality without Social Stratification," *Canadian Review of Sociology and Anthropology* 1 (February 1964), 5–16.

"Jews, Gentiles, and the New Establishment," *Commentary* 39 (June 1965), 83–86. Copyright © 1965 by the American Jewish Committee.

"How Important is Social Class?" *Dissent* 19 (Winter 1972), 278–85.

"Some Problems in Defining Social Power," *American Journal of Sociology* 73 (May 1968), 673–81.

"Economic Development and Democracy" and "Reply to Robert L. Heilbroner," *Dissent* 14 (November–December 1967), 723–33, 738–41.

"The Rhythm of Democratic Politics," *Dissent* (Winter 1974), 46–55.

"Politics and Ethics" from "Introduction," Dennis H. Wrong, ed., *Max Weber* (Englewood Cliffs, N.J.: Prentice-Hall, © 1970), 58–69.

"On Thinking about the Future," *The American Sociologist* 9 (February 1974), 26–31.

PRINCETON, N.J.   DENNIS H. WRONG
MARCH 1976

Contents

Skeptical Sociology

Prologue: On Skeptical Sociology

SOCIOLOGISTS are as much addicted to "labeling" as the people they study, so I feel constrained to justify my choice of the label "skeptical" to characterize the general perspective of these essays. C. Wright Mills defended his use of the term "sociological imagination" on the grounds that he needed "a counter term on which to stand," in view of his critical assaults upon the then-prevailing sociological approaches.[1] It is harder today to find a term that hasn't been corrupted or preempted for special purposes that are not necessarily my own. In the 1950s and early 1960s, as a critic of the dominant "positivistic" or "science-building" * sociology of the time, I sometimes used the term "humanistic" to describe the alternative approach I favored. I have always thought of myself, and have often been thought of, as standing in an area where two intellectual circles overlap: that of academic sociology and that of those writers and journals, predominantly literary, often regarded as constituting the world of the "New York intellectuals."

"Humanistic" perhaps characterizes the outlook of this latter world, and I still have no objection to the label if it is taken to mean no more than that the best sociology arises out of concerns shared with the humanities rather than from an effort to apply methodological prescriptions allegedly based on the natural sciences to the study of human affairs. Today, however, it is more widely recognized than

---

* I much prefer "science-building" to "positivistic" in view of the numerous and varying connotations that have become attached to positivism in both philosophy and social science over the past century and a half.

it was when many of these essays were written that sociology cannot be a sealed-off universe impermeable to outside political and cultural currents. Moreover, "humanistic" has acquired a certain self-congratulatory aura, a "more-caring-about-people-than-thou" flavor. This is doubtless partly due to the "humanistic psychology" movement, which not only extols emotion at the expense of reason but regards publicly expressed and even group-induced emotion as the measure of the genuinely "human"—a fashionable new therapeutic version of an oversocialized conception of man. Some sociologists also use "humanistic" as a virtual synonym for an *engagé* sociology aligned politically with the Left.

"Skeptical sociology" sounds like no more than a variant of "critical sociology," a term widely used to identify what is often seen as the major counter-tendency to that sociology which continues to invoke the model of science to legitimate itself. Critical theory originally referred to the revisionist Marxism of the Frankfurt School and is still often understood in this restricted sense. There is a certain appositeness in its having become popular in the early 1970s after the decline of the militant protest movements of the previous decade, for Frankfurt neo-Marxism was itself a response to the far greater and more tragic defeats of the Left earlier in the century: the failure of the Second International to prevent the First World War, the Stalinist perversion of Marxism into an instrument of tyranny, the coming to power of Hitler and the Second World War, and, perhaps most of all, the failure of the proletariat to fulfill the revolutionary mission assigned to it by Marx. Critical theory became a turning away from "praxis" in the wake of these disasters to a primary concern with "theory," though a theory that continued to cherish the ideal of "unity of theory and practice" as one of its hallmarks. It is not surprising to find young sociologists nowadays taking the same path after the collapse and corruption of the New Left of the 1960s.

I do accept fully two of the major tenets of the critical theorists: (1) that the sociologist, in contrast to the usual position of the physical scientist, is inescapably part of the social world he is studying and must "reflexively" take into account his own involvement with it and influence on it; (2) that the sociologist should stand in a critical relationship to existing society, refusing to regard established structures, institutions, and culture as exhaustive of historical possibility. Neither of these contentions, however, is the peculiar property of Marxism or neo-Marxism in any of their variants. Both have often been expressed by sociologists without appeal to the authority of the writings of Hegel, Marx, Lukács, or the Frankfurt philosophers. Nor have critical theorists monopolized the critique of "positivism" in sociology, especially if "positivism" is understood in the relatively precise sense in which Anthony Giddens has recently defined it rather than as a mere term of "opprobrium . . . used so broadly and vaguely as a weapon of critical attack . . . that it has lost any claim to an accepted and standard meaning." [2]

The core of critical theory's rejection of positivism in the social sciences has been the charge that positive science's acceptance of the impregnable "facticity" of what currently exists excludes awareness of what might be possible and therefore justifies the status quo. ("That which is cannot be true," as Herbert Marcuse approvingly quoted Ernst Bloch.) [3] This argument is often echoed by radical sociologists to charge so-called Establishment sociology, regarded as incurably positivist, with unconscious ideological bias. But it has little or no applicability to the views of many nonradical sociologists who do not delude themselves that they speak with the voice of impersonal scientific truth and who do not fail "to distinguish the side to which they are attached, from the *grounds* on which they are attached to it," [4] in the words of Alvin Gouldner. This is an apt formulation of the sociologist's ability to free himself from both the illusory claim of "value neutrality" and an inevitably blind partisanship. Consider, for example, Raymond Aron, Daniel Bell, Reinhard Bendix, Peter Berger, Ralf Dahrendorf, Ernest Gellner, Nathan Glazer, Robert Nisbet, Barrington Moore, Jr., John Rex, David Riesman, and Edward Shils, to mention only a dozen prominent names. Only in the loosest sense could any of these men be considered a positivist; none of them is a Marxist except in the ecumenical sense in which it may be conceded that "we are all Marxists now"; and, although they include liberals, conservatives, and democratic socialists, none of them is a revolutionary, nor, with the doubtful exception of Moore, a radical.

One is led to ask also whether the second tenet for sociologists that

I cited above must necessarily be interpreted, as it often is, to mean that sociologists should be political radicals of one or another Marxist persuasion. Critical theory was originally a code word for Marxism,* although its creators eventually came to accept their cryptic language at face value in recognition of the inadequacy of traditional Marxism to account for major developments in modern history, let alone provide a basis for "praxis" to deal with them through political action.[5] I sometimes have the impression that contemporary American admirers of critical theory are reversing this evolution, using critical theory as a road back to some fairly old-fashioned Marxist assumptions and at the same time invoking it as an intellectual credential to legitimate the belated appearance of "Marxists of the chair" in the American university.

But the contention that the sociologist should preserve a critical detachment from existing society need not imply total revolutionary rejection of it, nor even commitment to a utopian standard. Edward Shils, one of the few self-declared conservatives in contemporary sociology, has written that "the observations, insights and generalizations of sociology inevitably assert that things are not what they seem. They will impugn the grounds human beings adduce . . . to justify their conduct. . . . Sociology is agnostic vis-à-vis the order of being with which religions, authorities, and traditions purport to be in contact." [6] Nostalgia for the past that stops short of mythicizing it may be a source of detachment from the givenness of existing social structures as potent as the vision of a utopia. Several interpreters, in fact, have detected elements of historical nostalgia in the very utopianism of the older Frankfurt theorists themselves.[7]

The linkage between critical theory and Marxism, however tenuous it eventually became for several of the Frankfurt philosophers, can also impose intellectual and political blinders on their epigones among American sociologists. No doubt criticism, like charity, ought to begin at home, but it has become a truism that we live in an increasingly interdependent world. And the fact is that roughly a billion

---

* A possibly apocryphal story is told of a student of Marcuse's at Brandeis in the fifties who when visiting Trier, where Karl Marx was born in 1818, sent his teacher a postcard reading "I greet you from the birthplace of Critical Theory!"

and a quarter people, close to a third of the world's population, live under regimes that claim to Marxist-inspired. In contrast to the Western democracies, these regimes do not permit their sociologists to criticize them, although it is worth noting that Poland and Yugoslavia, at least, compare favorably in this respect with many of the world's non-Communist dictatorships. Nor are any of the subjects of Communist regimes free to express critical opinions of the societies in which they live. Yet if one counts those who vote with their feet, as the saying goes, it is striking that nowhere in the world are there large numbers of people clamoring to get into rather than out of Communist countries, which continue to prevent their subjects from leaving by means of figurative "iron curtains," actual Berlin Walls, and tight controls over emigration. Critical theory developed in part as a rejection of the orthodox Marxism first elevated to the status of a state religion in the Soviet Union. But it seems a mite parochial, to say the least, for its latter-day devotees to confine themselves to the analysis of the "late" or "high" or "neo" capitalism of the West, or of a monolithically conceived "Third World" allegedly victimized by American imperialism, while disdaining to pay much attention to the Communist third of the world that exhibits a praxis claiming derivation from Marxism itself—even if, unlike vulgar anti-Marxists and/or anti-Communists, one grants that it is not necessarily the only possible such praxis.

I have considerable sympathy with another major belief of critical theory that belongs properly to the philosophy of politics and history rather than to sociology as such: the affirmation of utopianism as an ultimate standard, of "utopian visions [as] less blueprints for action than sources of critical distance from the gravitational pull of the prevailing reality." [8] An insistence on utopian hopes as a final measure, however, must be tempered by awareness of the risk of their conversion into the ideological goals of revolutionary movements all too readily persuaded that "the urge to destroy is a creative urge" (Bakunin). Marcuse lost sight of this danger in the late 1960s. Adorno and Horkheimer, on the other hand, were compelled to repudiate their own student followers who had turned violently on them and on the Frankfurt Institute they had recreated after the war, inspiring Adorno's much-quoted remark that "when I made my theoretical model, I could not have guessed that people would try to realize it with Molotov cocktails."

The movements of the 1960s certainly confirmed in a very short time Péguy's famous observation that *"tout commence en mystique et finit en politique."* Yet fear of the destructive emotions aroused by utopianism need not lead to quietism or to a narrow technocratic pragmatism. Even after the chastening experience of the romantic revolutionism of the late sixties, the backwash from which is still powerful in our intellectual and cultural lives, I still believe that a utopian ideal should serve as a standard for evaluating limited and gradual historical changes, instituted through "piecemeal" reforms yet moving toward a goal, luminously present in the minds of the reformers, that truly transcends the status quo.[9]

In the last essay in this book I tell a story about how I mocked the possibility of graduate students' "making a revolution" in the very place, the Berkeley campus, where two years later the famous revolt began. I can match that story with another having to do with the "counterculture" of the sixties rather than with political radicalism. I recall telling a friend in 1960 about Norman O. Brown's *Life Against Death*,[10] published the year before and shortly to become one of the "in" books of the decade, which had strongly moved me with its radical Freudian vision of the abolition of repression and the transcendence of the discontents of civilization as the terminus of history. My friend replied somewhat impatiently, "But just how is all this going to be achieved? What exactly are we supposed to do?" I thought this a bit unimaginative, even philistine, and responded, "Well, of course, it's not a matter of organizing a political movement with the slogan 'abolish repression,' or 'end alienation now.' " Yet within a few years there was just such a movement with the appearance of the "flower people" and the psychedelic hippie culture that so powerfully shaped the outlook of the New Left—"the dreams of nineteenth-century poets polluted the psychic atmosphere of the great boroughs and suburbs of New York," as Saul Bellow put it.[11] Today all that seems to have happened a long time ago, but it revealed that the yearning to be "made new," the utopian greed for total change, is hardly confined to a few dissident intellectuals disenchanted with the "disenchantment of the world" that prevails in modern society.

Imperceptive as I may have been in failing to foresee what was about to happen (though who did?), I was nevertheless right to doubt that revolution was a real possibility in America and that repression and/or alienation could be abolished overnight by adopting flamboyantly publicized new "life-styles." However, the changes in recent years in attitudes toward sexuality, marriage and the family, and the position of women, for the most part not the result of political confrontations, are of greater significance in altering the texture of our lives than the failures and occasional limited successes of radical political movements. Progress toward the kind of transformation of human nature envisaged by Brown—if such a thing is conceded to be possible at all—still seems to me necessarily to take place by the slow diffusion of new values and outlooks through the fabric of personal relations, especially the attitudes of parents toward children and the sexes toward one another—the kind of gradual change implied by Brown's own metaphor of the "return of the repressed" as a historical process.

The increasing appointment of "token" blacks and women to high positions, the spread of beards, modestly longer hair, and informal dress even among corporation executives, the widespread use of marijuana by ordinary apolitical adolescents and many of their elders, the statement by a president's wife that she would not automatically condemn her daughter for a premarital affair—all these, slowly divested of their ritualized countercultural or generational aggressiveness, are legacies of the sixties. Small pumpkins, no doubt, after the apocalyptic hopes and fears of those years, but that is how cultural change usually takes place. Certainly the speed of change is accelerated by the media blanket we live under, but it still falls far short of revolution and, as frustrated radical activists are quick to perceive, soon ceases to pose even a symbolic threat to the survival of the "system" they denounce.

In the late 1950s, like others, some of whom later became famous as senior spokesmen for the New Left and the counterculture, I felt it important to insist upon the utopian dimension of human experience in face of the compulsive moderationism and the sense of restricted possibilities then evident in sociology as well as in other areas of our culture. The fifties, however, now appear to have been an aberrant period, one in which a postwar and a prewar mentality curiously coexisted. Over fifteen years later, the feverish political protests of the succeeding decade have abated in accordance with what I have called the rhythm of democratic politics,[12] but the cultural ferment is still being absorbed. The assertion of a utopian standpoint is no longer urgent or timely, and I find myself more deeply moved by Walter Benjamin's beautiful and profound image of the angel of history with "his face turned towards the past . . . which piles up a mountain of ruins before his feet. The angel would like to stay, awaken the dead, and make whole what has been smashed; but his wings are forced back by a storm . . . which irresistibly propels him into the future to which his back is turned, while the pile of ruins mounts up before him heavenwards. This storm is what we call progress." [13]

The relevance of the utopian perspective of critical theory to sociology, as distinct from the philosophy of history, must be qualified in two respects. The first I have already mentioned in arguing that the necessary self-distancing of the sociologist from the pressures of existing society can also result from his anchorage in the past. Much of classical sociology was animated by conservative sentiments and, while this has sometimes been overstressed, there is no reason to doubt that sociologists will continue to draw on a dual heritage of Enlightenment progressivism and Counter-Enlightenment disillusion.[14]

The second qualification has to do with the principled refusal of the original critical theorists to specify the utopian possibilities in the name of which they "negated" the present order. This position resembles that of Marx, who in creating his "scientific" socialism wished to avoid the utopian socialists' preoccupation with blueprints of the future society. In his last years, Max Horkheimer suggested that there was a relationship between critical theory's reservations about specifying the nature of utopia and the traditional Jewish prohibition on naming or describing God.[15] The negation of what exists in the name of an undescribed Kingdom of Freedom easily merges— especially at the level of "praxis"—into the existentialist-anarchist notion that the new order defines itself only in the process of the revolutionary struggle to create it, although Horkheimer and Adorno always expressed serious reservations about both existentialist philosophy and

the politics of anarchism. The avoidance of any effort to depict utopia is also notably congruent with the increasingly shadowy contours
of "socialism" as an ideal upheld by Western intellectuals who are
disillusioned by the totalitarian or authoritarian socialisms of the
Nazis, the Communists, and leftist dictatorships in the Third World.
Socialism nowadays is often invoked as little more than a "god-term,"
a set of abstract ideals against which to measure the deficiencies of
existing social orders.

The original critical theorists' view of utopia demands both too
much and too little of the sociologist. On the one hand, there is no
good reason why the sociologist should be committed to the neo-
Hegelian metaphysics of the Frankfurt philosophers, let alone its
religious nuances. Moreover, Marx may have had good reasons for
saying little about the social order he thought would replace capitalism, but it is hard to see why they should continue to apply a century
later to contemporary sociologists. On the other hand, theoretical
and comparative-historical work in sociology must attempt to show
the range of variation in social structures. The sociologist does not
thereby commit himself to the view that the historical record necessarily exhausts man's potentialities or powers of social creativity.* But
in revealing the enormous variety of the societies and cultures humanity has made, the comparative sociologist challenges the disposition to eternalize the present or to regard existing institutions as
grounded in transhistorical necessities. The sociologist is also concerned with exploring directly *the limits of the possible*, an enterprise
that may both broaden the prevailing consciousness of such limits
and suggest that there *are* limits, that some utopias will always be
"nowhere" in accordance with the literal meaning of the word.

Explorations of the limits of the possible unavoidably raise transhistorical questions and issues and thus go beyond a strictly historicist
sociology without, however, elevating the search for universal social
and historical laws into the primary objective of the social sciences.
Several of the essays here on human nature, social inequality, and

---

*Mills wrote: "What social science is properly about is the human variety, which
consists of all the social worlds in which men have lived, are living, and *might live*."
The Sociological Imagination (New York: Oxford University Press, 1959), p. 132. My
italics.

power originated as efforts to deal with such questions. For example: Does man have a biosocial nature that makes him less than infinitely malleable? Is a completely egalitarian society feasible, and if so, at what cost? What limits are there to the exercise of power in human societies?

The debate over the functional theory of inequality centering on the Davis-Moore theory first advanced in 1945 bore on one of these questions, one that has been a major concern of Western intellectuals at least since Rousseau: the possibility of a fully egalitarian society.[16] In most theoretical debates in sociology, the rival positions rarely make contact with one another except at the most superficial level: different ideological rhetorics are displayed or contrasting metatheoretical standpoints or "paradigms" (surely the word most abused by sociologists in the past decade) are pitted against one another in mock battle. The conflict between the "schools" seems spurious because the participants are usually talking about different matters altogether rather than asserting genuinely contradictory points of view on a clear-cut, substantive issue. This situation encourages the appearance of a master synthesizer who claims to demonstrate that the various perspectives of the schools really complement one another rather than being at odds, as is generally believed.*

The debate over the Davis-Moore theory was unusual in that, although these features were not entirely lacking, it involved important substantive issues that were clarified, with the result that the exchange led to modification and development of the views of the participants. Davis and Moore raised with exemplary clarity the central question of the limits to equality in human societies, which is why they initiated a discussion of greater coherence and significance than the controversies over functionalism itself that became commonplace in the 1950s and 1960s. The Davis-Moore debate remains a standard topic in textbooks on social stratification, even though it had wound down by about 1965. Many of the issues discussed in that debate are reflected in both the more recent concern over social policies aimed

---

* Talcott Parsons played this role in the 1940s and 1950s, as in a somewhat different way did Robert K. Merton. The leading candidate for master synthesizer of the 1970s is perhaps Jürgen Habermas.

at implementing greater equality and the revival of interest in equality on the part of political philosophers associated with the names of John Rawls and Robert Nozick. But social science, alas, is still so forgetful of even its recent past that this is rarely recognized.

I have mentioned the Davis-Moore debate because it exemplified substantive sociological theory at its best. It dealt with a transhistorical issue of undeniable ideological significance on which it brought to bear the historical record of primitive, traditional, and modern industrial societies. It encompassed ideological values, metatheoretical standpoints, and historically sensitive interpretations of social structures. It raised psychological questions about basic human motivations. It even inspired some behavioral research in the mode of what Mills called "abstracted empiricism." To be sure, the debate focused coherently on these matters because it dealt with a single issue, in contrast to so much of the sound and fury of theoretical argumentation in sociology. Yet its scope was considerably wider than that of what is usually called "middle range" theory.*

For the reasons I have indicated at some length, I remain skeptical about the currently popular label "critical sociology." In choosing instead "skeptical sociology" to characterize my outlook, I am aware that "skeptical" carries overtones of sophistry, shallow iconoclasm, and idle mockery. However, I do not believe that the sociologist

---

* Merton's most recent discussion of middle range theory, in a rejoinder to critics of the notion, seems to me to be so broad as to exclude very little and to obscure what would fall under "upper range" theory. He argues, for example, that, Robert Bierstedt to the contrary notwithstanding, Weber's *The Protestant Ethic and the Spirit of Capitalism* "is a prime example of theorizing in the middle range." This would seem to extend the middle range to encompass works that are macrosocial in scope but historically specific rather than confining it to limited ahistorical generalizations about such largely microsocial phenomena as deviance, small groups, and "role-sets," as Merton seemed to suggest in his earlier statements. Weber's study, he remarks, is middle range because "it deals with a severely delimited problem—one that happens to be exemplified in a particular historical epoch with implications for other societies and other times." But later he writes that "actual theories of the middle range . . . have great generality extending beyond a particular historical epoch or culture." I find myself simply unable to decide on the basis of these statements whether or not the Davis-Moore theory constitutes an example of middle range theorizing in Merton's sense. See Robert K. Merton, *On Theoretical Sociology* (New York: The Free Press, 1967), pp. 63-64.

should entirely dissociate himself from such attitudes, shorn of invidious adjectives. With part of his being he belongs to Joyce's "brood of mockers" and should steel himself to the danger that "the void surely awaits all them that weave the wind: a menace, a disarming and a worsting from those embattled angels of the church, Michael's host, who defend her ever in the war of conflict with their lances and their shields." [17] The sociologist must be prepared today to face not only the somewhat blunted lances of Stephen Dedalus's "crazy queen" but those of a host of creeds and doctrines striving to appease what Arthur Koestler once called the "obscene hunger for faith" that characterizes our age, including, of course, the various churches, sects, and theologies of Marxism.

But the skeptical sociologist is more than a debunker. It is sometimes hard to draw a clear line between corrosive cynicism and a tragic sense of the vanity of human aspirations, a stoical awareness of how pure intentions and lofty ideals produce consequences that are travesties of what they sought to realize. Max Weber—who for me, as for Raymond Aron, is *the* sociologist [18]—has been seen as standing on both sides of the line. Leo Strauss called him a "noble nihilist" [19] and others have described him both as a "cynical" and as a "tragic" realist. The skeptic, however, is not a nihilist or cynic in the sense of denying or denigrating all values; he is, rather, committed to intellectual integrity, to telling the truth, as his own chosen highest value. His tragic sense stems from his insight that this value is often subversive of other values that men must live by. With Freud, the skeptical sociologist bows to the reproach of his fellow men that he can "offer no consolation: for at bottom that is what they are all demanding— the wildest revolutionaries no less passionately than the most virtuous believers." [20] With Weber, he rejects all "academic prophecy, which does not clearly realize that in the lecture-rooms of the university no other virtue holds but plain intellectual integrity." [21] He refuses to bend his knowledge to the "uses of faith," * while simultaneously recognizing that his own role is necessarily a partial one cutting him off from total commitment to any human association or project.

---

* The reference is to the subtitle of Philip Rieff, *The Triumph of the Therapeutic: Uses of Faith after Freud* (New York: Harper Torchbooks, 1968).

In presenting one's own version of a sociological outlook, there is a temptation to attribute to it all the intellectual virtues in exactly the right proportions and to subtract from it the sins of dogmatism and false pride to which all outlooks are prone. I have no doubt succumbed to this temptation in describing a skeptical sociology. I shall try to be more specific and, inevitably, more parochial for a moment. The skeptical sociologist should resist the growing fragmentation of sociology into a stalemated pluralism of divergent "approaches" whose adherents talk only to each other. Ethnomethodologists, for example, are notorious for citing only one another's works, many of them unpublished and distributed through private networks. I have been told that when leading ethnomethodologists are invited to speak at some campuses, non-ethnomethodologists are not even informed of the visits. But ethnomethodology is not the sole offender. An elected council member of the newly organized Section on Marxist Sociology of the American Sociological Association found himself a minority of one when he proposed a session at the next annual meetings devoted to critiques of Marxism. Skeptical sociologists, though their sympathies may lie with the political Left, should never forget John Stuart Mill's insistence that liberals and radicals ought to wish for able and worthy conservative opponents against whom to test in debate the rationality of their own convictions and the subtlety of their reasoning powers. And why should there be a special section of the American Sociological Association devoted to "Marxist Sociology," which refers to a theoretical point of view rather than to a substantive field of interest? Efforts are also under way to organize a section on ethnomethodology. Perhaps there will soon also be sections on "neo-Marxist sociology," "symbolic interactionism," and "structuralism." (It is unlikely that there will be any on "bourgeois" or "capitalist" sociology, for there are probably not enough members willing to accept these labels to fill a seminar room—or a small cell in the Lubyanka!)

One dictionary meaning of "skepticism" is "universal doubt," a doubt that obviously must extend to the skeptic's own assumptions and role. Thus a skeptical sociologist is likely to be even more reflexive in scrutinizing his own sentiments and allegiances, without necessarily abandoning them, than a "critical" sociologist, whose targets may remain entirely external to him. But in choosing a title for a collection of essays, I have no intention of creating a new movement or tendency within sociology: skeptical sociologists may wryly recognize a kinship with one another under various disguises, but it would be self-defeating for them to organize as a group or even to adopt a common label. In the end, there can be no such thing as a skeptical sociology, only skeptical sociologists.

PART ONE
Human Nature and
the Perspective of Sociology

Introduction

ALL THE ESSAYS in this section were written with a polemical intent, directed against the leading assumptions of academic sociology and social criticism influenced by it that prevailed in the 1950s and early 1960s. I was not interested solely in critical demolition, however, for I also wished to present corrected versions of or alternatives to the ideas I assailed. Yet the first three articles, at least, were contributions to what was soon to become a widespread assault on both science-building and consensual sociology, an assault that by the mid-1970s had unmistakably triumphed.[1]

"C. Wright Mills and the Sociological Imagination" was originally printed in *Commentary* in 1959 under the title "The Failure of American Sociology." Unlike the other four essays in the section, it does not deal specifically with conceptions of human nature or of the relation of self to society, although it adumbrates the theme of an oversocialized conception of man that is the subject of the two following essays. Its discussion of Mills's now-famous polemic helps to locate the later articles in the context of the attack on conventional sociology that was building up steam at the time.

The second and third articles are clearly companion pieces. "The Oversocialized Conception of Man in Modern Sociology" is my most frequently cited and reprinted publication. It obviously owes the attention it has received to the strategic timeliness of its criticism of the then-prevailing conformist assumptions about human conduct in sociological theory, challenging these assumptions from a more social-psychological and less directly political standpoint than earlier attacks by Mills, Barrington Moore, Jr., Ralf Dahrendorf, and others. Since

I have added a postscript to "The Oversocialized Conception of Man" written especially for this volume, I shall say little more about it here. "Human Nature and the Perspective of Sociology" was originally projected as an answer to Talcott Parsons's rebuttal of the earlier article in *Psychoanalysis and The Psychoanalytic Review*.[2] The editor of this journal refused to open his pages to me for a counter-rebuttal, so in the end I dealt only briefly with Parsons's argument and chose instead to elaborate more fully on the thesis of the original article. Although it is often assumed today that Parsons's views totally dominated sociological theory in the 1940s and 1950s, this was very far from being the case, and in "Human Nature and the Perspective of Sociology" I attempted, *inter alia*, to assess other theoretical approaches—neo-Marxist conflict theory, historicism, symbolic interactionism—in relation to the oversocialized conception of man and the rival Freudian view of human nature that I favored.

The last two essays in this section are also companion pieces, although unlike the two preceding them they were not conceived as such. They critically examine two major themes in popular social criticism: the "quest for community" and the corollary or complementary "quest for identity."[3] The first drafts of both were written several years before their eventual publication in *Dissent*, so they stand closer in time to the relatively apolitical social criticism of the previous decade than the publication dates, 1966 and 1968, might suggest.

Both essays, unlike the two preceding ones, were addressed to a general intellectual audience rather than primarily to academic sociologists. Both examined not only the ideas of influential writers and thinkers, including though by no means confined to sociologists, but also the reception of these ideas by educated middle-class audiences and their rhetorical use as social criticism, which often ignores the tensions and contradictions among them. In one of the earliest studies of the new postwar suburbs—those alleged hotbeds of the compulsive search for community—William M. Dobriner remarked that an interviewed housewife who described her suburb to him in sociological jargon represented "the voice of sociology feeding back on itself through the voice of a corrupted respondent."[4] But more and more of our respondents have clearly been so corrupted. The diffusion of

sociological clichés and catchwords through many media to a widening segment of the population has itself become a social process significantly shaping the ethos and self-consciousness of the public. We have hardly had to await instruction in epistemology from the fashionable antipositivist philosophers of social science to be made aware of the difference between our relation to our subject matter and that of physicists or biologists to theirs. "The Idea of 'Community': A Critique" and "Identity: Problem and Catchword" were efforts to explore the impact of popularized social science on everyday values as a pervasive and ubiquitous occurrence, rather than treating "self-fulfilling" or "self-defeating" prophecies as no more than interesting curiosities.

An author's claim to discern a thematic coherence in a collection of essays on diverse subjects written for diverse audiences is no doubt properly to be viewed with suspicion. Nevertheless, I think there is a genuine link between the themes of the two last essays in this section and the two preceding ones. The critique of the oversocialized conception of man was, as I have indicated in the postscript to the original article, intended to complement the critique of the overintegrated conception of society developed by neo-Marxist and conflict theorists. The ideology of "community" involves the affirmation as a value of the consensus and social cohesion that were regarded as the defining attributes of society by the dominant sociological theories of the 1950s. Similarly, "identity" as a sought-after goal is congruent with the definition of man as essentially a "role-player" who finds the meaning of life in conformity to the "expectations" of others.* Yet in the rhetoric of social criticism, "community" and "identity" are presented as goals to be pursued rather than as inevitable results or achievements of social life. Rather than celebrating their comforting presence, social criticism deplores their absence under the "alienating" and impersonal conditions of modern life.

In "The Idea of 'Community': A Critique," I considered the ideology of community to be a successor or alternative to political protest, but the experience of the late 1960s showed that it was capable of sur-

---

* This statement applies only to the concept of "social identity," which, as my article emphasizes, is by no means to be equated with Erik H. Erikson's concept, nor, for that matter, with Allen Wheelis's. Both Erikson and Wheelis are, of course, psychoanalysts rather than sociologists.

viving the repoliticization of social criticism. There are curious continuities underlying the apolitical, conformist but "alienated" mood of young people at the end of the fifties—such as those described in Kenneth Keniston's first book [5]—and the sudden turn to frenetic political activism and the adoption of "countercultural" life-styles in the following decade. The early New Left extolled community and generational solidarity in opposition to the alienation and inauthenticity ("role-playing") of modern society. Both the New Left and the counterculture have declined as movements in the seventies, but have apparently been succeeded by a host of communalist sects, cults, and therapies which promise community, self-realization, and secure identity to their adherents. Critics have charged sensitivity training, encounter groups, and such new religions or quasi-religions as Scientology, Hare Krishna, and the Jesus people with artificially engineering consensus by means of authoritarian and psychologically manipulative techniques. Such accusations resemble those that were levelled in the 1950s against large organizations, suburban communities, the educational system, and the mass media. Yet one has the impression that people shift rather rapidly today from one movement or therapy to another, becoming followers of, say, Maharaj-Ji, dropping out, and then becoming attached to another guru or joining a new commune. Such restlessness suggests precisely the search for community and identity dissociated from commitment to any substantive values or group attachments that I discussed in "The Idea of 'Community' " and "Identity: Problem and Catchword." The quest persists whether it assumes conformist or nonconformist shapes in relation to the larger society. My two essays still seem to me, therefore, to possess contemporary relevance.

   I have updated some references and made minor corrections in all five essays in this section. In a few cases I have restored phrases and even sentences that were edited out of the original printed versions. I have incorporated into the text several of the long footnotes appended to "The Oversocialized Conception of Man in Modern Sociology."

ONE

C. Wright Mills and
the Sociological Imagination

COLLEGE STUDENTS, however unlettered, often possess what journalists call "the instinct for the jugular." Meeting a class one day which had just been reading C. Wright Mills's *White Collar*, I was asked on entering the room whether I agreed with the description of American professors as men "of typically plebian cultural interests . . . and a generally philistine style of life." I acknowledged that on the whole I did. Yet a reviewer of one of Mills's later books reported that academicians of his acquaintance thought *White Collar* profound and acute on salesgirls and business executives but wide of the mark on professors. I find my opposite reaction confirmed by Mills's new book, *The Sociological Imagination*,[1] a full-scale dissection of his academic colleagues and to my mind the best book he has yet written.

The new book is an attack on the dominant schools or "styles of work" in contemporary sociology for their failure to meet the demands of the "sociological imagination." Mills wishes by this phrase to indicate that quality of mind which fully perceives the intimate connection between the private and the public, between personal experience and the broader typicalities and specificities of this time and that place. Or, as he puts it repeatedly, "the sociological imagination is the ability to grasp history and biography and the relations between the two within society." The forerunners and founders of modern sociology had such a grasp, and we still read Tocqueville and Marx, Weber and Veblen. Contemporary sociologists honor their names but rarely follow their example. Those in search of a sense of themselves and their time, a search that led some of us to become professional sociologists in the thirties and the forties, are apt today to turn to nonsociologists, to writers as different as Hannah Arendt, Lionel Trilling, and W. H. Whyte, as well as to sociologists like David Riesman and Mills himself who are unlikely ever to become presidents of the American Sociological Association.

The condemnation of sociology that this suggests needs qualification on two counts. First, to expect professional sociologists to be the primary possessors of the sociological imagination would be to perpetuate an ancient intellectual imperialism which the humanities and the older social sciences have always rightfully resented. Mills himself makes it clear that he is using the phrase to refer to an ethos or intellectual ambiance, analogous to Newtonian mechanism" and "Darwinian ethics," rather than to an outlook that can or ought to be the exclusive property of a single discipline. Second, much of the work of contemporary sociologists in special areas such as criminology, population problems, or the study of voting trends is unquestionably valuable, as even the harshest critic of the field discovers when seeking comparable information about a foreign country where academic sociological research remains undeveloped. Yet sociology aspires to be more than a loose grouping of semiautonomous specialties—not to speak of the armory of research techniques plus an esoteric vocabulary that it is in danger of becoming.

Literary men and journalists who regularly sneer at the graceless verbosity and obsessive methodolatry of sociologists are likely to applaud much of what Mills says without paying very close attention to it. But Mills's point of view is not really theirs: he knows that "insight" or "literary sensibility" or an awareness that in some sense "Dostoyevsky said it all before and better" are not enough to assure even a limited understanding of history, politics, and society. Disciplined thinking, much plain fact-grubbing, unremitting exposure to the materials of contemporary and recorded history, the capacity to brood over and exploit one's personal experiences without crudely projecting them onto the universe—all this and more are necessary. Neither a personal gift of perceptiveness nor any easily teachable method can provide a short cut. The trouble with contemporary sociologists is that from the mixed ingredients of the sociological imagination they have extracted a few mental skills and thought-ways and set them up as the royal road to truth.

Max Weber, the one great man we sociologists can plausibly claim as our own, once wrote: "No sociologist should think himself too good, even in his old age, to make tens of thousands of quite trivial computations in his head and perhaps for months at a time." A social researcher, one of those whom Mills with his usual talent for phrase-making calls an "abstracted empiricist," once quoted this to me in justification of the narrow technicism of the quantifiers and tabulators. But Weber obviously didn't mean that "trivial computations" ought to be rushed into print and hailed as science or scholarship. And he went on to remark that such busywork is not worth the effort "if no idea occurs to his [the sociologist's] mind about the direction of his computations . . . [for although] the idea is not a substitute for work . . . work in turn cannot substitute for or compel an idea any more than enthusiasm can." [2]

I don't suppose that even the most hidebound empiricist would withhold verbal assent from that today. No one believes any longer that "the facts speak for themselves"; it is universally admitted that "theory" and "research" ought to be united. But what Mills labels Grand Theory, meaning chiefly the work of Talcott Parsons and his followers, not only has little or no intrinsic relation to the research routines and the processed questionnaire "data" of the empiricists, but is a very different thing from theory as we find it in the classical sociologists. Marx's "capitalism," Weber's "rationalization of life," or Veblen's "leisure class," ideas which, inclusive as they are, have clear historical referents linking them to the world as we know it, are usually surrounded by deprecatory quotation marks in the writings of the grand theorists. The latter prefer to deploy terms like "dysfunction," "role expectation," or "structural requisite"—highly abstract and formal concepts which at best amount to possible building blocks for theory rather than to theory itself. The ugliness of this jargon * would be a small price to pay if we had any assurance that it would

---

* Kathleen Nott writes: "Jargon is a parrotlike or mumbo jumbo imitation of the precise classifications of the physical and mathematical sciences. A language is a jargon when its references claim an objectivity, an agreement about definition, that does not exist." "Feeling and Ideology," *Partisan Review* 26 (Winter 1959), 68.

give us otherwise unobtainable answers to important questions. But when it is "applied" by Parsonians to the concrete social and historical world, we merely find translations of what more old-fashioned historians and social scientists tell us in English.

Grand theory and abstracted empiricism are degenerations of older intellectual traditions in which both found a proper and limited place. Mills's account of how such partial perspectives have become dominant in American sociology and how they are sustained and perpetuated by trends in American society amounts to a first-rate sociology of sociology itself. To appreciate it fully one must oneself be a sociologist, preferably a former graduate student at Columbia in the postwar years, for although Mills names a good many names, his book has some of the traits of a *roman à clef*. He is marvelously accurate at describing and recording the intellectual mannerisms, the falsely modest solemnities about the "hard and unrewarding demands of real science," the new academic types, and the new forms of career-making that prevail in the "research shops" of bureaucratic social science. To give the full flavor requires quotation. Mills writes of the younger men, exclusively "trained" in the new social science:

> I have seldom seen one of these young men in a condition of genuine intellectual puzzlement. And I have never seen any passionate curiosity about a great problem, the sort of curiosity that compels the mind to travel anywhere and by any means, to remake itself if necessary, in order to *find out*. These young men are less restless than methodical; less imaginative than patient; above all, they are dogmatic—in all the historical and theological meanings of the term. . . . They have taken up social research as a career; they have come early to an extreme specialization, and they have acquired an indifference or a contempt for "social philosophy"—which means to them "writing books out of other books" or "merely speculating." Listening to their conversations, trying to gauge the quality of their curiosity, one finds a deadly limitation of mind.[3]

Mills sees more clearly than previous critics the extent to which abstracted empiricism has robbed sociology of its traditional subject matter. Sociology has become "the methodological specialty"; the sociologist is now a tool-maker, a technician of research, possessing skills equally usable by advertising agencies, giant bureaucracies, and independent scholars. For a few years research money flows from corporations concerned over industrial morale; then a foundation becomes interested in, say, attitudes toward civil liberties and a whole new subfield springs into being appropriately labeled and discussed at a session of the September ASA meetings. At present, hospitals and mental health groups are providing jobs and research funds, so "medical sociology" and the "sociology of mental health" are burgeoning specialties. Now, the new research skills are indispensable for many purposes: it would, I think, be a gain to all concerned if those who wished to concentrate on elaborating and refining them were to secede from sociology and set up shop as a service discipline like statistics, accessible to all would-be users. Unfortunately, this is unlikely to happen. Nor can I share the optimism of some of my fellow members of what might be called the "humanistic underground" in American sociology, who think that abstracted empiricism will prove to be a passing fad. It is now, as Mills shows, too securely built into the very structure of American society as one of the instrumentalities of bureaucratic administration. Those of us, therefore, who still value understanding more than know-how may have to accept and wear with pride the labels "social philosopher," "journalist," or even "literature major," the latest appellation adopted by research technicians to describe their betters.

Mills's chapter on Talcott Parsons is less satisfactory than his discussion of empiricism. He makes much of the opaqueness of Parsons's terminology and effectively ridicules it by quoting huge globs and then "translating" them into a few brief and lucid sentences. I have no desire to defend Parsons's prose, which has to be read to be believed, but it does have more content than Mills's jibes suggest. Mills in fact implicitly concedes as much when he criticizes the conservative view of the social order that is embedded in Parsons's categories.

For Parsons, unlike most of his epigones, deals with real theoretical problems, especially in his earlier books. Why, given a secular Hobbesian or Darwinian view of man as simply a gifted animal, do men refrain from regular resort to fraud and violence in pursuit of their ends and maintain a viable society at all? Parsons answers that their very ends are acquired from other men and become shared moral values, "internalized" by processes with which psychoanalysis has made us familiar. But even if biological man is thus transformed into social man, why is society not rent apart by warring *groups*, each seeking to advance its own values and collective interests? To this, the "Marxist" problem, Parsons answers, more dubiously, that society has a tendency toward an equilibrium in which its component groups and institutions become harmoniously adapted to one another.

The trouble with Parsons's theory is that in trying to explain conformity and social stability, which become problematical once the assumption of an innate or God-given moral sense or Lockean "identity of interests" is abandoned, he manages to make their opposites appear even more problematical. That violence, revolution, and historical change occur at all becomes incomprehensible. In the terms of Parsons's theory, as Mills observes, "the idea of conflict cannot effectively be formulated. Structural antagonisms, large-scale revolts, revolutions—they cannot be imagined." At most they can be explained by individual psychopathology as "failures of socialization," which is not even adequate to account for the juvenile delinquent, let alone the reformer, the revolutionary, or the prophet.

Parsons reviewed Mills's *The Power Elite* at considerable length and it is instructive to compare Parsons on Mills with Mills on Parsons. Parsons challenges Mills's assumption that the exercise of power always imposes some deprivation on those subject to it. To him power is essentially "a facility for the performance of function in and on behalf of the society as a system" and he refuses to regard its expansive tendency and its openness to abuse as of more than secondary importance.[4] He does not even look on power as at best a necessary evil.

Mills is right, I think, to see tension and potential conflict between the goals of the power holders and their subjects as inescapable. But his pose as a tough-minded connoisseur of power inclines him to a neo-Machiavellian cynicism in which the "common values" stressed so heavily by Parsons are redefined as "master symbols of legitimation" which "justify or oppose the arrangement of power and the position within this arrangement of the powerful." This amounts to saying that values and ideologies are mere epiphenomena and that power interests alone are autonomous in history. Far from disposing of Parsons's oversocialized man and overintegrated society, such a view simply reinstates the original "problem of order" as it stood before Parsons tried to solve it. No true dialogue takes place between the two men, no dialectic of their ideas results—they succeed merely in negating one another.

If Mills reminds us of Pareto and Mosca in his conception of what is, Parsons rightly argues that Mills's notion of what might be implies "a utopian conception of an ideal society in which power does not play a part at all." [5] It is here that traces of ideological Marxism, or even of Leninism, are most evident in Mills's thinking. He could, of course, reply to Parsons that in refusing to view power as beneficient he at least avoids the mistake of reasoning as if utopia were already here. But the question of Mills's ideological preconceptions must be raised because readers who do not accept the diagnosis of contemporary America or of the cold war set forth in his earlier books may be inclined to look on his indictment of sociology with suspicion. Is he simply complaining that sociologists are not radicals and thus are not preoccupied with his own political concerns in their work?

Except for occasional lapses, I do not think Mills is vulnerable to this charge. Actually, most of the thinkers he praises as exemplars of the sociological imagination were by no means radicals themselves—Marx, Veblen, and possibly Mannheim are the only real exceptions—and several, notably Durkheim, Mosca, and Schumpeter, are usually classified as conservatives. Mills's liberal-radical outlook is most evident in his two final chapters. Since I share this outlook, much of what he says seems to me to be unexceptionable. For the most part he echoes, down to the phrasing, ideas he has developed at greater length elsewhere, although his particular views on American society and world politics are considerably muted.

Inevitably, it is partly this avoidance of detailed political programs and analyses that leads me in common with others (e.g., George Lichtheim) [6] to find *The Sociological Imagination* more impressive than its predecessors. But there is, I think, more to it than this. Mills is undoubtedly at his best in writing about what he knows at first hand—a further bit of evidence that sociological understanding differs only in degree from the understanding achieved by a good novelist or by any acute observer of the life around him. Moreover, Mills has always made his most telling points when he is opposing a point of view which has been stated with sufficient clarity and intelligence to make it impossible to dismiss it in its least convincing form. In taking on Parsons and Paul Lazarsfeld, Mills chooses the most able spokesmen for grand theory and abstracted empiricism respectively. As a result, his own arguments are sharper and more probing and the frequent lapses into rhetoric and journalistic purple patches that mar his other books are less in evidence.

Mills's gift is largely for synthesis, for sketching in the outlines of the whole, rather than for careful, close reasoning. His books are full of exciting vistas, imaginative suggestions pointing to overlooked connections in social life, but he invariably fails to follow these up in any rigorous fashion. For example, *The Power Elite* provides us with no more than a starting point for the analysis of power in American society: Mills tells us *who* the decision-makers and power-holders are, but, as I argued in the September 1956 issue of *Commentary*, he neglects to discuss in detail *what* sort of things they decide and what *interests* they serve. He seems to hold assumptions about these latter dimensions of power that remain hidden. Again, in *Character and Social Structure*, an advanced text in social psychology that Mills wrote with Hans Gerth several years ago, we are promised "a view of man as an actor in historic crises and of man as a whole entity" [7]—a prospect offering an exciting contrast to the usual hodgepodge of attitude studies and watered-down psychoanalysis that passes for social psychology. But, as Philip Selznick pointed out in an acute review,[8] the book does not live up to its promise: the authors are erudite in their use of wide-ranging historical illustrations, but they largely confine themselves to elaborating a set of concepts and definitions, an enterprise which, though more elegantly executed, does not differ in kind from what Mills condemns as "grand theory."

There is a striking discrepancy between Mills's own work and the admirable conception of what sociology ought to be advanced in *The Sociological Imagination*. To begin with, his books are surprisingly diffuse and repetitive if measured against the altogether fascinating discussion of his methods of work which he includes in an appendix entitled "On Intellectual Craftsmanship." And if there is one rule that Mills insists on again and again as an absolute prerequisite for the exercise of the sociological imagination, it is the necessity of thinking historically and comparatively. "Never think of describing an institution in 20th century America without trying to bear in mind similar institutions in other types of structures and periods," he writes. "The aim of classic social science requires that we seek a fully comparative understanding of the social structures that have appeared and now exist in world history." [9]

Yet, in spite of these exhortations, I find his own studies of contemporary America lacking in historical depth and comparative perspective. The only other societies he ever discusses in detail are early nineteenth-century America and Nazi Germany. He holds a somewhat idealized and Whitmanesque view of the former and his main, if not only, authority on Nazism is Franz Neumann's *Behemoth*, an excellent study of the prewar Hitler regime; but Mills seems unaware of the fact that Neumann later qualified or rejected many of its neo-Marxist conclusions. Does Mills think that contemporary Britain is ruled by a "power elite" resembling that of the United States? Or did the Labour Party seriously modify capitalist institutions and break the continuity with the past he finds in America? No answers to these queries can be found in Mills's books because, except for a passing reference to the superiority of the British civil service in *The Power Elite*, he never mentions England. And beyond a few comments on the brutalities of enforced industrialization, he has surprisingly little to say, even in *The Causes of World War III*, about Soviet Russia. Tocqueville maintained that he did not write a single paragraph of *Democracy in America* without having France in mind and, although he never mentions France as such, we know fully what he thought about his own country as well as about the United States. "One need not make explicit comparisons," [10] Mills observes. Indeed, but his own books do not pass the Tocqueville test. (But, then, how many do?)

And yet *The Sociological Imagination* is incredibly rich in ideas. It is impossible not to feel a sense of personal gratitude to Mills for having dispelled the air of make-believe that clings to contemporary sociology, the dominating pretense that its practitioners are skilled scientists when their work so often falls below the standards of the most old-fashioned kind of scholarship. The strange linguistic habits of the theorists and the "methodological inhibition" of the empiricists have a common source in the ambition to create a social science matching the natural sciences in its monopoly of an arcane and specialized expertise. Whatever one's view of the possibilities of ever achieving such a science (and my own is decidedly skeptical), one can be sure that neither physics nor biology would have advanced very far had they been guided solely by a like ambition.

But in his stress on the contemporary bureaucratic and ideological trends which currently sustain American sociology, Mills perhaps fails to recognize how venerable the ambition is. The following episode occurs in Nikolai Gogol's *Dead Souls*, a novel written in and about the Russia of the czars well over a century ago: Tchitchikov, Gogol's dealer in dead souls, has been asked to wait in the library of a vain and pretentious provincial landowner. "It was an immense apartment, the walls of which were lined with books from the floor to the ceiling. . . . There were six volumes in a row, entitled *Preliminary Introduction to the Theory of Thought in its General Aspect as a Whole, and in its Application to the Interpretation of the Organic Principles of the Mutual Distribution of Social Productivity.* Wherever Tchitchikov opened the book, on every page he found 'phenomenon,' 'development,' 'abstract,' 'cohesion,' and 'combination'; and the devil only knows what. 'No, all that's not in my line,' thought Tchitchikov." [11] He might almost have been glancing at a book by Talcott Parsons!

TWO

The Oversocialized Conception
of Man in Modern Sociology

GERTRUDE STEIN, bed-ridden with a fatal illness, is reported to have suddenly muttered, "What, then, is the answer?" Pausing, she raised her head, murmured, "But what is the question?" and died. Miss Stein presumably was pondering the ultimate meaning of human life, but her brief final soliloquy has a broader and humbler relevance. Its point is that answers are meaningless apart from questions. If we forget the questions, even while remembering the answers, our knowledge of them will subtly deteriorate, becoming rigid, formal, and catechistic, as the sense of indeterminacy, of rival possibilities, implied by the very putting of a question is lost.

Social theory must be seen primarily as a set of answers to questions we ask of social reality. If the initiating questions are forgotten, we readily misconstrue the task of theory, and the answers previous thinkers have given become conceptual prisons, degenerating into little more than a special professional vocabulary for situations and events that can be described with equal or greater precision in ordinary language. Forgetfulness of the questions that are the starting points of inquiry leads us to ignore the substantive assumptions buried in our concepts and commits us to a one-sided view of reality.

Perhaps this is simply an elaborate way of saying that sociological theory can never afford to lose what is usually called a "sense of significance"; or, as it is sometimes put, that sociological theory must be "problem-conscious." I choose instead to speak of theory as a set of answers to questions because reference to "problems" may seem to suggest too close a linkage with social criticism or reform. My primary reason for insisting on the need to hold constantly in mind the questions that our concepts and theories are designed to answer is to preclude defining the goal of sociological theory as the creation of a formal body of knowledge satisfying the logical criteria of scientific theory set up by philosophers and methodologists of natural science. Needless to say, this is the way theory is often defined by contemporary sociologists.

Yet to speak of theory as interrogatory may suggest too self-sufficiently intellectual an enterprise. Cannot questions be answered satisfactorily and then forgotten, the answers becoming the assumptions from which we start in framing new questions? I might convey my view of sociological theory more adequately by saying that it concerns itself with questions arising out of problems that are inherent in the very existence of human societies and that cannot be finally "solved" in the way that particular social problems perhaps can be. The "problems" theory concerns itself with are problems *for* human societies which, because of their universality, become intellectually problematic for sociological theorists.

Essentially, the historicist conception of sociological knowledge, central to the thought of Max Weber and ably restated by Barrington Moore, Jr., and C. Wright Mills,[1] is a sound one. The most fruitful questions for sociology always refer to the realities of a particular historical situation. Yet both of these writers—especially Mills—tend to underemphasize the degree to which we genuinely desire and seek answers to transhistorical, universal questions about the nature of man and society. I do not have in mind the formalistic quest for social "laws" or "universal propositions," nor the even more formalistic effort to construct all-encompassing "conceptual schemes." Moore and Mills are rightly critical of such efforts. I am thinking of such questions as, How are men capable of uniting to form enduring societies in the first place? Why and to what degree is change inherent in human societies, and what are the sources of change? How is man's animal nature domesticated by society?

Such questions—which are existential as well as intellectual questions—are the raison d'être of social theory, and men asked them long before the rise of sociology. Sociology itself is an effort, under unprecedented historical conditions, to find novel answers to them.

They do not lend themselves to successively more precise answers as a result of cumulative empirical research, for they remain eternally problematic. Thus social theory is necessarily an interminable dialogue. "True understanding," Hannah Arendt has written, "does not tire of interminable dialogue and 'vicious circles' because it trusts that imagination will eventually catch at least a glimpse of the always frightening light of truth." [2]

I wish briefly to review the answers modern sociological theory offers to one such question, or rather to one aspect of one question. It may be variously phrased as, "What are the sources of social cohesion?"; or, "How is social order possible?"; or, in social-psychological terms, "How is it that man becomes tractable to social discipline?" I shall call this question in its social-psychological aspect the "Hobbesian question" and in its more strictly sociological aspect the "Marxist question." The Hobbesian question asks how men are capable of the regulation by social norms and goals that makes possible an enduring society, while the Marxist question asks how, assuming this capability, complex societies manage to control and restrain destructive conflicts between groups. Much of our theory offers an oversocialized view of man in answering the Hobbesian question and an overintegrated view of society in answering the Marxist question.

A number of writers have challenged the overintegrated view of society in contemporary theory. In addition to Moore and Mills, the names of Bendix, Coser, Dahrendorf, and Lockwood come to mind. [3] My intention, therefore, is to concentrate on the answers to the Hobbesian question in an effort to disclose the oversocialized view of man which they seem to imply.

Since my view of theory is obviously very different from that of Talcott Parsons and has, in fact, been developed in opposition to his, let me pay tribute to his recognition of the importance of the Hobbesian question—the "problem of order," as he calls it—at the very beginning of his first book, *The Structure of Social Action.* [4] Parsons correctly credits Hobbes with being the first thinker to see the need to explain why human society is not a "war of all against all"; why, if man is simply a gifted animal, men refrain from unlimited resort to fraud and violence in pursuit of their ends and maintain a stable society at all. There is even a sense in which, as Coser and Mills have both noted,[5] Parsons's entire work represents an effort to solve the Hobbesian problem of order. His solution, however, has tended to become precisely the kind of elaboration of a set of answers divorced from questions that is so characteristic of contemporary sociological theory.

Hobbes's solution to the problem of order he saw with such clarity need not concern us in detail. As is well known, he postulated a "state of nature" in which men unrestrainedly "endeavour to destroy or subdue one another" when it serves their interests; rationally perceiving the perpetual insecurity that results, men enter into a social contract and establish a common power, the Leviathan of the state, to protect them from one another's aggressions by reserving for itself alone the use of force. Whatever interest his famous theory of the origin of the state may still hold for political scientists, it is clearly inadequate as an explanation of the origin of society. Yet the pattern, as opposed to the details, of Hobbes's thought bears closer examination.

The polar terms in Hobbes's theory are the state of nature, where the war of all against all prevails, and the authority of Leviathan, created by social contract. But the war of all against all is not simply effaced with the creation of political authority: it remains potential in human society, at times quiescent, at times erupting into open violence. Whether Hobbes believed that the state of nature and the social contract were ever historical realities (and there is evidence that he was not that simple-minded, even in the seventeenth century) is unimportant; the whole tenor of his thought is to see the war of all against all and Leviathan dialectically, as coexisting and interacting opposites.[6] As R. G. Collingwood has observed, "According to Hobbes . . . *a body politic is a dialectical thing*, a Heraclitean world in which at any given time there is a negative element." [7] The first secular social theorist in the history of Western thought, and one of the first to clearly discern and define the problem of order in human society long before Darwinism made awareness of it a commonplace, Hobbes was a dialectical thinker who refused to separate answers from questions, solutions to society's enduring problems from the conditions creating them.

How does contemporary sociological theory answer the Hobbesian question? There are two main answers, each of which has come to be understood in a way that denies the reality and meaningfulness of the question. Together they constitute a model of human nature, sometimes clearly stated, more often implicit in accepted concepts, that pervades modern sociology. The first answer is summed up in the notion of the "internalization of social norms." The second, more commonly employed or assumed in empirical research, is the view that man is essentially motivated by the desire to achieve a positive image of self by winning acceptance or status in the eyes of others.

The following statement represents, briefly and broadly, probably the most influential contemporary sociological conception—and dismissal—of the Hobbesian problem: "To a modern sociologist imbued with the conception that action follows institutionalized patterns, opposition of individual and common interests has only a very limited relevance or is thoroughly unsound." [8] From this writer's perspective, the problem is an unreal one: human conduct is totally shaped by common norms or "institutionalized patterns." Sheer ignorance must have led people who had the misfortune not to be modern sociologists to ask, "How is order possible?" A thoughtful bee or ant would never inquire, How is the social order of the hive or anthill possible? The opposite of that order is unimaginable when the insects' instinctive endowment insures its stability and a built-in harmony between "individual and common interests." Human society, we are assured, is not essentially different, although conformity and stability are there maintained by noninstinctive processes. Modern sociologists believe that they have understood these processes and that they have not merely answered but disposed of the Hobbesian question, showing that the question, far from expressing a valid intimation of the tensions and possibilities of social life, can only be asked out of ignorance.

It would be hard to find a better illustration of what Collingwood, following Plato, calls *eristical* as opposed to dialectical thinking: [9] the answer destroys the question, or rather destroys the awareness of rival possibilities suggested by the question which accounts for its having been asked in the first place. A reversal of perspective now takes place, and we are moved to ask the opposite question: How is it that violence, conflict, revolution, and the individual's sense of coercion by society manage to exist at all, if this view is correct? [10] Whenever a one-sided answer to a question compels us to raise the opposite question, we are caught up in a dialectic of concepts which reflects a

dialectic in things. But let us examine the particular processes sociologists appeal to in order to account for the elimination of the war of
all against all from human society.

The Changing Meaning of Internalization

A well-known section of *The Structure of Social Action*, devoted to
the interpretation of Durkheim's thought, is entitled "The Changing
Meaning of Constraint." [11] Parsons argues that Durkheim originally
conceived of society as controlling the individual from the outside by
imposing constraints on him through sanctions, best illustrated by
codes of law. But in Durkheim's later work he began to see that social
rules do not "merely regulate 'externally' . . . they enter directly into
the constitutions of the actors' ends themselves." [12] Constraint,
therefore, is more than an environmental obstacle which the actor
must take into account in pursuit of his goals in the same way that he
takes into account physical laws: it becomes internal, psychological,
and self-imposed as well. Parsons developed this view that social
norms are "constitutive" rather than merely "regulative" of human
nature before he was influenced by psychoanalytic theory, but
Freud's theory of the superego became the source and model for the
conception of the internalization of social norms that today plays so
important a part in sociological thinking. However, the use some
sociologists have made of Freud's ideas might well inspire an essay
entitled "The Changing Meaning of Internalization," although, in
contrast to the shift in Durkheim's view of constraint, this change has
been a change for the worse.

Internalization has imperceptibly been equated with "learning," or
even with "habit-formation" in the simplest sense. Thus when a
norm is said to have been "internalized" by an individual, what is
frequently meant is that he habitually both affirms it and conforms to
it in his conduct. The whole stress on inner conflict—on the tension
between powerful impulses and superego controls, the behavioral
outcome of which cannot be prejudged—drops out of the picture.
Yet this conflict is central to Freud's view, for in psychoanalytic
terms to say that a norm has been internalized (or introjected to
become part of the superego) is to say no more than that a person will
suffer guilt feelings if he fails to live up to it, not that he will in fact
live up to it in his behavior.

The relation between internalization and conformity assumed by most sociologists is suggested by the following passage from a textbook: "Conformity to institutionalized norms is, of course, 'normal.' The actor, having internalized the norms, feels something like a need to conform. His conscience would bother him if he did not." [13] What is overlooked here is that the person who conforms may be even more "bothered," that is, subject to guilt and neurosis, than the person who violates what are not only society's norms but his own as well. To Freud, it is precisely the man with the strictest superego, he who has most thoroughly internalized and conformed to the norms of his society, who is most wracked with guilt and anxiety. [14]

Paul Kecskemeti, to whose discussion I owe initial recognition of the erroneous view of internalization held by sociologists, argues that the relations between social norms, the individual's selection from them, his conduct, and his feelings about his conduct are far from self-evident. "It is by no means true," he writes, "to say that acting counter to one's own norms always or almost always leads to neurosis. One might assume that neurosis develops even more easily in persons who *never* violate the moral code they recognize as valid but repress and frustrate some strong instinctual motive. A person who 'succumbs to temptation,' feels guilt, and then 'purges himself' of his guilt in some reliable way (e.g., by confession) may achieve in this way a better balance, and be less neurotic, than a person who never violates his 'norms' and never feels conscious guilt." [15]

Discussions of "deviant behavior" have been compelled to recognize these distinctions between social demands, personal attitudes toward them, and actual conduct, although they have done so in a laboriously taxonomic fashion. [16] They represent, however, largely the rediscovery of what was always central to the Freudian concept of the superego. The main explanatory function of the concept is to show how people repress themselves, imposing checks on their own desires and thus turning the inner life into a battlefield of conflicting motives, no matter which side "wins" by dictating overt action. So far as behavior is concerned, the psychoanalytic view of man is less deterministic than the sociological. For psychoanalysis is primarily concerned with the inner life, not with overt behavior, and its most fundamental insight is that the wish, the emotion, and the fantasy are as important as the act in man's experience.

Sociologists have appropriated the superego concept, but have separated it from any equivalent of the Freudian id. So long as most individuals are "socialized," that is, internalize the norms and conform to them in conduct, the Hobbesian problem is not even perceived as a latent reality. Deviant behavior is accounted for by special circumstances: ambiguous norms, anomie, role conflict, or greater cultural stress on goals than on the approved means for attaining them. Tendencies to deviant behavior are not seen as dialectically related to conformity. The presence in man of motivational forces resisting social discipline is denied.

Nor does the assumption that internalization of norms and roles is the essence of socialization allow for a sufficient range of motives for conformity. It fails to allow for variable "tonicity of the superego," in Kardiner's phase.[17] The degree to which conformity is the result of coercion rather than conviction is minimized.[18] Either someone has internalized the norms, or he is "unsocialized," a feral or socially isolated child, or a psychopath. Yet Freud recognized that many people, conceivably a majority, fail to acquire superegos. "Such people," he wrote, "habitually permit themselves to do any bad deed that procures them something they want, if only they are sure that no authority will discover it or make them suffer for it; their anxiety relates only to the possibility of detection. Present-day society has to take into account the prevalence of this state of mind."[19] The last sentence suggests that Freud was aware of the decline of "inner-direction," of the Protestant conscience, about which we have heard so much. So let us turn to the other elements of human nature that sociologists appeal to in order to explain away the Hobbesian problem.

Man the Acceptance-Seeker *

The superego concept is too inflexible, too bound to the past and to individual biography, to be of service in relating conduct to the pres-

---

* In many ways I should prefer to use the neater, more alliterative phrase "status-seeker." However, it has acquired a narrower meaning than I intend, particularly since Vance Packard appropriated it, suggesting primarily efforts, which are often consciously deceptive, to give the appearance of personal achievements or qualities worthy of deference. "Status-seeking" in this sense is, as Veblen perceived, necessar-

sures of the immediate situation in which it takes place. Sociologists therefore rely more heavily on an alternative notion, here stated—or, to be fair, overstated—in its baldest form: "People are so profoundly sensitive to the expectations of others that all action is inevitably guided by these expectations." [20]

Robert Cooley Angell [21] points out the ambiguity of the term "expectations." It is used, he notes, to mean both a factual prediction and a moral imperative, e.g., "England expects every man to do his duty." But this very ambiguity is instructive, for it suggests the process by which behavior that is nonnormative and perhaps even "deviant," but nevertheless "expected" in the sense of being predictable, acquires over time a normative aura and becomes "expected" in the sense of being socially approved or demanded. Thus Parsons's "interaction paradigm" provides leads to the understanding of social change and need not be confined, as in his use of it, to the explanation of conformity and stability.

Parsons's model of the "complementarity of expectations," the view that in social interaction men mutually seek approval from one another by conforming to shared norms, is a formalized version of what has tended to become a distinctive sociological perspective on human motivation. Ralph Linton states it in explicit psychological terms: "The need for eliciting favorable responses from others is an almost constant component of [personality]. Indeed, it is not too much to say that there is very little organized human behavior which is not directed toward its satisfaction in at least some degree." [22]

When values are "inferred" from this emphasis and then popularized, it becomes the basis of the ideology of "groupism" extolling the virtures of "togetherness" and "belongingness" that have been attacked so savagely by recent social critics. David Riesman and W. H. Whyte, the pioneers of this current of criticism in its contemporary guise, are both aware, as their imitators and epigones usually are not,

---

ily confined to relatively impersonal and segmental social relationships. "Acceptance" or "approval" convey more adequately what all men are held to seek in both intimate and impersonal relations according to the conception of the self and of motivation dominating contemporary sociology and social psychology. Nevertheless, I have been unable to resist the occasional temptation to use the term "status" in this broader sense.

of the extent to which the social phenomenon they have described is the result of the diffusion and popularization of sociology itself.[23] As a matter of fact, Riesman's "inner-direction" and "other-direction" correspond rather closely to the notions of "internalization" and "acceptance-seeking" in contemporary sociology as I have described them. Riesman even refers to his concepts initially as characterizations of "modes of conformity," although he then makes the mistake of calling them character types. But his view that all men are to some degree both inner-directed and other-directed, a qualification that has been somewhat neglected by critics who have understandably concentrated on his empirical and historical use of his typology, suggests the more generalized conception of forces making for conformity found in current theory.[24] However, as Gutman and I have observed: "In some respects Riesman's conception of character is Freudian rather than neo-Freudian: character is defined by superego mechanisms and, like Freud in *Civilization and Its Discontents*, the socialized individual is defined by what is forbidden him rather than by what society stimulates him to do. Thus in spite of Riesman's generally sanguine attitude towards modern America, implicit in his typology is a view of society as the enemy both of individuality and of basic drive gratification, a view that contrasts with the at least potentially benign role assigned it by neo-Freudian thinkers like Fromm and Horney." [25]

The insistence of sociologists on the importance of "social factors" easily leads them to stress the priority of socialized or socializing motives in human behavior. It is frequently the task of the sociologist to call attention to the intensity with which men desire and strive for the good opinion of their immediate associates in a variety of situations, particularly those where received theories or ideologies have unduly emphasized other motives such as financial gain, commitment to ideals, or the effects on energies and aspirations of arduous physical conditions. Thus sociologists have shown that factory workers are more sensitive to the attitudes of their fellow workers than to purely economic incentives; that voters are more influenced by the preferences of their relatives and friends than by campaign debates of the "issues"; that soldiers, whatever their ideological commitment to their nation's cause, fight more bravely when their platoons are intact and they stand side by side with their "buddies."

It is certainly not my intention to criticize the findings of such studies. My objection is that their particular selective emphasis is generalized—explicitly or, more often, implicitly— to provide apparent empirical support for an extremely one-sided view of human nature. Although sociologists have criticized past efforts to single out one fundamental motive in human conduct, the desire to achieve a favorable self-image by winning approval from others frequently occupies such a position in their own thinking. The following "theorem," in fact, has been openly put forward by Hans Zetterberg as "a strong contender for the position as the major Motivational Theorem in sociology": [26] "An actor's actions have a tendency to become dispositions that are related to the occurrence of favored uniform evaluations of the actor and-or his actions in his action system." [27]

Now Zetterberg is not necessarily maintaining that this theorem is an accurate factual statement of the basic psychological roots of social behavior. He is, characteristically, far too self-conscious about the logic of theorizing and "concept formation" for that. He goes on to remark that "the maximization of favorable attitudes from others would thus be the counterpart in sociological theory to the maximization of profit in economic theory." [28] If by this it is meant that the theorem is to be understood as a heuristic rather than an empirical assumption, that sociology has a selective point of view which is just as abstract and partial as that of economics and the other social sciences, and if his view of theory as a set of logically connected formal propositions is granted provisional acceptance, I am in agreement. (Actually, the view of theory suggested at the beginning of this paper is a quite different one.)

But there is a further point to be made. Ralf Dahrendorf has observed that structural-functional theorists do not "claim that order is *based on* a general consensus of values, but that it *can be conceived of in terms of* such consensus and that, if it is conceived of in these terms, certain propositions follow which are subject to the test of specific observations." [29] The same may be said of the assumption that people seek to maximize favorable evaluations by others; indeed this assumption has already fathered such additional concepts as "reference group" and "circle of significant others." Yet the question must be raised whether we really wish to, in effect, define sociology by such partial perspectives. The assumption of the maximization of approval from others is the psychological complement to the sociological assumption of a general value consensus. And the former is as selective and one-sided a way of looking at motivation as Dahrendorf and others have argued the latter to be when it determines our way of looking at social structure. The oversocialized view of man of the one is a counterpart to the overintegrated view of society of the other.

Modern sociology, after all, originated as a protest against the partial views of man contained in such doctrines as utilitarianism, classical economics, social Darwinism, and vulgar Marxism. All of the great nineteenth and early twentieth century sociologists saw it as one of their major tasks to expose the unreality of such abstractions as economic man, the gain-seeker of the classical economists; political man, the power-seeker of the Machiavellian tradition in political science; self-preserving man, the security-seeker of Hobbes and Darwin; sexual or ibidinal man, the pleasure-seeker of doctrinaire Freudianism; and even religious man, the God-seeker of the theologians. It would be ironical if it should turn out that they have merely contributed to the creation of yet another reified abstraction in socialized man, the status-seeker of our contemporary sociologists.

Much of the work of Thorstein Veblen, now generally regarded as a sociologist, was, of course, a polemic against the rational, calculating *homo economicus* of classical economics and a documentation of the importance in economic life of the quest for status measured by conformity to arbitrary and shifting conventional standards. Early in his first and most famous book Veblen made an observation on human nature resembling the one that looms so large in contemporary sociological thinking: "The usual basis of self-respect," he wrote, "is the respect accorded by one's neighbors. Only individuals with an aberrant temperament can in the long run retain their self-esteem in the face of the disesteem of their fellows." [30] Whatever the inadequacy of his psychological assumptions, Veblen did not, however, overlook other motivations, to which he frequently gave equal or greater weight.

Of course, an image of man as acceptance seeker is, like all the others mentioned, valuable for limited purposes so long as it is not taken for the whole truth. What are some of its deficiencies? To begin with, it neglects the other half of the model of human nature presupposed by current theory: moral man, guided by his built-in superego and beckoning ego-ideal.* In recent years sociologists have been less interested than they once were in culture and national character as backgrounds to conduct, partly because stress on the concept of "role" as the crucial link between the individual and the social structure has directed their attention to the immediate situation in which social interaction takes place. Man is increasingly seen as a "role-playing" creature, responding eagerly or anxiously to the expectations of other role-players in the many group settings in which he finds himself. Such an approach, while valuable in helping us grasp the complexity of a highly differentiated social structure such as our own, is far too often generalized to serve as a kind of ad hoc social psychology, easily adaptable to particular sociological purposes.

But it is not enough to concede that men often pursue "internalized values," remaining indifferent to what others think of them, particularly when, as I have previously argued, the idea of internalization has been "hollowed out" to make it more useful as an explanation of conformity. What of desire for material and sensual satisfactions? Can we really dispense with the venerable notion of material "interests" and invariably replace it with the blander, more integrative "social values"? And what of striving for power, not necessarily for its own sake—that may be rare and pathological—but as a means by which men are able to *impose* a normative definition of reality on others? That material interests, sexual drives, and the quest for power have often been overestimated as human motives is no reason to deny their reality. To do so is to suppress one term of the dialectic between conformity and rebellion, social norms and their violation, man and social order, as completely as the other term is

---

* Robin M. Williams, Jr., writes: "At the present time, the literature of sociology and social psychology contains many references to 'conformity'—conforming to norms, 'yielding to social pressure,' or 'adjusting to the requirements of the reference group.' . . . ; the implication is easily drawn that the actors in question are *motivated* solely in terms of conformity or non-conformity, rather than in terms of 'expressing' or 'affirming' internalized values . . ." (his italics). "Continuity and Change in Sociological Study," *American Sociological Review* 23 (December 1958), 630.

suppressed by those who deny the reality of man's "normative orientation" or reduce it to the effect of coercion, rational calculation, or mechanical conditioning.

The view that man is invariably pushed by internalized norms or pulled by the lure of validation by others ignores—to speak archaically for a moment—both the highest and the lowest, both beast and angel, in his nature. Durkheim, from whom so much of the modern sociological point of view derives, recognized that the very existence of a social norm implies and even creates the possibility of its violation. This is the meaning of his famous dictum that crime is a "normal phenomenon." He maintained that "for the originality of the idealist whose dreams transcend his century to find expression, it is necessary that the originality of the criminal, who is below the level of his time, shall also be possible. One does not occur without the other." [31] Yet Durkheim lacked an adequate psychology and formulated his insight in terms of the actor's cognitive awareness rather than in motivational terms. We do not have Durkheim's excuse for falling back on what Homans has called a "social mold theory" of human nature. [32]

Social but Not Entirely Socialized

I have referred to forces in man that are resistant to socialization. It is not my purpose to explore the nature of these forces or to suggest how we ought best conceive of them as sociologists. That would be a most ambitious undertaking. A few remarks will have to suffice. I think we must start with the recognition that *in the beginning there is the body.* As soon as the body is mentioned the specter of "biological determinism" raises its head and sociologists draw back in fright. And certainly their view of man is sufficiently disembodied and nonmaterialistic to satisfy Bishop Berkeley, as well as being desexualized enough to please Mrs. Grundy.

Am I, then, urging us to return to the older view of a human nature divided between a "social man" and a "natural man" who is either benevolent, Rousseau's Noble Savage, or sinister and destructive, as Hobbes regarded him? Freud is usually misrepresented as the chief modern proponent of the dualistic conception which assigns to the social order the purely negative role of blocking and redirecting man's "imperious biological drives." [33] I say "misrepresented" because, although Freud often said things supporting such an interpretation, other and more fundamental strains in his thinking suggest a different conclusion. John Dollard, certainly not a writer who is oblivious to social and cultural "factors," saw this in the 1930s: "It is quite clear," he wrote, "that [Freud] does not regard the instincts as having a fixed social goal; rather, indeed, in the case of the sexual instinct he has stressed the vague but powerful and impulsive nature of the drive and has emphasized that its proper social object is not picked out in advance. His seems to be a drive concept which is not at variance with our knowledge from comparative cultural studies, since his theory does not demand that the 'instinct' work itself out with mechanical certainty alike in every varying culture." [34] So much for Freud's "imperious biological drives"!

When Freud defined psychoanalysis as the study of the "vicissitudes of the instincts," he was confirming, not denying, the "plasticity" of human nature insisted upon by social scientists. The drives or "instincts" of psychoanalysis are not fixed dispositions to behave in a particular way; they are utterly subject to social channeling and transformation and could not reveal themselves in behavior without social molding, any more than our vocal cords can produce articulate speech if we have not learned a language. To psychoanalysis man is indeed a social animal; his social nature is profoundly reflected in his bodily structure. [35]

But there is a difference between the Freudian view, on the one hand, and both sociological and neo-Freudian conceptions of man on the other. To Freud man is a *social* animal without being entirely a *socialized* animal. His social nature is itself the source of conflicts and antagonisms that create resistance to socialization by the norms of any of the societies which have existed in the course of human history. "Socialization" may mean two quite distinct things; when they are confused an oversocialized view of man is the result. In one sense socialization means the "transmission of the culture," the particular culture of the society an individual enters at birth; in the other the term is used to mean the "process of becoming human," of acquiring uniquely human attributes from interaction with others. [36] All men are socialized in the latter sense, but this does not mean that they have been completely molded by the particular norms and values of their culture. All cultures, as Freud contended, do violence to man's socialized body drives, but this in no way means that men could possibly exist without culture or independently of society.[37] From such a standpoint, man may properly be called, as Norman Brown has called him, the "neurotic" or the "discontented" animal, and repression may be seen as the main characteristic of human nature as we have known it in history.[38]

But isn't this psychology? And have not sociologists been taught to foreswear psychology, to look with suspicion on what are called "psychological variables" in contradistinction to the institutional and historical forces with which they are properly concerned? There is indeed, as recent critics have complained, too much "psychologism" in contemporary sociology, largely, I think, because of the bias inherent in our favored research techniques. But I do not see how, at the level of theory, sociologists can fail to make assumptions about human nature.* If our assumptions are left implicit, we will inevitably presuppose a view of man that fits our special needs; when our sociological theory overstresses the stability and integration of society we will end up imagining that man is a disembodied, conscience-driven, status-seeking phantom. We must do better if we really wish to win credit outside of our ranks for special understanding of man, that plausible creature † whose wagging tongue so often hides the despair and darkness in his heart.

* "I would assert that very little sociological analysis is ever done without using at least an implicit psychological theory." Alex Inkeles, "Personality and Social Structure," in Robert K. Merton et al., ed., *Sociology Today* (New York: Basic Books, 1959), p. 250.

† Harry Stack Sullivan once remarked that the most outstanding characteristic of human beings was their "plausibility."

Postscript 1975

I SOMETIMES reflect ruefully that nothing else I have ever written has attracted anything like as much notice as "The Oversocialized Conception of Man in Modern Sociology." This situation is familiar enough for authors of a single successful and influential book but has a certain comic, even humiliating aspect when what is involved is a mere article that hit the target with one resonant phrase. Few people seem aware of the existence of a companion article, for it has never been reprinted and is rarely cited.[1] (It was published, to be sure, in a journal with a far lower circulation among sociologists than *The American Sociological Review*.) "The Oversocialized Conception of Man," by contrast, has been widely reprinted in several languages; it has contributed a phrase to the vocabulary of sociology; and its major thesis, though inevitably often misrepresented, has by now been virtually absorbed into the conventional wisdom of the discipline. I hope therefore that it will not be thought to be sheer vanity on my part if I attempt a reassessment in light of an intellectual situation in sociology that is very different from the one that prevailed fourteen years ago when the article was first published.

In 1961, structural-functional theory, most frequently associated with the work of Talcott Parsons, who had given it its full name, still seemed to be the dominant mode of sociological theorizing, although a counter-tendency was already fully visible by the end of the 1950s in the work of C. Wright Mills, Barrington Moore, Jr., Ralf Dahrendorf, Reinhard Bendix, Lewis Coser, and several others. This tendency came to be called "conflict theory" (the label was chiefly Ralf Dahrendorf's) and it obviously had broad affinities with the Marxist tradition. Nevertheless, none of the writers I have mentioned considered himself a Marxist, nor do any of them today, all of them except Mills being alive and still at work. Most of them, including Mills, were more Weberian than Marxist. The now-familiar brunt of their attack on Parsonian structural-functionalism was that its view of society minimized the importance of group conflict, coercive power, and material interests and overemphasized consensus, legitimate authority, and moral values.

All these writers were primarily concerned with the macrosocial level of group and inter-institutional relations, with "structure" rather than "milieu" in Mills's terms. None of them were social psychologists concerned primarily with human nature. Much as I agreed with them in 1961 (and still do), there seemed to be something incomplete about their theorizing, something that failed to go beyond a reaction against the consensual bias of structural-functionalism. Parsons himself rather complacently remarked on this in 1962, observing that "the 'Opposition' has much less of a coherent theory than the 'Establishment.' " * Structural-functionalism, especially in its Parsonian version, possessed a powerful, well-developed theory of human nature based on the idea that "the internalization of social norms" is the most important feature of the socialization process, thus linking, as Durkheim had not, a consensual view of society with a conforming and "role-playing" view of individual personality. Not only did the conflict theorists of the 1950s lack a systematic social psychology of their own, but some of them—notably Gerth and Mills in *Character and Social Structure*—subscribed to conceptions of socialization that scarcely differed from those of Parsons and his fellow functionalists.†

I decided, therefore, that the attack by the conflict theorists on the

---

* Talcott Parsons, "Individual Autonomy and Social Pressure: An Answer to Dennis Wrong," *Psychoanalysis and The Psychoanalytic Review* 49 (Summer 1962), pp. 70–79. This response to my article also seems to be scarcely known, having been published in a lay psychoanalytic rather than sociological journal.

† Ernest Becker argued, in effect, that Mills held an oversocialized conception of man in "Mills' Social Psychology and the Great Historical Convergence on the Problem of Alienation," in Irving Louis Horowitz, ed., *The New Sociology* (New York: Oxford University Press, 1964), pp. 112–116.

overintegrated conception of society in Parsonian theory needed to be complemented by an attack on the oversocialized conception of man that provided the psychological underpinnings of the theory. I originally conceived of the paper as a kind of companion piece, a social-psychological counterpart, to Ralf Dahrendorf's "Out of Utopia," [2] and, appropriately enough, the two articles have been reprinted side by side in readers several times. For substance I turned to Freud— not, however, to the bowdlerized Freud of Parsons or of the neo-Freudian psychoanalysts who were so popular among sociologists in the 1930s and 1940s, and on whose writings I had myself been raised intellectually (e.g., Karen Horney, Erich Fromm, Abram Kardiner, Harry Stack Sullivan). The main shaping influences on my 1961 essay were a rereading of Freud himself and three brilliant books of the late 1950s that were critical of the neo-Freudians and that moved in a far wider intellectual and cultural ambience than most previous interpreters of Freud (the majority of whom had been practicing psychoanalysts): Herbert Marcuse's *Eros and Civilization*, Norman Brown's *Life against Death*, and Philip Rieff's *Freud: The Mind of the Moralist*.

So much for the intellectual context of the late 1950s and early 1960s, when "The Oversocialized Conception of Man" was conceived and written. Today, all has changed: "the coming crisis of sociology" rather belatedly announced by Alvin Gouldner in 1970 has come and gone; the former sociological "mainstream" has been diverted into a number of smaller rivulets; the "Establishment" sociological theory with which Parsons identified himself as late as 1962 has been disestablished, although the victorious "Opposition" remains as diversified as he then thought it to be. A young British theorist, Herminio Martins, recently observed that "functionalism 'dies' every year, every Autumn term, being ritually executed for introductory teaching purposes, its life-cycle somewhat resembling the gods of the ancient Near East. . . . The demolition of functionalism is almost an initiation rite of passage into sociological adulthood or at least adolescence. If functionalism did not exist—or had not existed—it would have had to be invented." [3]

Martins goes on to remark on the paradox that none of the competing post-functionalist successor sociologies is innocent of what was almost invariably the major count in the indictment of functionalism: its alleged neglect of dynamics, process, history, and temporality, and its corollary overemphasis on statics, structure, synchrony, and timelessness. Indeed, Martins argues, the successor sociologies are more atemporal and ahistorical than functionalism itself ever was—let alone recent functionalism, which has made attempts in several directions to overcome the defects pointed to by its critics. He mentions Goffman's dramaturgical approach, neo–symbolic interactionism, Homan's neobehaviorism, ethnomethodology, Schutzian social phenomenology, cybernetics systems theory, and French structuralism as the leading cases in point. Most of these schools have two features in common: they exemplify what Martins calls a "cognitivist revolution" and a "microscopic reaction." Adapting his terminology somewhat, one might describe nearly all of them as "cognitivist microsociologies."

The major theorizing of these approaches revolves around such concepts as "receiving and storing information," "typification," "reciprocity of perspectives," "indexicality," "linguistic codes," "defining the situation," "labeling," and "presentation of self." All these concepts refer to processes of knowing rather than of desiring, willing, or feeling (or, in Goffman's case, to controlling or manipulating what others can know, "impression management"). Berger and Luckmann's influential book is subtitled "A Treatise in the Sociology of Knowledge." [4] Aaron Cicourel's recent work appears to have moved towards a redefinition of ethnomethodology as "cognitive sociology." [5] Back in 1963, in the companion article to "The Oversocialized Conception of Man," I noted and criticized the cognitivist bias of symbolic interactionism, referring especially to Goffman but also quoting a statement by the father of symbolic interactionism, George Herbert Mead, to the effect that the self is "essentially a cognitive rather than an emotional phenomenon." [6]

Most of the new approaches have also largely concerned themselves with microsociological problems, with "milieu" rather than with "structure." They have focused on the world of "everyday life" and face-to-face interaction; the research they have inspired has explored such circumscribed social situations as the jury room, the doctor's office, fleeting encounters on the street between strangers, and telephone conversations.

A fourfold table suggests itself (at least to anyone who was a graduate student in sociology at Columbia in the late 1940s and early 1950s). One can readily identify current theoretical approaches that are both cognitivist without being microsociological and the reverse. French structuralism, for example, perhaps the most recent entry in the theoretical sweepstakes, is determinedly cognitivist but by no means primarily microsociological. Homans's "exchange theory" or "social behaviorism," on the other hand, is microsociological but not exclusively cognitivist in view of its acceptance of a simple hedonistic psychology of motivation.

But what of Marxism, surely the most trendy tendency in the sociological academy today? Whatever else Marxism may be, it can hardly be described in any of its varieties as concerned primarily with the minutiae of face-to-face interaction—with how people break off telephone conversations or reserve seats in bars when they have to go to the bathroom. The conflict theorists of fifteen or twenty years ago, as I have noted, had affinities with Marxism, though usually "mediated" through Max Weber, and they were unmistakably macrosociological in their concerns. Marxism is obviously a macrosociology, or at least aspires to be. How does it fit into our designation of the postfunctional successor sociologies as cognitivist and microsociological?

I think we can find a kinship, if not identity, between the cognitivist character of so much contemporary theory and the prevalent tendency to favor *voluntaristic* versions of Marxism over the deterministic ones that were dominant in the past. One might almost describe the presently fashionable brands of Marxism as "consciousness raising." The young Marx rather than the old, the Hegelian Marx rather than the economist, the idealistic Marx (in both the popular and the philosophical meanings of idealism) as against the positivistic and evolutionist Marx are most prominent in contemporary academic Marxism. Perhaps the most resonant phrase among younger sociologists over the past decade has been "the social construction of reality." The phrase, of course, is of phenomenological rather than of Marxist origin. The two authors of the book with that name are, it so happens, moderately conservative politically, but as a slogan it crystallizes both the voluntarism and the world-changing aspirations of Western Marxism. The link between Marxism and the apparently quite distinct cognitivist microsociologies now becomes apparent: to Berger and Luckmann "the social construction of reality" refers to the cognitive meanings and definitions, or "typifications," used by social actors, and underlines their freedom to *create* such meanings. This freedom manifests itself most directly in the microsocial interactions of "everyday life." As Anthony Giddens has argued:

> The leading forms of social theory, it is asserted, have treated man as *homo sociologicus*, the creature rather than the creator of society, as a passive recipient of social influences rather than as an active, willing agent who injects meaning into an otherwise featureless moral universe. If the charge is in some degree warranted, the inferences which are drawn from it—that the most vital aspects of social existence are those relating to the triviata of "everyday life," whereby the individual shapes his phenomenal experience of social reality—easily rationalize a withdrawal from basic issues involved in the study of macro-structural social forms and social processes.*

But the emphasis on cognitivism and voluntarism in everyday life carries with it the suggestion that what is true of that restricted sphere can be extended to the macrosocial world of institutions, just as in the 1950s some positivist and strongly empiricist sociologists hoped that a grasp of the laws underlying behavior in small groups might eventually be extended to apply to—and "solve"—the problems of war and peace among nations. If we are free to "construct" or negotiate over the social reality we encounter most immediately, then we are also free to change the world, to conceive of and will into being a new world closer to our heart's desire, to make the leap from the Kingdom of Necessity to the Kingdom of Freedom at the level of "structure" and not merely "milieu." And the source of our freedom lies in our cognitive powers.

---

* Anthony Giddens, *The Class Structure of the Advanced Societies* (London: Hutchinson, 1973), p. 15. The opening sentence of the quotation clearly refers to what has been a widely accepted version of the critique of an oversocialized conception of man. The popularity of this version undoubtedly accounts for the continuing popularity of the phrase.

Now, at long last, I am ready to revisit the oversocialized conception of man. The 1961 paper was, as I have indicated, intended to complement at the social-psychological level the attacks on an overintegrated conception of society by the conflict theorists. Contemporary theory, as Martins and Giddens have stressed, tends to be ahistorical, cognitivist, and voluntaristic. None of these three attributes can be said to characterize Freud's thought: he saw biography, or life-*history*, as the key to understanding human beings; his theory is motivational rather than cognitivist; and he was scarcely a voluntarist, although the famous "psychic determinism" of his thought has sometimes been overemphasized. (He did, after all, believe that "where id was, there shall ego be" represented a realistic, attainable goal for men.)

In invoking Freud once more, I have no wish to sanctify every word of the Master as sacred dogma, in the manner of so many of his followers. What is crucial to Freud can, I think, be summed up in three propositions that I am prepared to put forward here as slogans: (1) *Life begins at zero.* (2) *In the beginning is the body.* (This is the only one of the three that was asserted in the 1961 article.) (3) *The child is father to the man.*

No doubt these are a bit vague and flashy, as slogans usually are. With regard to the first, I don't care to specify at what point after conception the "zero" at which life begins occurs, thus avoiding the possible ire of either, or both, the pro- and antiabortion movements. Nor, obviously, is the slogan meant to rule out the possibility of prenatal influences on personality, a subject long speculated about by both "old wives" and psychologists. The third proposition or slogan is obviously sexist and might be revised to read *The child is parent to the person*, which is nicely alliterative if lacking the authority of Wordsworth. In further deference to the feminist movement, let me stress that "in the beginning is the body" is *not* equivalent to the usual understanding of "anatomy is destiny."

Psychoanalysis is still alone among social psychologies in taking these three propositions with the absolutely literal seriousness that they require, however doctrinaire and reductive the details of psychoanalytic application of them may be. To the extent that this is so, Herminio Martins's paradox that the successor sociologies to func-

tionalism fail to remedy the alleged major defect of functionalism—
its neglect of time and change in society—is paralleled by the failure
of the successors to the now-discredited oversocialized conception of
man to remedy the defects of that sociological perspective: the neglect
of biography, of the motivational depths and complexities of the
human heart, and of the somatic, animal roots of our emotional
lives.

THREE

Human Nature and the Perspective of Sociology

WHAT ROLE does a conception of human nature play in sociological theory? What role should it play, if any? To what extent does a sociological perspective in general, and the perspective of structural-functional sociology in particular, encourage sociologists to construct an implicit or explicit idea of human nature that is dangerously selective and one-sided? Where and how does this construction need correction? (And I stress *correction* rather than total abandonment.)

By an idea of human nature I mean a set of assumptions about motives, mental and emotional capacities, and psychic mechanisms which are regarded as universal or panhuman, as descriptive of all men living in human societies, whether primitive or civilized, ancient or modern. In accordance with at least one general usage of the term among social scientists,[1] I understand "human nature" to include those universal human qualities resulting from the shaping of man's psyche by his contacts with others; by—in other words—the primary socialization that all men undergo, in the absence of which we would consider them human only in an anatomical and not in a psychological or behavioral sense. The term, therefore, need in no way carry the connotations of "biological determinism" that are habitually read into it by some sociologists.

Even if it is granted that we may speak of a universal human nature without thereby becoming biological determinists, to raise the issue of the idea of human nature implied by contemporary sociologists suggests immediately big and abstract questions about the relation between psychological theory and sociological theory, the dubiety of so-called "psychological explanations" of social facts, and the rival sins of excessive "psychologism" and "sociologism." I do not find it profitable to approach the subject on this level. Professor Talcott Parsons has contended that in my criticism of sociologists for holding an oversocialized view of man I was uttering a commonplace no one would care to deny if all I meant to argue was that sociological theory should be "articulated with" psychological theory.[2] But that was not my intention, which is why I chose to speak of the concept of "human nature" rather than of psychological theory, and of sociological questions rather than of sociological theory.

In preference to engaging in the kind of metatheoretical discussion that concerns itself with integrating (or "articulating") the conceptual language of different disciplines, I think it more fruitful to examine directly the role that psychological assumptions actually play in sociology. These assumptions may not be drawn from psychological theory at all: they may be based on common sense; they may, as I think is usually the case in the writings of the dogmatically antipsychological human ecologists, imply a model of rational man resembling that of classical economic theory; or they may rest on a kind of sociological psychology assuming the dominance of those psychological motives and mechanisms that most conveniently serve the purposes of sociological explanation. It is this latter form of "psychologism" with which I am chiefly concerned.

The point to be made is that we are no less guilty of psychologizing when we use a psychology that is tailor-made to accommodate our sociological purposes than when we short-circuit the task of explanation by invoking "instincts" or "innate needs" to account for observed conduct. Assumptions that all behavior reflects "internalized values," or manifests the desire to win approval from "significant others," or expresses a "self-concept" formed in interaction with one's "reference group," are no less psychological because they resemble empty boxes that can be filled with quite different sociological contents and thus allow for far wider variation in the actual human behavior we observe than older, often rigid and ethnocentric notions of instinct.

Several critics have pointed out that the concept of "values" is often put to the same fallacious explanatory uses as "instinct" in the familiar example of accounting for the prevalence of wars by referring to man's "aggressive instinct" and then citing the same prevalence as evidence for the existence of the instinct.[3] Thus regularities of conduct—for example, frequent ceremonies of obeisance to a political ruler—may be taken as evidence of a "value system" strongly emphasizing loyalty to the polity (to "system goals" in Parsons's language), while other regularities—for example, resistance to foreign influences—are then explained as consequences of the value system. The circularity is less crudely obvious than in the instinct example, but "values" no less than instincts are treated as the prime movers from which any and all behavior necessarily follows. If the initial characterization of a value system, inferred from verbally stated norms, sacred books, or official ideologies, turns out to be consistently violated or ignored in actual behavior, sociologists frequently explain such behavior by referring to "operative" values or "expectations" that are "nonverbal" as distinct from the verbalized official code.

It may be argued that "values" are not psychological entities in the sense that instincts, conditioned reflexes, or unconscious drives clearly are; that a value system is by definition a social fact, a "normative orientation" shared by the members of a collectivity rather than an instigator to action rooted in biology or in the idiosyncracies of individual biography. However, if a contemporary sociologist is asked to explain just how a value system effectively motivates or "pressures" individuals to act in a given way, he is at no loss for an answer and, unlike Durkheim, will not have to resort to misleading metaphors about "collective currents" that somehow insinuate themselves into individuals. He will immediately refer to the process of "internalizing social norms" or to the shaping of the individual self by the "expectations" of others. In short, he will invoke a psychology that his interpretation in terms of common values has presupposed all along.

Now it should be clear from my earlier remarks that it is not my purpose to brand contemporary sociologists as guilty of the Durkheimian sin of psychologism and to insist that they should forthwith expunge all psychological assumptions from their writings. I cannot conceive of any sociological theory or interpretation, as distinct from sheer description and reporting of data, that does not rely at least implicitly on such assumptions. And I do not think many sociologists wish to confine themselves to reporting that their research shows, say, a given index of socioeconomic status to be the closest correlate of marital stability or family size and to leave it at that without making any further effort "to locate," in William J. Goode's words, "the mechanisms and processes by which the economic creates its sociological effects." [4] Methodological purists, frequently drawn from the ranks of the so-called "hard" subdisciplines of demography and ecology, sometimes demand that sociologists so limit themselves,[5] but it is doubtful that many will follow this advice and give up the search for "intervening variables" of a psychological nature to complete their interpretations.

My objection to current sociological uses of psychology is essentially twofold: first, that sociologists resort too readily to explanations depending on psychological assumptions without realizing they are doing so because the psychology they employ is so adaptable to sociological aims. Second, that this psychology is an inadequate one which abstracts certain motives and mechanisms of obvious sociological relevance from the total context of human nature, with the result that its use blinds sociologists to alternative possibilities for interpretation of the particular data they are examining.

It is important to specify the kinds of demands a sociological perspective makes on a construct of human nature. There are, I think, three main criteria which a psychology must satisfy to be sociologically usable, that is, to play a part in answering the questions sociologists typically ask about human conduct.[6] Such a psychology must be able to account for *conformity* to social norms and for the sharing of goals and values; it must relate psychological processes going on within individuals directly to *action*, or overt conduct; and it must be *situationist* in the sense of emphasizing as influences on behavior the features of the immediate external situation of the individual.* Let us examine each of these in turn.

---

* I use the term "situationist" in much the same sense as Gardner Murphy in *Personality: A Biosocial Approach to Origins and Structure* (New York: Harper and Brothers, 1947), pp. 866–79. See also the contrast Philip Rieff draws between Freud's approach and that of social psychology as exemplified by John Dewey in *Freud: The Mind of the Moralist* (Garden City, N.Y.: Doubleday, Anchor Books, 1961), pp. 31–35.

The Criterion of Conformity

The sociologist's point of departure is an established social structure—a group, an organization, a society. Thus he tends to be initially concerned with those attributes of human nature which sustain *consensus, conformity,* and *role behavior.* He must assume his subjects to have undergone a process of socialization rendering them responsive to group demands. John Dollard in 1935 accurately stated the sociologist's angle of vision on the relation between individual and society when he suggested as a way of "posing the psychological problem in an altogether new form" that we ask as a primary question "how a new person is added to the group." [7] He called this the "group-plus-one hypothesis." While it has little ring of novelty today, it succinctly catches the essence of the sociologist's demands on a concept of human nature and the narrow angle of approach they represent.

A more recent writer, the psychologist Alfred Baldwin, observes of Talcott Parsons: "One consequence of his approach is that personality theory is not intrinsically very important to him. His real commitment is to the problem of stability and change in a complex social system, not to the conceptualization of individual personality. . . . From such a viewpoint the most relevant features of individual personality are those that affect his social functioning." [8]

Baldwin, somewhat confusingly, identifies Parsons's approach both with that of "the" sociologist in general and with "functional sociology." He is correct, I believe, in equating major attention to psychological processes sustaining social conformity with the sociological perspective per se.* But the tendency of structural-functional sociologists to stress the primacy in society of consensus on values over conflicts of interest and to define society itself as a "boundary-main-

---

* Leon Bramson relates the "anti-individualism" of sociology to its origins in conservative social thought. He observes of nineteenth-century conservatives: "Even individuality, they declared, is social, nurtured within the context of a group of like-minded individuals." *The Political Context of Sociology* (Princeton, N.J.: Princeton University Press, 1961), p. 14. Rieff, on the other hand, finds in Freud ideological overtones of the liberal's traditional defense of the individual against the claims of society in *Freud: The Mind of the Moralist,* pp. 275–80, 370–79.

taining system" with built-in processes preserving its equilibrium, inclines them to reliance on a generalized view of man as a thoroughly oversocialized, conformist creature. In this sense an over-socialized view of man complements the overintegrated conception of society in structural-functional theory that has been so roundly—and, I think, effectively—criticized for its relative neglect of change, group conflict, and the role of coercion as opposed to consent in human society.

But what about the psychological assumptions of the antifunctional theorists concerning social change and conflict? Frequently, they adopt an antipsychological stance and contrast "values" with "objective conditions" allegedly giving rise to conflicting interests, as if the notion of "interests" did not itself ultimately require elucidation in psychological terms. Or else their denial that society is a self-equilibrating system in the structural-functional sense merely leads them to stress socialization in subgroups within total societies that are at odds with one another, as opposed to being united by an overarching, shared value system. Thus a Marxist view which treats the individual as the creature of his economic class and reifies "history" as an all-determining entity in the same manner that Parsonians reify the "social system" ultimately presents a conception of human nature that is no less oversocialized than that of structural-functionalism. Nor can one find important differences between the social psychologies of Talcott Parsons and such antifunctionalist sociologists as Hans Gerth and C. Wright Mills.[9] At best, an emphasis on the realities of group conflict and changes in social structure makes antifunctionalist sociologists less disposed to appeal to the successful or unsuccessful socialization of individuals when trying to account for conformity or deviation, stability or change. They do not, however, customarily make use of a more adequate psychology.

Another group of nonfunctionalist sociologists, those whose approach is primarily historical rather than conceptual and analytic, tend to avoid psychologizing entirely by dealing with "values" and "interests" in the concrete forms they assume in particular historical settings. Thus I do not believe any generalized conception of human nature is presupposed by Max Weber's studies of the Protestant ethic or bureaucracy. The superior richness and sense of life communicated to us by historians and historicist sociologists no doubt result from their reliance on little more than a common-sense psychology.[10] But we cannot remain satisfied with this today; even the historians are demanding more. If in the end we can never achieve a satisfactory understanding or explanation of man in society without immersing ourselves in particulars of history and biography that escape the net of our general concepts, our task as sociologists, nevertheless, is to generalize, to compare and contrast, and we cannot with an easy conscience stop short at the borders of the psychological.

Yet granting that all sociology starts with the reality of the solidary group and its impact on the individual, it need not presuppose a human nature consisting solely of group-sustaining forces. The impact of the group on what Dollard calls "the organic motors of action" of the individual can be conceived of as creating counterforces to conformity within the individual which become permanently available for mobilization, under appropriate conditions, in deviant and rebellious conduct. Such an idea in no sense implies the existence of fully developed and autonomous biological impulses that are inherently antisocial, of a "natural man" capable of existing apart from a social and cultural environment. Dollard puts forward as one of his criteria for an adequate theory of personality that "the organic motors of action ascribed must be socially relevant. . . . The organic properties which we assume as the basis of the life of the individual in the group must be of such a kind that they will submit to social elaboration." [11] This criterion applies to the psychological roots of conformity and deviation alike; *both* conforming and antinomian impulses represent an integration of biological drives and social pressures. Both, therefore, are social in nature, although only conformist motivation is the product of the internalization of social norms or the molding of the self by the expectations of others.

In accusing sociologists of selectively emphasizing psychological mechanisms promoting conformity, am I charging them with ignoring the plain fact that deviation from norms is as universal as conformity? Certainly not— most sociologists are clearly no less aware of the *fact* of deviant behavior than structural-functional theorists are of the fact of historical change. The trouble in both cases is that their concepts, or rather the presuppositions buried in their concepts, make it difficult for them to account for these obvious and massive facts. Hence the intense concern among contemporary sociologists with developing an adequate theory of "deviant behavior," both a general theory and special theories of such particular forms of deviation as political radicalism, delinquency, mental illness, and the like. Not so very long ago, when American sociology was still primarily concerned with what used to be called "social pathology," the more sophisticated minds within the field regularly insisted that it was as important to explain the conformity of the majority as to explain crime, prostitution, divorce, and so forth. We need, they argued, a sociology of conformity as well as of disorganization or maladjustment, a sociology of the regular and the everyday that we take so much for granted as well as a sociology of the bizarre, the pathological, and the socially problematic. The former, in fact, should have clear priority over the latter in the light of our aspirations to become a comprehensive science.

The wheel seems to have swung full circle, and we have accounted so thoroughly for conformity, for the shaping of man by the norms and values of his society, that deviation—both in act and in impulse—has become theoretically problematic. And we are, therefore, immensely attracted to theories of deviant behavior defining it as an expression of the divergent values of particular deviant subcultures existing within our society. Such theories require no revision of our accepted view of human nature as "normatively oriented."

The notion that deviants are just subcultural conformists, however, has come under sharp attack from several acute observers and interpreters of juvenile delinquency.[12] Yet I think the theoretical problem is largely created by our tendency to give preferential status to motives and mechanisms sustaining conformity. By presupposing implicitly a conformist psychology, we fail to give equal weight to universal motives and mechanisms resisting conformity. We have available a set of intervening psychological variables adequate to account for conformity but none similarly helpful in explaining deviation and rebellion. Thus we are forced to use our ingenuity to devise ad hoc and special case theories of the latter. I happen to believe there are such variables available in psychoanalysis, a psychology possessing the dialectical subtlety we need in order to recognize that man is both a conforming and a rebellious animal, but it is not my purpose in this paper to argue on behalf of psychoanalysis per se.

The Criterion of Action

The sociologist is primarily interested in overt conduct because a group or social structure *is* no more than a set of observable interactions among individuals, "a system of action" in Parsonian terminology. Not that the sociologist may not agree with Durkheim that "society exists only in the minds of individuals." But the translation of inner, mental processes into open, observable actions constitutes his focus of attention. He need not be much interested in the mental processes for their own sake, that is, apart from their effect on the "social functioning" of the individual, as Baldwin puts it. In contemporary social theory the concept of "role" clearly refers to overt behavior, standing for the crucial behavioral link between mind and society, between the individual and the group. The notion of "functional imperatives" or "prerequisites" suggests that certain things must be *done*, certain actions performed, if a social structure is to continue in existence, no matter how variable the motivations underlying these actions may happen to be. *How* the relevant activities are carried on is the sociologist's problem, clearly involving attention to overt behavior, to what goes on outside the skin of individuals.

Although I believe psychoanalysis provides the most adequate view of man available to us, the sociologist's focus on action makes him justifiably indifferent to a great deal that is of enormous importance to the psychoanalytic diagnostician of individual personality. One of Freud's most heralded achievements, for example, was his grasp of the symptomatic significance of minor habits and gestures of everyday behavior previously dismissed as trivial or accidental. Yet slips of the tongue, tics, and postural habits, whatever their importance as clues to unconscious motivations, *are* trivial from the perspective of the sociologist, who here shares the common-sense view. Nor are such evanescent and rarely communicated mental phenomena as dreams and fantasies of any sociological significance as such, although the general psychoanalytic conception of human nature, attained in part by closely studying them, is of great significance to the sociologist. As has often been noted, the psychoanalyst seeks the private meaning of behavior that is often insignificant from the standpoint of chief concern to the sociologist.[13] And such behavior is likely to be freighted with private meanings precisely because it is not subject to normative regulation or to social control through the interplay of expectations in social interaction.

Robert S. Lynd's reference to the "too-inner drama of Freudianism" expresses the typical sociological perspective.[14] Insofar as psychoanalysts overgeneralize *their* special perspective on human nature—and they do, they do!—I am fully prepared someday to write a paper for presentation to a gathering of psychoanalysts entitled "The Overinternalized Conception of Man in Modern Psychoanalysis." The deepest insight of psychoanalysis is that wishes, feelings, fantasies, and reveries are as important as acts and external events in forming and expressing the character of men. But in some professional and intellectual circles in our largest cities, there has grown up an "analysand culture," shared by both doctors and patients, which treats dreams, expressive gestures, and the emotional tone of personal relations as token of a reality superior to that of our everyday actions in coping with one another and the world. Action becomes no more than "acting out"; we "relate" to people emotionally, instead of being inescapably involved with them in objective social roles; the goal of life becomes the quest for "insights" and living is viewed as mere raw material to be worked over on the couch; all life's crises lead back to the couch for resolution, and often enough the cloistered drama in the analyst's office robs the real-life drama of its force and tragedy.* This error is the reverse of the sociologist's; where the latter is prone to define man as an oversocialized role player, the psychoanalyst too readily ignores the requirements of the objective social world.

The Criterion of Situationism

The need of sociologists for a situationist psychology follows from their stress on action as opposed to the inner life. Social structures

---

* As Erik H. Erikson observes of psychoanalysts: "When a devotional denial of the face, and a systematic mistrust of all surface are used as tools in a man's work-life, they can lead to an almost obsessional preoccupation with 'the unconscious,' a dogmatic emphasis on inner processes as the only true essence of things human, and an overestimation of verbal meanings in human life." *Young Man Luther* (New York: W. W. Norton, 1958), p. 152.

link individuals together in chains of role relationships, the action of one eliciting a response from another which changes the situation for the first actor, and so on. Inevitably, the sociologist's concentration on such recurring webs of interaction leads him to minimize the roots of behavior in individual biography. At most he need assume only a past experience sufficient to socialize the individual to the extent of endowing him with a general desire for the approval of others or with a self-image to protect and enhance, sensitizing him to the particular expectations of others in different group situations. Equipped with these broad dispositions, the individual is ready to become a cooperative role-player, subtly adjusting his conduct to the multiple demands directed at him in the variety of groups in which he participates. He does not even need the ballast of a built-in superego composed of internalized norms.

Several symbolic interactionist writers have pointed out that "role-playing" in the Meadian sense is a quite different matter from role-playing in the Linton-Parsons sense of the patterning of individual conduct according to the fixed prescriptions of preexisting roles.[15] To symbolic interactionists, social interaction is essentially spontaneous and creative processes rather than conformity to established norms and role expectations—"role-making" rather than "role-taking." Such a view avoids the conformist implications of both the Linton-Parsons version of role-playing and the internalization concept while at the same time satisfying the three criteria for a sociologically adequate psychology I have described. It accounts for the process by which the individual comes to share the normative outlook of others, it is attentive to action rather than to solipsistic inner processes, and it is thoroughly situationist in emphasis. A major theme of symbolic interactionist theory (and a realized achievement in the best research of the school) is an insistence on the sociologist's obligation to pay extremely close attention to what actually goes on in interaction. The symbolic interactionists subject interaction to a "close" reading analogous to the approach to poetry and fiction of the "textual" critics of literature.

Yet notwithstanding these very considerable virtues, there remains a sense in which the symbolic interactionists also hold an over-socialized conception of human nature. For they necessarily see all conduct as controlled by the self and as an expression of the self. And the self is, of course, ultimately a social product containing the built-in reflection of common experience and consensus. Mead taught us that the self is an object of which we become cognitively aware by means of the "taking-the-role-of-the-other" process implicit in language. But to Mead "self-consciousness rather than affective experience with its motor accompaniments, provides the core and primary structure of the self, which is thus essentially a cognitive rather than an emotional phenomenon." [16] The purely cognitive nature of the Meadian self, its lack of any motivational energies of its own, is frequently overlooked by symbolic interactionists. Nor are they correct in defining the Meadian "I" as a dynamic principle of individuality to be set against the conformist "me": the "I" and the "me" are merely the Kantian "subject" and "object" of knowledge viewed in the context of active experience rather than as static "forms" of thought, the "me" serving as object rather than a phenomenon of the external world.

True, an affective aspect is easily added to Mead's cognitive self when it is observed that the self is an object invested with supreme emotional significance by the individual. Moreover, the content of self-feeling clearly results from "the reflected appraisals of others" (Sullivan). The self, emerging in the individual's experience with the secure acquisition of language in early childhood, "traps," as it were, emotional energies and affects which were originally in a literal sense "self-less." Harry Stack Sullivan relates Meadian self-cognition to emerging motivational "self-dynamisms," which is why he so often turns out to be the sociologists' favorite psychiatrist. But by treating all conduct as self-referential, the symbolic interactionists ignore the existence of motivations antedating the birth of the self in the individual's life-history, motivations which persist "behind" it or "under" it as constituents of his inner life.

Herbert Blumer is, nevertheless, correct in criticizing efforts to explain social interaction by immediately invoking deep-lying "motives" or "attitudes" within the individual when no adequate description has been presented of the unfolding process of interaction. [17] Yet for a complete theory of human nature, a cross-sectional, situational view of interaction, important though it is, remains insufficient. We need also a longitudinal, genetic, and biographical perspective to account for motivational constants which cannot be understood by even the most subtle and faithful scrutiny of the interaction situation alone.

In emphasizing that the self reflects diverse reference groups and "situated roles," [18] the symbolic interactionists, to be sure, endow the individual with inner resources to resist the demands of any particular group or role. In fact, their best work often consists precisely of richly detailed accounts of the ways men use these resources to evade and subvert institutional controls. Symbolic interactionists are not guilty, therefore, of suggesting that men are conformist automatons—the implication one finds so often in structural-functional writers with their overriding interest in stability and "tension management." Nevertheless, symbolic interactionists still see resistance to social demands and expectations as essentially a by-product, though an inevitable one, of socialization. The essence of man is "the presentation of self in everyday life," even though it is recognized that the social world is discontinuous and permits individuality and some resistance to social control to flourish in the interstices between roles and institutions.* Instead of successful "tension management" imposed by the imperatives of the social system, "impression management" under the dominance of the self, a theatrical impresario cannily sizing up its audience, becomes the compelling social reality. Both views, though in different ways, present an oversocialized conception of man.

In short, if stress on the internalization of social norms makes man appear to be all "superego," symbolic interactionism gives us a subtle and rich psychology of the "ego." But we need also a conceptual equivalent of the "id," one that locates the source of human energies in the body and in the universal experiences of infancy while avoid-

---

* Reviewing a book of Erving Goffman's, William Caudill asks: "Does the self about which Goffman speaks have an inner part or is it solely defined by patterns of social control?" He proceeds to indicate his dissatisfaction with Goffman's view on the grounds that "if life entails being against something, if it is seen as a game in which one is always busy presenting a front, then there is little time to integrate the part of the self that faces outward with that which faces inward, or even to conceive of a reconciliation between these two." Review, *American Journal of Sociology* 68 (November 1962), 366–69.

ing the reductionist and biologically mythical modes of explanation on which psychoanalysis has too often relied.

The Limits of Scientific Abstraction

Since I have argued that sociologists have a legitimate need for a psychology meeting the three criteria of being able to account for conformity, stressing action over purely intrapsychic experience, and attributing causal significance to the actor's immediate external situation, why should there be grounds for complaint in the fact that they have borrowed psychological assumptions from various sources which satisfy these criteria? Why, indeed, shouldn't sociologists even postulate an oversocialized model of man as a heuristic principle serving analogous purposes to the model of rational man in economic theory? Perhaps they merely need to be reminded and cautioned now and then that their model is an abstraction failing to describe real men in their full-bodied actuality, and my critical remarks perhaps amount to no more than such an admonition.

This is more or less the view taken by Talcott Parsons in his rejoinder to my original article. To respond to it adequately would require critical dissection of his entire conception of scientific theory in general and its relevance and application to sociology in particular. At the risk of appearing arbitrary and dogmatic, I shall content myself here with asserting that I reject Parsons's view that sociological theory should strive to imitate the logical structure and degree of abstraction of theoretical physics, most closely matched in the social sciences by neoclassical economic theory. This rejection also implies a rejection of Parsons's definition of sociology as a special discipline confined to the study of "the place of institutionalized values and the integrative operation of normative systems through social control." [19]

I do not believe these are productive paths for sociology to follow, and it does not seem to me that they were the paths followed by most of the past thinkers we all acknowledge as outstanding sociological theorists—Marx, Tocqueville, Weber, Cooley, Mead, Simmel, Veblen, or Mannheim. These men, unlike Parsons, did not deliberately set out to create a science of sociology patterned on the physical sciences as interpreted to them by the philosophers and logicians of scientific method. If they succeeded in creating a new discipline, they did so in the same way the British acquired their empire—in a fit of absentmindedness. Or, in other words, as a by-product of seeking answers to the substantive questions and problems preoccupying them. If taking the great theorists of the recent past as my guide to what sociological theory ought to be makes me a "historical empiricist," as Parsons charges, I plead guilty, yet the role of what Weber called the "historical individual" is precisely what is at issue between the rival views of the nature of sociological theory.

Weber's concept of *Wertbeziehung*, or value-relevance, implies recognition of the fact that our major interest in the subject matter of sociology is not abstract and quantitative to the degree that characterizes our interest in the physical world or even in economic phenomena. It is often overlooked that in seeing the objects of the social sciences as "constituted for us by our values," Weber did not have in mind merely the general properties or attributes of human actions to which we attach significance in the light of a "value system" that is universalistic in its implications. He also regarded particular entities—*this* man, *this* institution, *this* nation—as objects constituted for us by our acts of valuing, in exactly the same sense that the deification of secular authorities may be considered "relevant" to the values of transcendental religion, or the facts of economic exploitation of the values of humanitarian socialism. In other words, "historical individuals" *are themselves values* and in part determine what constitutes relevant or significant knowledge in the social sciences, which differ in this respect from the generalizing natural sciences. In Weber's own words: "The 'points of view' which are oriented toward 'values,' from which we consider cultural objects and from which they become 'objects' of historical research, change. Because, and as long as they do, new facts will always be becoming historically 'important.' . . . This way of being conditioned by 'subjective values' is, however, entirely alien in any case to those natural sciences which take mechanics as a model, and it constitutes, indeed, the distinctive contrast between the historical and the natural sciences. . . . The concept of the 'culture' of a particular people and age, the concept of 'Christianity,' of 'Faust,' and also—there is a tendency to overlook this—the concept of 'Germany,' etc., are individualized value-concepts formed as the objects of *historical* research, i.e., by relation with value-ideas." [20]

Such a view need not, however, reduce the sociologist to a historical empiricist. Weber's own immense work suggests the contrary. The sociologist, unlike the monographic historian, is committed to the systematic comparative study of historical social structures. His goal, however, is not merely to arrive at overarching general laws or conceptual schemes, but rather to elucidate the similarities *and* the differences between social structures by examining them comparatively. Nor does he eschew entirely transhistorical problems and questions. The very question I have been discussing, the nature of human nature, is obviously a transhistorical issue. Sociology must be defined by the questions it asks, both those that are transhistorical and those that our contemporary history "places on the agenda" [21] for us. A subtle interplay between transhistorical problems and their embodiment in the structure of the historical individuals we directly confront is the hallmark of the work of the great theorists of the recent past. The requirements of this interplay make the abstract, logically formal models we find in physics of only secondary relevance to our particular enterprise. It therefore seems to me a grave error if sociologists create a model of human nature—even if they do so with heuristic intent—that is, in effect, a caricature.

FOUR

The Idea of "Community": A Critique

THE "LOSS OF COMMUNITY" in modern society has become a major theme in contemporary social criticism. One could even say that the discipline of sociology begins with a concern over the decline of such traditional forms of association as small towns, neighborhoods, religious congregations, and social classes in the wake of that great wave of "creative destruction" (Schumpeter) we call the Industrial Revolution. Books with titles such as *The Quest for Community* or *The Eclipse of Community* have a contemporary resonance extending far beyond the circle of social scientists or even the educated public. [1] Used as a counterconcept to "mass society," "anomie," "rootlessness," and similar terms, "community" replaces more politically focused labels of the past. Emphasis on the erosion of traditional ties that once bound men together becomes central to most sociological thinking that goes beyond the technicism of fact-finding and/or abstract theory-building.

The intellectual prestige of sociology since World War II is largely the result of a decline in political faith among Western intellectuals. One of the most influential sociological interpretations of extremist political movements defines them as efforts to create a new "community of ideology" to supplant traditional group allegiances that have been destroyed by rapid social change. Students of totalitarianism have shown how the psychic dependence of militant supporters on the movement frees its leaders from bondage to the manifest ideology that is the movement's ostensible raison d'être. Totalitarian leaders possess, therefore, a flexibility of political maneuver that is unavailable to power-seeking groups demanding less than total commitment from their supporters. The paradox of totalitarian movements is that they are able to combine a fanatical following of "true believers" with a political strategy that is almost entirely opportunistic and in no way constrained by an official creed. Totalitarian movements are "orthodoxies without doctrines," as Raymond Aron once said, because their unity is founded on the community of ideology they create rather than on any definitive political goals affirmed by their ideology.

European writers who have described modern industrial society as a "mass society" in which men are lost and rootless have seen it as inherently prone to produce destructive, ideologically fanaticized mass movements. This alleged political consequence of mass society, however, has never had much plausibility when applied to America. Impressed by the stability of the American political order, an influential group of political sociologists in this country has denied that the United States is a mass society and characterized it instead as "pluralist." But these writers slur over the fact that America remains the classic land of "mass culture," impersonal large-scale bureaucracy, and population mobility. As Hannah Arendt remarks, the American body politic "has at least endured to the present day, in spite of the fact that the specifically modern character of the modern world has nowhere else produced such extreme expressions in all nonpolitical spheres of life as it has in the United States." [2]

To recognize the search for community as a major force in American life need not commit us to accepting apocalyptic theories of mass society that see totalitarianism as the inevitable outcome. Tendencies that have elsewhere found expression in organized mass movements may be contained by the American political system; but they exist nonetheless, manifesting themselves in nonpolitical forms. Commitment to an "ideology of community," rather than the attempt to create a "community of ideology," has been a characteristic American response to mass society, although it is, of course, by no means peculiarly American. Even the recent political activism of young people has combined political goals like civil rights and world peace with heavy rhetorical emphasis on such nonpolitical concerns as the

overcoming of alienation, sexual freedom, and the need for generational solidarity.

Since awareness of loss of community in modern society is over a
century old, we need to recognize that responses to this awareness
have become part of the same social reality we seek to understand.
The increasing popularity of sociological accounts of our plight has
created an ideology of community that shapes our social relations, or
at least our consciousness of them, in much the same way that popular Freudianism shapes our psychological self-awareness.

We need go back only as far as the 1930s to find a change in the
conditions and institutions alleged to be responsible for our "lack of
community." In that decade leading social critics complained of the
competitiveness of men under capitalism, their ruthless pursuit of
wealth and success, and their preference for "making good" over
"being good," to use a phrase of Margaret Mead's. The goal of success was held to be demoralizing when all are urged to pursue it
under circumstances where opportunities are highly unequal. These
indictments of American society were clearly influenced by socialism
in its various forms and by the New Deal. Changes in the structure of
the economy achieved by political means were looked to for the creation of a community that would substitute fraternal cooperation for
divisive competition. With varying emphases, these themes are central to the writing of the 1930s of such social scientists as Margaret
Mead, the Lynds, Ruth Benedict, Abram Kardiner, Robert K. Merton, Lawrence Frank, and others.

Today, at least on the surface, the complaints seem to be just the
opposite. There is too much "community," not enough individualism, too much conformity to others and sensitivity to their feelings
rather than indifference; too great a readiness to participate in collective tasks as opposed to sturdy independence. David Riesman has
argued that middle-class Americans today are more like the Zuni Indians, described and idealized by Ruth Benedict in her *Patterns of
Culture,* than like the status-proud Kwakiutl, whom she, like Thorstein Veblen before her, saw as caricaturing American competitive
values. Business organizations are criticized—by William H. Whyte,
for example—not for ruthless exploitation, but for being big happy

families eager to transform their employees into self-satisfied "organization men." If the critics of the 1930s were futuristic in outlook, hopeful for a new social order, the critics of the 1950s were nostalgic, looking back to a more individualistic past.

The contrast between these two styles of criticism is bewildering. Is it just that the fashionable values of intellectuals have changed? Or have Americans taken to heart the earlier criticisms and overdone it in trying to rectify them? Daniel Bell has argued for the latter theory:

The early theorists of mass society condemned it because in the vast metropolitan honeycombs people were isolated, transient, anonymous to each other. Americans, sensitive as they are to the criticisms of others, took charge to heart and, in building the postwar suburbs, sought to create fraternity, communality, togetherness, only to find themselves accused of conformity.[3]

Although Bell is correct in maintaining that the American middle class has responded anxiously to its critics, he too readily dismisses the critics' complaints as stemming merely from the ideological bias of "European sociology." The receptivity of the audience indicates that an exposed nerve has been touched. Very often the critics combine the older themes attributing the absence of community to competitive and hostile men with the new-style complaints about the smothering conformism of life in suburbia in apparently contradictory ways. However, as Bell acknowledges, the various targets of criticism are dialectically related. The ethic of conformism, the search for suburban oases, and the loyalties of organization men are responses to the conditions described by the earlier critics: urban anonymity, social and geographical mobility, and the values of competitive individualism, which have long been characteristic of America and have by no means disappeared.

A number of different emphases in recent social criticism center around the themes of loss of community and conformity.

Writers who are not professional social scientists frequently confine themselves, in the name of individualism, to a straightforward attack on all contemporary forms of group life, from suburban togetherness to the "engineered consent" of the mass media and the imposed uniformity of authoritarian political movements. Present-day targets are simply latter-day versions of Babbit and Main Street, and the critics remain in the tradition of the revolt against village, church, and provincial bourgeoisie that initiated a new trend in American writing some decades ago. This critical perspective is not based on an ideology of community. It merely asserts with refreshing directness the need for protecting individuality from any social pressures. It is often essentially aesthetic in outlook, defending the antinomianism of the creative artist as an ultimate value. Sometimes it becomes nostalgic in tone, idealizing the smalltown and nineteenth-century past, overlooking the tyrannies of Main Street, and picturing our grandfathers as firm, principled "characters" in contrast to the flabby herdmen of today. It then contributes to an indigenous American nostalgia which, in the absence of any systematic conservative ideology, is exploited by promoters of right-wing causes.

This brand of social criticism, while blunt, often zestful in its assaults on institutions and fashions, and always needed, has limitations from the point of view of both the professional sociologist and the social critic who has learned from the sociologists. For the sociologist, the relation between individual and society is always a crucial problem. Sociology itself began with the sense of a disturbance in the relation between individuals and society created by the modern political and technological revolutions. The sociologist's very definition of man asserts that he is profoundly shaped by the group, by the dominant values of society; in consequence the sociological critic cannot, without violating his professional conscience, confine himself to affirming the values of individualism and personal autonomy while failing to consider the social context in which these values might be realized. To see the community merely as something to be resisted, as the source of false identities which stifle an essentially private self, is to deny that men live in communities as naturally as fish in water and that their private selves are necessarily closely intertwined with selves shaped by public pressures.

Accordingly, critics influenced by sociology locate the source of individual malaise in the fragmentation and disorder of modern society rather than in society's demands for conformity as such. At its most simplistic, such as an approach stands in direct opposition to the moral and aesthetic defense of the individual against the claims of so-

ciety, to which I have just referred.[4] Though the more perceptive
sociological critics, such as David Riesman, Erich Fromm, and
W. H. Whyte, have assigned part of the blame for contemporary
conformism to the popularity of vulgarized versions of social science,
these writers themselves are sociologically sophisticated and are not
content merely to reassert the values of individualism in face of the
imperatives of modern social organization. By singling out "status-
seeking" as a major target of criticism, they often manage to combine
the anticapitalist attack on competitiveness of the 1930s, the moral-
aesthetic defense of individuality against pressures toward conformity,
and the more recent indictments of suburban and organizational
groupism. The compulsive quest for status weakens community by
pitting people against one another as competitors while at the same
time encouraging frantic conformity to the shifting group fashions
that set the terms on which status is granted. Unlike the material acquisitiveness condemned by the critics of the thirties, competition for
status both unites and divides people, creating what Riesman (bor-
rowing a term from William Graham Sumner) has labeled "antago-
nistic cooperation." Hence the prevalence of judgments such as the
following:

In the desert of the suburb, community life has lost whatever vestiges of
meaning it ever had for Americans: if any community life exists at all, it
exists frantically at the synthetic level of the club and church; it has a tinny
quality betraying a lack of conviction on the part of all concerned. Nowhere
is there more consciousness of the need for community; nowhere does this
consciousness of need reveal more clearly its hopelessness.[5]

The diagnosis of our discontents put forward by these critics is
often a convincing and powerful one. Their sociological realism saves
them from the kind of purely romantic protests against modern life
that refuse to recognize social necessities as distinct from the demands of the individual psyche. But because they no longer believe
in the political solutions favored by their predecessors of the thirties,
the specificity of their diagnosis stands in marked contrast to the extreme vagueness of their prescribed remedy.

In general terms, the restoration of a "true" or "organic" community is seen as the ultimate remedy. The goal is a community which

will bind men together in intimate, fraternal relations and at the same time allow individuality to flourish. "It almost seems as if community in the anthropological sense is necessary before human maturity or individuation can be achieved, while this same maturity is, in turn, a prerequisite for community," as Maurice Stein says.[6] The call for the recreation of community maintains a link between contemporary sociology and the conservative critique of modernity first formulated in the aftermath of the French Revolution.[7] For, "if there is one thing certain about the 'organic community,' it is that it has always gone," as Raymond Williams remarks.[8] Some convince themselves, like George Orwell, that it was there in their childhoods, other locate its last incarnation in the vanished rural village or small town, in nineteenth-century bourgeois society, in the medieval commune, or in the polis of the ancient world. Others, like Stein, go all the way back to primitive societies to discover models of community "in the anthropological sense."

These nostalgic excursions into history end in remarkably similar exhortations. Bewailing the disappearance of organic community, the literary critic F. R. Leavis, writing in 1932, concludes: "We must beware of simple solutions . . . there can be no mere going back . . . the memory of the old order must be the chief incitement towards a new." [9] Nearly thirty years later, Maurice Stein, a sociologist, strikes the identical note: "There is little to be gained by sentimentalizing about primitive life or advocating a return to it in any form. We are far too deeply committed to urban-industrial civilization even to think of abandoning it now." [10] The problem is seen as that of realizing community under the new conditions of urban-industrial mass civilization.

The trouble, however, is that this insistence on community as a value apart from its concrete manifestations produces precisely the aborted forms of striving for group adjustment that the social critics themselves condemn. The anxious audience reads the critics and, made self-conscious about community, strives to sink roots in the suburbs, to define occupational groups as devoted brotherhoods, and to stress the importance of belongingness in child-rearing. Made aware of the loss of community, the audience tries to create out of whole cloth a social ethic and a true community. The effort is analogous to that of those Americans who have made popular psychiatry the basis of a personal ethic, becoming self-conscious, even hypochondriacal, about their "mental health," which comes to be seen as the goal of life instead of as the by-product of a life with meaningful goals. The error lies in conceiving of community as a kind of end in itself, apart from the particular activities and functions that actually bind people together, and apart from those values that constitute a truly shared vision of life. As Ortega once pointed out, "People do not live together merely to be together. They live together to do something together."

Thus the social critics who deplore status-seeking and the mechanical kind of community of our Park Forests paradoxically perpetuate the conditions they complain of when they reassert the values of true community and stable identity. They end up providing their audience with a new and updated ideology of community, reminding one of books on child-rearing that tell parents not to rely on books on child-rearing but to be "spontaneous." The very willingness to follow the prescribed antidote is a symptom of the disease, and indeed aggravates it. Even status-seeking, the target of attack most closely linking the older criticism of ruthless individualism to the newer charges of overconformity, receives a kind of sociological warrant (as in Vance Packard's book, *The Status Seekers*, which has been aptly described as a pornography of social class in America). For status requires validation by others and implies shared values in a way that money or power as goals do not. But the emphasis is on the sharing of values rather than on their content.

The ideology of community thus provides the basis for a popular social criticism that influences its audience in ways that provide new material for the critics to assault. Just as psychoanalytic therapy, which originally presupposed a stable social world with relatively fixed moral standards incorporated into the patient's superego, is now itself often expected to provide the values and life-goals the individual feels he lacks, so sociology is looked to in the hope that it will itself remedy the loss of community. The result is that clichés about group "integration," "role-playing," "identity," "belongingness," "participation," and "we-feelings" fill the vacuum.

Consequently, instead of a genuine conformity based on shared values, we find conformism—the belief, rarely articulated as such, that one should act, think, and feel as others do for the sake of doing so. Instead of a status system in which individuals are rated according to stable dominant values, we find status-seeking, in which status itself becomes a value no matter what the terms on which it is awarded. Instead of loyalty to families, churches, local communities, occupational associations, and other established groups with multiple purposes and often deep roots in the past, loyalty attaches itself to functional organizations, thus making a specialized, collective instrumentality an end in itself. Erich Kahler's distinction between a community and a collective is relevant here: "Collectives develop through the joining of pre-established individuals for some specific purpose. Collectives are established by common ends, communities derive from common origins." [11] To Max Weber, the modern mood of "disenchantment of the world" resulted from the spread of bureaucracy, the proliferation of functional organizations organized to pursue limited goals and lacking the aura of sacredness traditionally associated with family, church, and nation. But Weber did not anticipate the "organization man" who strives to invest bureaucracy with intrinsic value and give it the loyalty usually given to these older forms of association.

The achievement of community, like the achievement of mental health (or, for that matter, of happiness, as John Stuart Mill argued a century ago), cannot come from pursuing it directly but only as a byproduct of the shared pursuit of more tangible goals and activities. Community may result from the concrete forms of political, economic, familial, and cultural association among men, but it cannot be willed into existence by exhorting people to immerse themselves in group activity and to find greater significance in their social identities. The inevitable failure of the ideology of community to deliver the elusive good it promises then gives rise to a social criticism that at its worst simply becomes a counter-ideology making a shibboleth of "nonconformity" or exploiting a romanticized version of an allegedly more individualistic American past.

The failures and inconsistencies of recent social criticism suggest that there are limits to what we are entitled to expect from social science in general, and sociology in particular, as a source of remedies for our deeper discontents. Sociology can analyze the events and processes that have destroyed older values and forms of community; it cannot create new ones. Only moral, religious, and political inspiration can do that.

FIVE
Identity: Problem and Catchword

LIONEL TRILLING'S STORY "Of This Time, Of That Place" begins with a young English professor assigning to his freshman class as their first theme an essay on "Who I am and why I came to Dwight College." The first of the student papers the professor examines is that of a tall, gawky, badly dressed but passionately if confusedly eloquent boy who has previously caught his attention. It begins: "I think, therefore I am, but who am I? Tertan I am, but what is Tertan? Of this time, of that place, of some parentage, what does it matter?" After puzzling a few minutes over the strange mixture of fractured syntax and verbal richness in Tertan's essay, Professor Howe picks up a second student paper and proceeds to read: "I am Arthur J. Casebeer, Jr. My father is Arthur J. Casebeer and my grandfather was Arthur J. Casebeer before him. My mother is Nina Wimble Casebeer. Both of them are college graduates and my father is in insurance. I was born in St. Louis eighteen years ago and we still make our residence there."

Trilling's story was published in 1943 before the terms "identity" and "identity crisis" had joined "neurosis," "alienation," and "mass society" as semantic beacons of our time, verbal emblems expressing our discontent with modern life and modern society. Erik H. Erikson, the creator of "identity" as a distinctive psychoanalytic and so-cial-psychological concept, has brought together in revised and re-worked form all of his major papers on the subject.[1] Commenting on the promiscuous popularity the concept has achieved, he observes that adolescents these days know that "they are supposed to have" an identity crisis and compares the "strenuous overtness" of their search for identity with the earlier emergence into general awareness of sexual wishes that formerly remained unconscious and gave rise to hysterical symptoms.[2] Almost unavoidably, one today sees Trilling's two student protagonists as having arrived, tentatively at least, at contrasting solutions to the problem of identity. Tertan rejects the socially established coordinates of time and place and even of family, and seeks a deeper, more individual, and at the same time less history-bound definition of himself. Casebeer, while "less interesting" than Tertan, "at least knows who he is," reflects Trilling's professor. The contemporary reader is likely to see Tertan as a seeker after "authentic selfhood," a quest that for him, as Trilling brilliantly shows, verges on the psychotic; Casebeer, on the other hand, is obviously a conformist, a square, a budding "organization man," who buries his true self by identifying himself totally with his social roles as scion of the Casebeer family, son of college graduates and a potential graduate himself, heir of a respected businessman, urban Midwesterner.

Such a facile response to the contrast between the two students is little more than an ideological reflex, doing scant justice to the subtlety and moral ambiguity of Trilling's exploration of Tertan's fate. I call it "ideological," and use the word pejoratively, because "identity crisis," "authentic selfhood," and "conformism" belong to a whole language of social criticism that has recently become widely diffused in our society, reaching well beyond academic, literary, and psychoanalytic circles. "Alienation," "anomie," "mass society," "the loss of community," "the overdeveloped society," "organization man," "status-seeking," "soulless bureaucracy" are other terms in this language. I am not objecting to these terms as such—we owe most of them to our greatest thinkers in the social sciences, and they have become popular precisely because they truly convey something of the quality of life in modern society and express live historical emotions. What E. V. Walter has said of the idea of mass society applies more broadly to our language of fundamental social criticism as a whole:

It cultivates the muddle ground between fact and supposition that is frequently occupied by metaphysic and myth. . . . It is a sensitive indicator of changes dimly perceived, and perhaps it is a protoscientific formulation of truth, bringing to consciousness features of reality not yet substantial enough to be grasped by the methods of science.[3]

But this language is able, because of the evocative power it possesses, to elicit indiscriminate negative responses to modern life. Nowadays its separate words frequently blur into a general hum of lamenta-
tion about the fate of man in modern society, in which each
individual word loses its conceptual clarity in contributing to an
overall tonal effect. Any stick to beat a dog with. That each concept
has a rich and varied intellectual and ideological pedigree is forgotten. That the accusations leveled at modern society are inconsistent
with each other is overlooked. Thus our society is charged with destroying the primordial bonds of community among men, while at
the same time it is pilloried for promoting conformity and "togetherness"; man is said to be alienated, rootless, and drifting in contemporary America; but simultaneously he is too tightly controlled by giant
bureaucracies and manipulated by the mass media. Our consump-
tion-centered economy encourages Americans to retreat into a
"privatized" life of affluence in which they are apathetic about public
affairs, yet modern society is also seen as the seedbed of fanatical
mass movements whose followers willingly submerge their private
lives in dedication to a collective goal.

Now all of these charges may be true, and their inconsistency apparent rather than real. Different charges may describe the behavior
and attitudes of different segments of the population, or there may be
a temporal dialectic in which a particular response when played out
is succeeded by an alternative reaction to basically unchanged conditions. But popular social criticism, indiscriminately brandishing as
weapons such terms as "alienation" or "materialism," rarely dispels
the impression of inconsistency by systematically analyzing these possible connections between the various counts of the indictment
drawn up against American society. A word like "alienation," with its
peculiarly rich sociological and philosophical heritage, has become
virtually shapeless in its current intellectual usage. And now the same
fate threatens "identity crisis," initially defined and analyzed so carefully and acutely by Erikson.

I do not think the solution is to abandon words that have become
blurred as a result of wide and rapid circulation. The history of the
social sciences sufficiently attests to the disastrous consequences of efforts to create a hygienic "scientific" vocabulary free of all ideological

overtones. And anyway, communication between social scientists and a larger public is so rapid and extensive today that even the most arid neologisms quickly reach a wide audience. As Erikson notes, the classic psychoanalytic terms are themselves subject to changing historical connotations "which range from what Freud called the 'age-old ideologies of the Super-Ego' to the influence of contemporary ideologies." [4] Far from advocating the avoidance of "richly suggestive terms," he suggests that "an awareness of the changing connotation of its most important terms is one of the requirements of a 'self-analytic' psychosocial orientation." [5]

What we must try to do is to restore something of the analytical precision of the original terms, while simultaneously taking into account the resonance they have acquired, as their creators obviously could not. By analyzing the very cheapening process to which the language has been subject as an intellectual and social phenomenon in its own right, we may be able to arrest it and thereby advance the debate over the situation of man in our time.

Why do people suffer from identity crisis or identity confusion in modern industrial society? One common answer is that society fails to provide them with stable roles in which they can take pride and invest a large portion of their emotional energy and self-respect. Work roles are increasingly perceived as routines that fail to relate the worker to the larger community in any significant way. The emphasis placed by our advanced, "tertiary-stage" industrial economy on the consumption of trivia and on time-killing leisure pursuits makes many occupational activities seem intrinsically debasing—one thinks of advertising executives, cocktail waitresses, or change-makers in Nevada gambling casinos. The difficulty of achieving stable identity is increased by the sharp discontinuities in the life-cycles of Americans that result from rapid social change, from mobility, and from an imposed age-graded schedule of involvement in successive specialized and segregated institutional milieus—school, college, military service, work. Moreover, exposure to the mass media means exposure to constantly shifting fashions in life-styles. Even traditional sexual and familial roles become ambiguous, while depressions, wars, and cold wars destroy continuity of understanding between generations.

The diagnosis is familiar. In effect, it equates identity with social identity and delineates the features of modern industrial society that prevent the establishment of firm, preferably life-long, social identities. Social identity is the social-psychological counterpart of social role—the role viewed from the perspective of its incumbent rather than in relation to the larger system of roles to which it belongs. The failure of society to provide the individual with "secure anchorage," as it is often put, in a social role is seen as the cause of the anxieties and identity crises from which we suffer. True, it is a sociological commonplace that men play many social roles in modern society. But they are likely to lack firm attachment to any one of them, nor do they possess a secure total status in society cutting across their various "situated" [6] or segmental roles, such as that of "aristocrat" or "peasant" in the more rigidly stratified society of the past. Thus some social analysts have treated the decline of hereditary social classes and the increase in mobility aspirations as the major cause of the individual's uncertain identity in modern society. [7] Earlier writers, including Durkheim, more often stressed the decline of a common, deeply experienced religious faith uniting people who differed widely in status, wealth, occupation, and even language.

When viewed in this manner, the concept of identity becomes almost a synonym for "identification," with which it shares a common linguistic origin. At most, social identity is the result of successful identification with another person, group, social role, or movement. Sociologists have perhaps preferred to adopt the term identity, not merely because it is briefer and more economical—such considerations hardly seem to have influenced their terminological habits in general—but because it lacks the special psychoanalytic connotation of identification. However, even in psychoanalytic theory, identification is a socializing mechanism, in fact the primary socializing mechanism through which the superego itself is shaped and stabilized.

Yet Erikson rejects the equation of identity and identification from the standpoint of psychoanalytic theory. [8] He regards identity-formation as a distinct mechanism that "begins where the usefulness of identification ends." [9] Identity is the unique selection made by the individual from all the significant identifications of his past. "It arises from the selective repudiation and mutual assimilation of childhood identifications and their absorption in a new configuration." [10] Erikson goes on to observe that identity requires confirmation by the society to which the individual belongs. He makes it plain, however, that he does not mean confirmation of the individual's membership in a group or recognition that he has attained a new social role, but rather confirmation of the unique being that the individual has forged out of the identifications of his childhood and adolesence. Identity to Erikson means personal identity and is something more than mere social identity or the subjective reflection of a social role.

Personal identity is roughly synonymous with individuality. An important connotation that it has in common with individuality is that of referring to an objective attribute of the person rather than solely to the idea he has of himself. Identity, therefore, is not the same thing as "self-concept" or "self-image," although many writers have dealt with it as if it were. Self-image is more changeable than identity, lacking the "genetic continuity" Erikson ascribes to the latter.[11] Also, self-image is closer to consciousness, whereas identity, while including "the conscious sense of individual identity," refers also to an "unconscious striving for a continuity of experience." [12] If I understand Erikson correctly, identity includes both what the person really is—how in psychoanalytic terms his ego has synthesized his previous identifications and social roles—and his perception of himself, whether positive or negative.

That a sense of identity is something more than a favorable self-conception needs stressing, because identity has tended to become a value-charged, almost a charismatic term, with its secure achievement regarded as equivalent to personal salvation. It has acquired the same aura that clings to "mental health" or "normality" in popular usage. Even the experiencing of identity crisis is interpreted as a mark of spiritual depth: Erikson reports that "on occasion I find myself asking a student who claims that he is an 'identity crisis' whether he is complaining or boasting." [13] Yet, surely, one may wryly or ruefully accept one's identity. A sense of identity may include a regretful recognition of limits: recognition that the self one has become precludes some experiences, some kinds of mastery, has closed off what were once open possibilities as now lying beyond the range of personal capability. Opportunities for mobility and the array of life-styles popularized by the mass media are often held responsible for delaying the achievement of secure personal identity by keeping modern men in a state of perpetual adolescence, fostering an illusory sense of limitless possibilities that survives well into the adult years.

Existentialist discussions of identity appear to be sharply at variance with the sociological perspective that stresses the lack of consensus, the fragmented social structure, and the discontinuities in individual growth of modern society. Existentialist writers are primarily concerned with personal identity. Far from seeing identification with a social role as a prerequisite for identity, they see it as the ultimate death of authentic selfhood. To Sartre, the man who identifies himself totally with his social role is guilty of "bad faith" in seeking to destroy the freedom of his "being-for-itself" by grasping at an illusory "being-in-itself." Such men have handed their lives over to others when they imprison themselves in the "dance of the grocer, of the tailor, of the auctioneer, by which they endeavour to persuade their clientele that they are nothing but a grocer, an auctioneer, a tailor." [14] Their betrayal of identity lies in their effort to be their social role in the same way that "this inkwell is an inkwell, or the glass is a glass." [15] Sartre calls the man who thus tries to escape from his freedom and individuality a *salaud*—a French colloquialism which, it seems to me, is most accurately translated in this usage as "square."The square is he who fails to realize the arbitrariness, the humanly invented character, of all social codes. He is blind to the fact that his social role is truly a role in the theatrical sense— something one plays at, not something that exhausts the definition of what one is.

Writers influenced by existentialism complain that modern society, far from preventing identity-formation by failing to provide secure social roles, depersonalizes the individual by forcing him into standardized roles and treating him as an altogether replaceable integer in a mass. He becomes the mere appendage of a technical-bureaucratic machine. Political propaganda, mass production, and the mass media presuppose a public that is merely an aggregate of identical consumers or "little men," and thus they promote conformism. Such protests are, of course, by no means confined to existentialists. Like existentialism, however, they stem from an antinomian, romantic individualist tradition that sees social controls and collectively imposed patterns of conduct as the enemies of personal identity. This tradition appears to be directly at odds with the sociological critique that regards identity as the result of anchorage in a group or social role and condemns the atomization, rootlessness, and anomie of modern life. Yet popular social criticism borrows freely from both perspectives, seemingly unaware of the contradictions between them. In its purer forms existentialism, however, purports to describe not merely man as victimized by modern society, but the human condition in general. Thus the justification for appropriating the language of existentialism for attacks on the specifics of contemporary life is doubtful. For to the existentialist all social roles, all institutions, mores, and group loyalties are threats to personal identity, the rituals of the tribesman and the allegiances of serf and nobleman as much as the "alienated" work routines of the organization man or the frantic sociability of the suburban housewife. All social identities are masks, false-faces that stifle the lonely freedom and uniqueness of the person. As John Schaar observes: "With all its richness of sociological and psychological detail, the philosophical theory of alienation refuses to concede that alienation can be reduced to an exclusively sociological problem and understood solely in sociological terms." [16]

If one similarly pushes the sociological critique of modern society to its limits, it is hard to see why the writers who make use of it so frequently deplore conformism, organization men, and the search for roots in suburbia. For if identity is the result of firm group attachments and rootedness in established social roles, what is wrong with efforts to create a master loyalty to the corporation or the suburban community? Was the feudal vassal's loyalty to his liege different in kind from that of the modern executive to his company? For that matter, why object, now that religious faith has lost its hold over men, to establishing a new consensus based on a secular ideology interpreted by a priesthood of state officials? Indeed, both David Riesman and William H. Whyte have understood, unlike many of those who parrot them, that other-direction as a way of life and managerial efforts to create loyal organization men owe a great deal to popularization and application of the findings and principles of modern social science.

Ultimately, there is a fundamental moral and philosophical conflict between the antinomian individualist and the sociological positions. But having drawn as sharply as possible the contrast between their critical perspectives on modern society, I shall now explore the sense in which both are true and complement one another.

Social analysts have often observed that greater individuality, a heightened sense of identity, and a richer inner life may flourish where social constraints are more binding than they are under the regime of aimless freedom enjoyed by so many contemporary Americans. Maurice Stein remarks that: "It almost seems as if community in the anthropological sense is necessary before human maturity or individuation can be achieved. . . ." [17] Although David Riesman has frequently protested such an interpretation, readers of *The Lonely Crowd* have often understood it as an attack on other-direction and a eulogy of inner-direction. Yet our Victorian grandfathers were models of inner-direction, while the entire modern movement in the arts, social sciences, psychiatry, education, child-rearing, and attitudes toward sexuality has been an assault on the repressiveness, narrowness, intolerance, and hypocrisy of the codes by which they lived.

Erikson observes that "the concept or at least the term identity seems to pervade much of the literature on the Negro Revolution in this country." [18] While he concerns himself chiefly with problems of black identity, he also recognizes that the survival of racial oppression poses a challenge to white identities and provides opportunities to reshape them: "There is, in fact, more than poetic justice in the historical fact that many young white people who feel deeply deprived because of their family's 'culture' find an identity and a solidarity in living and working with those who are said to be deprived for lack of such culture." [19] The attitude of some writers and intellectuals toward the black man is also instructive. Norman Mailer and Jack Kerouac are only the most extreme and most publicized celebrants of the greater vitality, inner freedom, and personal integrity often attributed to black life and personality.

Yet black writers have protested, like Ralph Ellison, that the black is the "invisible man," or, like James Baldwin, that "nobody knows my name." Black identity in America is, of course, a negative identity in Erikson's terms, and (though we need not accept the romanticism of Mailer and Kerouac) for that very reason it may be less stifling of personal identity than approved roles for some of its bearers. Under the worst conditions of oppression in the South it often became no more than a self-conscious mask worn in encounters with whites.

The fragmentation of the original civil rights movement, however, reflects (among other things) growing conflict between the claims of personal and social identity among blacks themselves. The civil rights movement initially seemed to promise visibility and identity to blacks as individual human beings. Its failures and the shift in the focus of protest from segregation in the South to conditions in the urban ghettos of the North have intensified efforts by blacks to replace a negative group identity with a positive one, efforts that seemed exotic and cultist even a few years ago when the Black Muslims first received national publicity. Today someone like Ralph Ellison, with his passionate insistence on his right to his own individuality as it has been shaped by the cultural resources of Western civilization as a whole, strikes black power militants as being positively old-fashioned and out of touch—if they do not simply dismiss him as an Uncle Tom.[20]

Hereditary statuses, precisely because they represent an unalterable social fate for the individual, may threaten personal identity less than statuses that are subject to the tensions and agonies of choice and for which the individual, having chosen, must prepare himself in advance by what sociologists have called "anticipatory socialization."[21] Also, frequent and intimate personal contacts between members of different social classes and status groups have often been the rule where status rank is hereditary, as Philippe Ariès and Philip Mason have recently shown to have been the case in medieval Europe and eighteenth-century England, respectively.[22] Thus in contrast to the nagative racial identities of modern times, the person of low social rank in these societies was less likely to become invisible and nameless behind a derogatory stereotype.

A sense of personal identity is more easily safeguarded by formal manners and strict rules of etiquette governing one's relations with others than by the ready friendliness, lack of reserve, and casual intimacy with strangers that have long been recognized as character-

istically American. The rigid artificiality of formal manners permits
the individual to maintain his inner life intact behind the barrier they
present and gives an unmistakable significance to breakthroughs to
intimacy (recall the meaning of achieving a linguistic "thee-thou"
relationship with someone in the great nineteenth-century European
novels). In America, on the other hand, quite apart from the blatant
commercial exploitation of pretended intimacy (pseudo-*Gemein-
schaft*, as Merton has called it),[23] an apparently intimate rapport
is established so quickly that one cannot be certain it means anything
beyond the moment.

Considerations such as these have been advanced by ideological
conservatives in defense of hereditary social hierarchies and restrictions on personal freedom. As has often been pointed out, much of
both the language and the substance of modern social criticism is
derived from, or is at least continuous with, the conservative critique
of democracy and equality developed in the aftermath of the French
Revolution. And the usual riposte by defenders of contemporary
American life is to label the critics reactionaries whose nostalgia for
the past prevents them from enthusing over the vastly increased opportunities for freedom and individuality made available to all men,
rather than to an upper-class elite alone, by democratization and
technical progress. This rebuttal is unconvincing, not merely because
analysts who hold a wide variety of theoretical and ideological positions agree on essentially the same diagnosis of the ills of American
society, but because the fact that greater freedom and individuality
are possible under conditions of relative classlessness, democratic culture, and high living standards is not the same as their actual realization. Moreover, if these values have truly been maximized, how does
one account for the swelling chorus of discontent? To attribute complaints about modern life to disgruntled conservatives, disillusioned
ex-Marxists, literary snobs, Europeans with an aristocratic bias or,
more generally, "alienated intellectuals," is to ignore the resonance
of the complaints in much wider circles. After all, books of social
criticism have been best-sellers and have often found an audience
among the very groups whose way of life they attack—suburbanites,
junior executives, the metropolitan middle class in general.

Conservatives and radicals, to be sure, often agree that equality of opportunity and material abundance have led to identity crisis, dehumanization, and cultural mediocrity rather than to freer, more creative, and more individualized lives for the majority of the population. Comparing two recent philosophical works analyzing modern technological society—Hannah Arendt's *The Human Condition* and Herbert Marcuse's *One-Dimensional Man*—one is struck by the underlying similarity of outlook shared by the authors in spite of obvious contrasts between their theoretical positions. Arendt is full of misgivings about the world created by modern science and technology when contrasted with the preindustrial societies of classical antiquity and medieval Christendom, where men preserved a sense of limits in a world they did not regard as entirely of their own making; she fears that "it is quite conceivable that the modern age—which began with such an unprecedented and promising outburst of human activity— may end in the deadliest, most sterile passivity history has ever known." [24] Marcuse, too, is aware of the loss of psychological depth in our "one-dimensional" world dominated by a purely functional rationality of anonymous and impersonal social controls, in which even the formerly explosive, reality-transcending energies of sexuality and artistic creativity are tamed in the service of a system that becomes all the more difficult to challenge because it tolerates them. But Marcuse insists that man must complete his "technological project" by realizing the historical alternative to the present: "the planned utilization of resources for the satisfaction of vital needs with a minimum of toil, the transformation of leisure into free time, the pacification of the struggle for existence." [25]

Arendt is more concerned with what has been lost in the passage from the stable, stratified, faith-centered societies of the past, while Marcuse's central aim is to reassert the liberating potentialities of science and technology—including social science—that have been used to create weapons of destruction, useless consumers' goods, and bureaucratic monoliths. The thrust of Arendt's argument is "conservative" while Marcuse's is "radical," although such simplifying labels do both writers an injustice.

Personal identity may have been less threatened by the more custom-bound societies of the past in which social institutions and norms retained an aura of sacredness than by today's self-evidently man-made world of technological rationality and planned social organization. But we cannot—even if we wished to—restore the mystery and absolutism of social control for the sake of enhancing identity, nor for the sake of anything else. What Max Weber called the "disenchantment of the world" applies to the realm of society as well as to the realm of nature:

There are no mysterious incalculable forces that come into play but rather . . . one can, in principle, master all things by calculation. . . . One need no longer have recourse to magical means in order to master or implore the spirits, as did the savage, for whom such mysterious powers existed. Technical means and calculations perform the service.[26]

Social science itself has made no small contribution to the demystification of social processes and, like the physical sciences, it has often been used to promote ends and to justify moral and political creeds at odds with those cherished by its creators. George Orwell once remarked that, even if one concedes the truth of the most extreme accusations of ugliness and human and natural destructiveness made against machine civilization, nevertheless one cannot travel to London by ox-cart with automobiles whizzing past and planes droning overhead, at least not in the same spirit that was possible before the invention of modern transportation. Consciousness of the existence of alternatives that are faster and mechanically more efficient alters the experience, no matter how intensely the wider social consequences of the alternatives may be deplored. Thus, Orwell argued, the self-conscious effort of medievalist and agrarian ideologues to eliminate modern technology from their lives and to live by handicrafts, relying on human and animal labor power only, is absurd.[27]

The same applies to efforts to recreate social ties and identities that have the emotional power of the prebureaucratic past. Thus those sociologists who argue for the necessity of stable social roles, binding consensus, and firm intermediate group loyalties are not in the end inconsistent when many of them refuse to applaud contemporary conformism, organization men, suburban sociability, and the "engineered consent" of the mass media or of totalitarian methods of control. The loyalty of the executive to his company is ultimately either a compulsive, willed loyalty or a qualified and provisional one that is different in kind from the loyalty of the vassal to his liege. We have lost the capacity to believe, or even to achieve a "willing suspension of disbelief," in the transcendental authority of society, just as we some time ago lost the capacity to believe in supernatural authority—which Nietzsche understood when he proclaimed the death of God. Nor is the existentialist who asserts that all socially imposed conduct is alienating as ahistorical as he appears to be. For he knows that only in the modern world of demystified, instrumentalized social structures could he gain such insight into the human condition.

Social identity no longer provides a protective barrier for personal identity. Nor does it destroy personal identity by eliminating choice and the possibility of "role distance." [28] With the important exception of racially persecuted minorities and the underclass of the permanently poor and unemployed, the absorption of individuality by social role is not an irresistible process but one that depends on the complicity of the individual himself: he chooses to be an eager role-player, to wear the uniform of the organization man, the happy consumer, or the hippie. We know now that even totalitarian regimes are less successful in reshaping men in their own ideological image than we once thought. The existentialist insistence that man makes himself by his choices has never been more apposite than to the situation of modern man. Yet the existentialist, while actively engaging himself in protests against social injustice and political oppression, usually describes only in negative terms the social order that might encourage men to make the most authentic choices. The sociologist, on the other hand, has been unable to advance much beyond specifying the formal requirements such an order must meet: minimal consensus, a degree of continuity in socialization, the regulation of potentially destructive group conflicts, etc. Can we create a society that does not mythologize its own processes of social control and allows men to choose their own identities without making life appear a senseless routine?

PART TWO
Social Stratification and Inequality

Introduction

"THE FUNCTIONAL THEORY of Stratification: Some Neglected Considerations" was a contribution to the debate over functionalism or structural-functionalism in sociology.* Like other critics, I called attention to the neglect by functionalists of power, group conflict, and historical change and tried to show that failure to consider them made functional theories of stratification, and the Davis-Moore theory in particular, especially vulnerable. Today the article possesses greater significance, I think, as an analysis of inequality in human societies than as a contribution to the antifunctionalist polemic.

I was just as concerned with criticizing the critics of the Davis-Moore theory, several of whom themselves used functionalist arguments, as with adding to the growing critical literature on functionalism in general and the Davis-Moore theory in particular. Most readers saw the article as a further specification of the antifunctionalist case against the theory, although one, Celia Heller, interpreted the second sentence as a qualified defence of Davis and Moore.[1] She was right, but she failed to note that it was a "defence" that considered the valid claims of the theory to be so general and abstract that they told us little of value about actual inequalities in historical societies; they were not even inconsistent with most models of egalitarian utopias proposed by socialists. I viewed the theory as "true

---

* Perhaps, in deference to the renewed prestige of German social-science scholarship, it ought to be called the *Functionalismusstreit*.

but trivial," as it were, a judgment applying to many other sociological generalizations favored by functionalists. I regret, however, that in the second sentence I failed to put quotation marks around "functionally necessary" as I did elsewhere in the article. Better still, I should have written "unavoidable" or "inevitable" instead of "functionally necessary," for I agree with Celia Heller's argument that stratification may be "a *consequence* of complexity" in social organization without being, as Davis and Moore claimed, "a necessary *condition* for complexity." [2] Kingsley Davis himself might well accept this reformulation, for, presumably by coincidence, the very issue of the *American Sociological Review* in which my article appeared featured his well-known presidential address to the American Sociological Association, "The Myth of Functional Analysis," in which— fourteen years after the publication of the article on stratification he had coauthored with Wilbert Moore—he argued for the elimination of the term "function" from sociological analysis and substitution of the language of causal analysis. [3]

"The Functional Theory of Stratification" was the first primarily theoretical article that I submitted to a scholarly journal, and I tried to cram into the text or long footnotes virtually every idea I had on the subject of stratification that I thought at all significant. (I have incorporated most of the longer footnotes into the text in the present version.) The second article in this section, "Social Inequality without Social Stratification," elaborated on two of the arguments advanced in "The Functional Theory of Stratification." The first, touched on only briefly in the opening section of the earlier article, was that stratification refers essentially to a hierarchy of relatively cohesive *groups* rather than of unequally "rewarded" individuals or social roles. The second argument was the issue of "meritocracy": whether the full achievement of equality of opportunity should be considered identical with "classlessness" or whether it would produce new group conflicts and tensions even though those arising from hereditary inequalities were eliminated.

"Social Inequality without Social Stratification" was the lead article in 1964 in the very first issue of the *Canadian Review of Sociology and Anthropology*, the official journal of the Canadian Association of Sociology and Anthropology. In 1973, I was honored by an invitation from the CASA to participate in a panel discussion of my article at the association's annual meetings. My fellow panelists were two young radical sociologists, who proceeded to attack the article on fairly predictable "Marxist" grounds. They charged me, among other things, with equating "class" in thoroughly un-Marxist fashion with "consciousness" instead of with "objective economic determinants" or "production relations"; with believing, like "bourgeois" sociologists such as W. Lloyd Warner, that I had refuted Marxism by showing that class was not a reliable predictor of much human behavior, thus overlooking that Marxism was a theory of change that could be tested only in the long run by the appearance or nonappearance of historically decisive class conflicts; and with asserting a trend toward meritocracy that recent research by Christopher Jencks and others had disproved.

These arguments, whatever their possible applicability to others, seemed to me to have been tagged onto my article without any consideration of what I had actually said. I pointed out that the familiar issue of "objective" versus "subjective" definitions of class, invoked by both critics, was misleading, because even if "consciousness" was made a defining criterion of class, it had to be "consciousness" *of* something outside of itself, whether common material interests, position in the relations of production, access or lack of it to social power, or a shared style of life. I noted that class consciousness was central to Marx's notion of *Klasse für sich* and that Marx himself had sometimes used the term "stratum," or simply occupational labels, for groups such as the peasantry which he elsewhere characterized as *Klassen an sich*, thus plainly indicating that in his view "an aggregate of people which satisfies the economic criteria of a social class becomes a class in the full meaning of this term only when its members are linked by the tie of class consciousness" *—a use of the term almost identical with my own.

* Stanislaw Ossowski, *Class Structure in the Social Consciousness* (New York: The Free Press of Glencoe, 1963), pp. 72–73. I cited Ossowski on this point because my two critics had invoked him as an authority on Marxist class theory in several other connections.

I mentioned that I had first heard the argument that Marxism should be evaluated as a theory of historical dynamics rather than of the influence of class at a single point in time nearly thirty years before from S. D. Clark, one of my undergraduate teachers at the University of Toronto, as well as shortly afterward from Robert K. Merton and C. Wright Mills in graduate school at Columbia. My critics seemed a bit discomfited to hear this, for they evidently regarded Clark and Merton as conservative old fogeys utterly blind to illumination from Marxism. (Clark, who was in the audience, grinned broadly.) More important, I pointed out that I had argued in the article almost the reverse of what my critics charged, contending that class was undeniably a major determinant here and now of much human conduct, especially voting behavior, but that classes as mobilized groups appeared to be declining in importance as political and historical actors, or agents of change, in contrast to the role they had played in the early bourgeois-capitalist era. The protest movements of the 1960s were for the most part not class-based, but appealed to groups sharing either racial, ethnic, national, sex, or age or generational bonds. The difficulty in America of disentangling these various group characteristics, including class, from one another as influences on outlook and behavior is discussed in the last essay in this section.

Criticism of meritocracy, both as a goal and as a reality in some organizations—e.g., elite universities—became commonplace in the late sixties, and today many social critics have rejected the traditional liberal ideal of equality of opportunity in favor of what has been called "equality of results." But this theme had not yet become visible in the early sixties even among sociologists, and one of the aims of "Social Inequality without Social Stratification" was to speculate about possible undesirable consequences of a fully institutionalized equality of opportunity, drawing on Michael Young's brilliant satire, The Rise of the Meritocracy, which I had previously reviewed favorably [4] but which had escaped the notice of American sociologists. Far from claiming that meritocracy was imminent, I described it as "only dimly adumbrated in our present imperfectly affluent society" and noted that income distribution in the United States had become more unequal in the 1950s. As an ideal, however, meritocracy was still largely unchallenged by American liberals; and if one took a long view, from, say, the beginning of the century, a trend toward meritocracy had obviously occurred in capitalist societies. My critics themselves recommended just such a long view in assessing the value of Marxist theories of class conflict.

The last two essays in this section deal concretely with American society rather than with issues in stratification theory. "Jews, Gentiles, and the New Establishment" was a review of E. Digby Baltzell's *The Protestant Establishment: Aristocracy and Caste in America.* The theme of meritocracy is again discussed, this time with reference to criticisms of meritocracy raised from a classically conservative rather than a left-liberal point of view. I also reviewed somewhat critically Baltzell's extensive discussion of anti-Semitism and Jew-Gentile relations in America, subjects on which I had previously written myself.[5] In fact, I adapted the last three paragraphs from a recent essay of my own.

"How Important is Social Class?" was written at the request of the editors of *Dissent* and was printed not only in that journal but in a massive anthology of commissioned essays on blue-collar workers.[6] The editors asked me to discuss the relation between class and ethnic loyalties among American workers, and hoped that my views would provide some sort of contrast to those of Andrew M. Greeley, one of the main students and apostles of the "new ethnicity," who was also a contributor to the anthology.

I may have disappointed them in this expectation, for they changed my original dull but descriptive title, "Class and Ethnicity in American Politics," to "How Important is Social Class?" And, indeed, I used the essay as an occasion to revisit some of the issues raised in "Social Inequality without Social Stratification" in addition to dealing with the assigned subject. I was bothered by the fact that, although I had argued for the increasing obsolescence of the concept of class in the earlier article, I still found it indispensable in trying to understand the realities of American culture and politics. The essentially Weberian rather than Marxist view that classes—in America at least—are groups sharing common life-chances which give rise to a diffuse similar outlook determined by their market position in the national economy, is my final resting-place. This article deals much too briefly with the issues that it raises, but it also relates the discussion of class to the problem of "community" and defense against anomie that is the subject of the two last articles in the previous section.

SIX

The Functional Theory of Stratification: Some Neglected Considerations

NEARLY FIFTEEN YEARS after its original publication, the issues raised by Kingsley Davis and Wilbert E. Moore in their article "Some Principles of Stratification" * are still being debated by sociologists. Critics of the authors' thesis have succeeded in showing that there are a great many things about stratification that Davis and Moore have failed to explain, but they have not succeeded in seriously denting the central argument that unequal rewards are functionally necessary in any and all societies with a division of labor extending much beyond differences in age and sex. On the other hand, the extreme abstractness and limited relevance of the Davis-Moore theory to the concrete historical world have been only partially recognized by its authors and their critics alike. Moreover, several of the theory's assumptions have yet to be made explicit, and a number of additional implications have been ignored by participants in the debate.

The Definition of Stratification

Walter Buckley's criticism of the Davis-Moore theory largely centers on the question of how stratification should be defined.[1] He accuses Davis and Moore of confusing *social differentiation*, the existence of specialized roles or of a division of labor, with *social stratification*, which he defines as a system of unequally privileged groups mem-

---

*Kingsley Davis and Wilbert E. Moore, "Some Principles of Stratification," *American Sociological Review* 10 (April 1945), 242–49. An extended and revised version of the theory which, as Davis has complained, the critics have largely ignored, appears in Kingsley Davis, *Human Society* (New York: Macmillan, 1949), 366–78.

bership in which is determined by the intergenerational transmission of roles, or of opportunities to attain them, through kinship affiliation. Davis has replied that what is or is not to be called stratification is purely a terminological question, provided that a distinction is made between the hierarchy of unequally rewarded roles and the way in which particular individuals are recruited in each generation to fill them.[2] Three relevant types of social organization, however, should be distinguished:

First, there is the existence of role differentiation or division of labor itself, irrespective of whether or how the roles are ranked and their incumbents unequally rewarded. This is what is usually called "social differentiation." Its causes and consequences, as Durkheim's famous study illustrates, can be discussed independently of the logically separable questions of how and why "horizontal" or "lateral" differences in position are transformed into "vertical" differences in rank.

Second, there are unequal rewards distributed among the various roles making up the division of labor. The Davis-Moore theory tries to explain the ubiquity and inevitability of unequal rewards wherever role differentiation is highly developed.

Third, there is the tendency, a result of kinship loyalties, for roles and opportunities to attain them to be passed on from one generation to the next, giving rise to enduring classes or strata monopolizing certain roles and exhibiting a greater or lesser degree of solidarity and a common style of life.

Buckley accuses Davis and Moore of confusing the second and third types of social organization, but he himself confuses the first and second. The Davis-Moore theory, if it achieves nothing else, surely provides sound arguments for regarding the existence of a hierarchy of roles as a problem in its own right. Consider that Buckley's terminology would require him to describe an army which recruited all of its officers from the lower ranks as a differentiated but nonstratified organization. And the same description would apply to the Catholic Church, where celibacy rules prevent the intergenerational transmission of roles. Admittedly, these types of hierarchy differ in important respects from hereditary class systems; if the term "stratification" is to be confined to the latter, however, another term is needed to distinguish armies, celibate priestly orders, and other bureaucracies from precivilized tribal societies, collegial bodies, parliaments, and similar nonhierarchical social structures. They might usefully be called "ladder hierarchies" to distinguish them from "class hierarchies." But Davis and Moore are concerned with hierarchy per se; such a distinction is only tangentially relevant to their argument.

The Functional Necessity of Stratification

What the critics of the Davis-Moore theory fundamentally object to is that in their view "the theory implies an assumption that any scheme of stratification is somehow the best that could be had, that the prevailing distribution of rewards comes into being somehow because it is 'functionally necessary.' " [3] The charge, repeated in some form by all of the critics, that Davis and Moore are "defending" or "justifying" the status quo, any status quo, rests on finding this implication in the theory. Yet it is not a logically correct implication, although it has never been explicitly disavowed by the authors.

All that the Davis-Moore theory actually asserts is that *if* the more important, highly skilled, and physically and psychologically demanding positions in a complex division of labor are to be adequately filled both from the standpoint of numbers and of minimally efficient performance, then there must be *some* unequal *rewards* favoring these positions over others. This proposition rests on certain assumptions about human nature. The important thing to note, however, is that it in no way denies that a particular distribution of rewards prevailing in a given historical society may vastly exceed the minimum inequalities necessary to maintain a complex division of labor.* Nor does it deny that some roles that are unimportant, unskilled, and pleasurable may be highly rewarded, provided only that they do not compete so successfully with roles possessing the opposite attributes

---

*Davis and Moore recognize the independent variability of the scale of rewards, or what they call "the magnitude of invidious differences," in listing it as a distinct "mode of variation" of stratified systems: "Some Principles of Stratification," 248–49. See also the lucid discussion by Ralph Ross and Ernest van den Haag in *The Fabric of Society* (New York: Harcourt, Brace, 1957), pp. 121–22.

that they reduce the quantity or quality of candidates for the latter below some minimum level.* Nothing in their theory requires Davis and Moore to disagree with Tumin's claim that the "sacrifices" made by those who undergo professional training are overrewarded,[4] nor with Simpson's contention that such roles as personal servant or kept woman may be highly rewarded although they make little contribution to society. Davis and Moore are committed solely to the view that there must be unequal rewards; *how* unequal these need to be or how strictly they must be apportioned according to functional importance and skill are separate questions the answer to which are not deducible from the theory.

The particular scale of unequal rewards prevailing in a society is likely to shape people's expectations and sense of distributive justice so that they will oppose efforts to alter it, even though no general sociological principle rules out a viable society in which the range of inequality might be far narrower. Notions of "fair price," "deserved recognition," and "proper return for services" may be invoked to protest increased taxation of large incomes, cuts for manual workers, or even changes in wage and salary differentials between occupations differing in skill, responsibility, and traditional prestige.

Belief in the *legitimacy* of the existing scale of rewards, however, should be distinguished from the *power* possessed by threatened groups to resist any reduction in the size of their shares. The incumbents of the more functionally important and skilled roles are able to fight back by threatening withdrawal of their services if faced with a proposed redistribution of rewards. This follows directly from the Davis-Moore principle viewed from a somewhat different perspective from that of its authors. Significantly, Davis and Moore have not formulated their theory in a way that focuses attention on the power element in stratification. They argue that unequal rewards are necessary to attract individuals into the more important and skilled positions, yet they neglect to observe that once these positions have been filled, their very importance gives their incumbents the power not

---

* "Actually a society does not need to reward positions in proportion to their functional importance. It merely needs to give sufficient reward to insure that they will be filled competently." (And, it should be added, in sufficient numbers.) Davis, *Human Society*, p. 368.

only to insist on payment of expected rewards but also to demand larger ones. This power is inherent in the positions. The unequal rewards in wealth and prestige "attached to" the positions also give their incumbents greater opportunities to influence the general distribution of rewards in society and to protect or augment their own privileges. A further consideration is that the incumbents of the most highly rewarded roles are relatively few in number, a fact that, as Michels and Mosca have taught us, facilitates collective organization and solidarity, which are preconditions for the effective exercise of social power.

Yet the history of left-wing parties and of labor movements in modern times demonstrates that the more numerous but individually less powerful occupants of the less-rewarded positions may organize to offset the initial power advantage of the privileged. By doing so they have succeeded often enough in effecting a redistribution of rewards in their favor. But the difficulties in organizing and maintaining solidarity among relatively poor, uneducated, apolitical, and geographically scattered majorities are formidable. That is why, as G. L. Arnold writes of the industrial worker, " 'Solidarity' is for him what 'honor' was to the feudal order, and 'honesty' for the bourgeois: a claim which is felt as absolute because the existence of the individual depends on it." [5]

Reformist and revolutionary governments striving to alter the existing scale of rewards have often been forced to modify their egalitarian programs when confronted with the resistance of privileged groups. The threat or reality of a flight of capital has sometimes been employed to compel moderation of the policies of governments committed to greater economic equalization. The British Labour Party was forced to make concessions to the medical profession when socializing health services in England. Even unorganized lower strata may by passive resistance and what Veblen called "calculated withdrawal of efficiency" succeed at least in slowing up the pace of drastic changes imposed on them by centralized authorities: the Soviet regime from its earliest days repeatedly has made concessions to the peasants in the interests of higher agricultural productivity and has also found it expedient to restore "capitalist" incentives and wage differentials in industry.

These examples illustrate the eternal difficulties faced by reformers and utopians in making the leap from history into freedom. The progressive departure from egalitarian practices in the Soviet Union since the Revolution may indicate the "functional necessity" of maintaining a certain scale of unequal rewards in societies in the early stages of capital accumulation.[6] But neither the resistance aroused by efforts to modify existing inequalities in any society nor the possible need for wide inequalities in societies experiencing rapid industrialization justifies the conclusion that a more equal distribution of rewards is in principle incompatible with the maintenance of a complex division of labor.

Freud, in observing the social pathology of everyday life, spoke of a "narcissism with respect to minor differences," and students of bureaucratic organization confirm its reality when they report the immense significance people often attach to the door which is used to enter the place of work, the size and location of desks, the exact shade of cordiality of the boss's salutation, and so on. But can *all* differences be abolished, even those that are trivial in comparison with the inequalities we usually have in mind when discussing historical class systems? Davis and Moore answer in the negative; a simple negative answer is all that their theory implies and all that any sociologist is entitled to mean in characterizing a "classless society" as a "sociological monstrosity" or a "contradiction in terms." [7]

It is worth noting that most egalitarian reformers in Western history have been concerned with narrowing the range of inequality and creating wider equality of opportunity rather than with the establishment of total equality of condition, the abolition of any system of unequal rewards altogether. And those who have favored the latter, notably sectarian Christian communists and Israeli kibbutzniks, have been willing to pay the price set by Davis and Moore: foregoing the advantages of an elaborate division of labor and committing themselves permanently to an agrarian way of life. Marx relegated the achievement of his ideal society based on the principle "from each according to his quality, to each according to his need" to the "higher phase" of Communism when the state will have withered away, an economy of abundance will have been realized, and a division of labor will no longer be necessary.[8] However difficult it may be to imagine technological innovations radical enough to make possible such a society,* there is nothing in its conception that violates the Davis-Moore principle. Moreover, the Marxist slogan refers only to *material* rewards. By recognizing different kinds of rewards, Davis and Moore do not rule out the possibility of a differentiated society in which complete income equality exists provided only that inequality of "psychological income" remains.†

The Davis-Moore theory, then, is formulated at so high a level of generality that it fails to rule out the "functional" viability of the many utopian models of egalitarian societies which have been advanced by visionary thinkers since medieval times and even earlier. Although this may be regarded as evidence of the theory's undeniable validity, one may be disposed to conclude that, like other generalizations about the "universal functional prerequisites" of societies, it explains so little about concrete class structures, social inequalities, and the ways in which they arise and change, that the theory's value is limited.

Yet by recognizing, if only implicitly, the separability of types of reward, the Davis-Moore theory is superior to other functionalist theories of stratification which tend to subsume all rewards under prestige or "differential evaluation." [9] Such theories require the questionable assumption that there is a single value consensus in society. But there are always roles which *must* carry high material rewards to attract people to them in compensation for their abysmally low pres-

---

*And, barring the Malthusian problem which Marxists have so notoriously slighted, such a society is not so difficult to imagine as it once was in view of the prospects of automation. However, as Meyer remarks: "Marx and Engels . . . had an idealized and quite premature conception of modern industrial society as a push-button shop, without realizing the complex technical demands such a society would make." Alfred G. Meyer, *Marxism: The Unity of Theory and Practice* (Cambridge: Harvard University Press, 1954), p. 81. See also Barrington Moore, Jr., *Political Power and Social Theory* (Cambridge: Harvard University Press, 1958), p. 137.

† Thus Walter Buckley is in error in suggesting that the Davis-Moore theory asserts that "some persons' incomes must always be greater or less than others.'" "A Rejoinder to Functionalists Dr. Davis and Dr. Levy," *American Sociological Review* 24 (February 1959), 84–85. Tumin has noted the possibility of emphasizing one type of reward "to the virtual neglect of others." "Some Principles of Stratification: A Critical Analysis," *American Sociological Review* 18 (August 1953), 392.

tige—for example, hangmen, prostitutes, professional criminals. The independent variability of types of reward also helps to account for social change: that wealth or power can be gained in certain roles, even though the existence of these roles may be deplored by prevailing mores and the resulting prestige judgments, encourages the spread of new activities, the rise of "new men" to foster them, and ultimately the development of new values, ideologies, and prestige rankings imposed by ascendant classes.

To avoid the "fallacy of misplaced concreteness," the Davis-Moore theory must be challenged on the ground of its psychological assumptions. Tumin is the only critic who has done so.[10] He suggests that motives other than desire for the prestige and material rewards attached to important and skilled roles might be institutionalized and might insure competent role performance at less cost to society than unequal rewards. He mentions "joy in work" and "social duty" as possibilities. However, as Davis has pointed out in his rejoinder, Tumin blurs the distinction between prestige and esteem, between incentives for striving to attain positions and incentives for conscientiously fulfilling their duties once they have been attained. The motives Tumin mentions conceivably might induce people to carry out properly the duties of their positions, but, even if men were angels, the need for some selective system to allocate them to these positions in the first place would still exist. That exactly the right number of would-be doctors needed by society would feel an inner call to cure the ill at exactly the right time, or that individuals, however beneficent their intentions, would spontaneously distribute themselves among positions in exactly the right proportions is, to put it mildly, an improbable supposition.

Tumin's point in his reply to Davis that sociology should not "shut the door on inquiry into alternative possible social arrangements" [11] is well taken, but he fails to propose any alternative to the Davis-Moore positional reward mechanism for recruiting individuals to their roles. If we overlook the probability that the tendency to make invidious comparisons both of unlike tasks ("prestige") and of performances of like tasks ("esteem") is rooted in the nature of the self, we may concede that intrinsic job satisfaction and social duty might insure high levels of performance in a static society where roles are ascribed at birth. But this does not appear to be what Tumin has in mind.

Earlier, in his original article, Tumin suggests that "a system of norms could be institutionalized in which the idea of threatened withdrawal of services . . . would be considered as absolute moral anathema." This observation, in common with his proposed motives for conscientiousness, indicates his exclusive concern with behavior *after* the various roles in a division of labor have been filled. But Davis and Moore are concerned with explaining how they come to be filled in the first place. As I have previously argued, they neglect the power to secure and enhance rewards that accrues to role incumbents once they have been recruited and trained. Tumin, however, makes the reverse error.

In a later article, "Rewards and Task-Orientations," [12] Tumin also overlooks this crucial distinction, contending that parents perform their child-rearing tasks with dedication in the absence of expectations of unequal rewards; but, even if this be the case, motives for having children and for caring for them once they are born may be of a different order. And there is no assurance, of course, that people will reproduce at the rate which is optimal for society.

The Problem of Equality of Opportunity

Davis and Moore see stratification as a sorting mechanism allocating the more talented and ambitious individuals to the more socially important and demanding roles by means of differential rewards which serve as incentives. Their model, as several critics have noted, is a special case of the market mechanism or price system of classical economic theory. And just as the conditions for the "perfect" functioning of the market mechanism are never met by actual economies, so the stratification system never fully performs its imputed social function in actual societies.

In *Human Society* Davis has attempted to modify the theory to take into account the evident fact that differential rewards do not function as a selective mechanism for talent and industry when roles are ascribed to individuals at birth. [13] His arguments, which have been largely ignored by his critics, are worth examining in some detail. He begins by observing that the institution of the family limits the operation of the stratification system by giving to the children of the incumbents of roles in one generation relatively or absolutely greater opportunities to attain the same roles in the next generation. He shows in an analysis of the Indian caste system, however, that despite its overwhelming emphasis on inherited status, the system cannot entirely preclude individual mobility because of caste fertility and mortality differentials, eventual changes in the physical environment giving rise to new roles and destroying old ones, and a number of other considerations.[14] He reiterates the distinction between the hierarchy of positions and the way in which individuals are recruited to them, pointing out that "the low estate of the sweeper castes in India, as compared with the priestly castes, cannot be explained by saying that sons of sweepers become sweepers and the sons of Brahmins become Brahmins." Since "there is a tendency for sweepers to have a low status in every society," Davis concludes that "the functional necessity behind stratification seems to be operative at all times, despite the concurrent operation of other functions." [15]

Now this argument actually does no more than assert that *over time but not necessarily "at all times"* differential rewards will operate as a selective mechanism. It lacks, but requires, a distinction analogous to that between the short run and the long run in economic analysis. By neglecting to make this distinction explicit, Davis understates the degree to which highly rewarded roles may be filled almost exclusively by ascription "in the short run" or "at any given time." Where inheritance of position generally prevails, the existence of a system of unequal positional rewards favoring the important and skilled roles, far from reflecting a "functional necessity" that is currently "operative," can be understood only with reference to the past, to the events which shaped the system at the time when the society was developing a differentiated social structure.

Thus we arrive at the paradoxical conclusion that the Davis-Moore theory, especially when it is applied to rigid caste societies, is often a better theory of social origins than of contemporary functioning—an odd conclusion indeed in view of the antihistorical bias of functional explanations. The high estate of Brahmins can be explained, in terms of the theory, only if we assume that the promise of unequal rewards was once necessary to attract men to the priesthood before the hierarchy of positions had hardened into a hierarchy of hereditary strata. The truth of Schumpeter's assertion, alien to the spirit of functional analysis, is thus confirmed: "Any theory of class structure, in dealing with a given historical period, must include prior class structures among its data; and . . . any general theory of classes and class formation must explain the fact that classes coexisting at any given time bear the marks of different centuries on their brow. . . ."[16]

Schumpeter, like Davis, insists on the ubiquity of mobility, even in relatively stagnant societies where legal and customary barriers between classes appear to be impassable. However, as in all his writings, including his technical economic works, Schumpeter's approach is fundamentally historical: he clearly differentiates between a cross-sectional or short-run view of economies and social structures and a long-run view that takes into account changes in the position of families and firms within stable structures and, ultimately, changes in the structures themselves. Schumpeter sees the lineal family rather than the individual as the "true unit" of class and of mobility within and between classes; it may take generations for representatives of a family line to inch their way upwards in the class hierarchy to the point where an apparently secure hereditary class position is achieved. By looking at mobility in terms of family lines and generations, Schumpeter avoids the rival errors of viewing class position as entirely hereditary and immobile, on the one hand, and, on the other, of regarding existing inequalities as reflections of the actual distribution of ability and effort in the population. Lacking a truly historical perspective, the Davis-Moore theory, even in Davis's revised version of it, leaves itself open to the charge of committing the latter error, although Davis's later qualifications implicitly take into account time and change as crucial variables.

American sociologists often stress the "dysfunctions" of the inequalities of opportunity that result from the inheritance of positions. When able and energetic individuals are prevented from competing for the most important and highly rewarded positions, the "efficiency" or "productivity" of society is alleged to suffer. This argument is a major one used by the critics of the Davis-Moore theory. However, Davis and Moore themselves accept the argument when they insist that the function of unequal rewards is to allocate talent to the position where it is most needed and answer their critics by claiming that this function can never be entirely suppressed. Yet for some important roles requiring subtle skills and character traits, hereditary ascription may actually be a more efficient way of recruiting candidates. Some administrative and leadership roles are perhaps best filled by those who are "to the manner born," who have been subjected to a process of character-molding beginning in infancy and preparing them for later assumption of their roles. Obviously, this does not apply to activities requiring genuinely scarce genetic aptitudes—for example, mathematics and music. But such roles are largely technical and are usually, as Davis and Moore point out, less highly rewarded than administrative positions—requiring "skill in handling people" or "capacity to make decisions," qualities which probably do not depend on rare genetic talents falling outside the range of endowment of the average man.

It is strange how insistence on the alleged "inefficiency" of unequal opportunities often leads sociologists to stress genetic endowment, the importance of which they are disposed to minimize in other connections. I suggest that this argument is another instance of the dangerous proclivity of contemporary social scientists to find "factual" or "instrumental" reasons for supporting views they ultimately favor on ethical grounds.[17] Nevertheless it is true, in a society with a growing population and an expanding economy, that barriers to full equality of opportunity may lead to shortages in the supply of candidates for important positions. But this situation, clearly applicable to engineers, physical scientists, doctors, and other professionals in the United States today, does not necessarily imply deficiencies in the role performance of those who are the beneficiaries of unequal opportunities. Nor should it be generalized to apply to all social orders where inequality of opportunity prevails, notably to static agrarian societies with caste-like stratification systems. The proponents of the view that inequality of opportunity is "dysfunctional" fail to distinguish between its effects when the *shape* or *profile* of the stratified occupational system is changing and under conditions where pure mobility alone is at issue.[18]

Actually, societies face three distinct problems in "allocating" and motivating their members: first, the number of candidates for important roles must be sufficient; second, their talents and aptitudes, innate or previously acquired, must not fall below a certain level; and third, once they have been trained and have assumed their roles, they must be induced to do their best. A solution to one of these problems is not necessarily a solution to the others.

If we wished to raise the intellectual level of the American academic profession, for example, two exactly opposite policies might prove effective. We might stop paying professors anything at all, with the result that only men with a genuine love of learning and a profound dedication to the pursuit of truth would be willing to become mendicant scholars. Or we might raise professorial salaries so that the academy could compete with business and the highly paid professions in attracting able and ambitious men. Both of these policies might lead to greatly improved academic performance, but only the second would insure an adequate supply of would-be professors to staff American colleges and universities.[19]

In hereditary class societies the desire for esteem rather than for prestige must suffice to motivate individuals to perform their roles competently. This is not, of course, strictly true: important political, bureaucratic, and military roles may be filled only from the ranks of a hereditary upper class, but not all members of the class fill such roles. Thus prestige incentives may be effective in inducing feudal princes to strive to become and to remain the king's first minister, Junker landlords to seek to be generals, etc. This situation necessitates the familiar distinction between the "elite," those necessarily few men who possess actual decision-making powers, and the "ruling class," the larger stratum from which the elite is recruited. Monopolizing the positions carrying high rewards, a ruling stratum is always subject to the temptation to become absentee owners embracing the values of Veblen's leisure class, which make a virtue of "functionless" activity and elevate what have previously been viewed as rewards for performance into criteria of worth in their own right. One of the patterns of conspicuous leisure described by Veblen is precisely the phenomenon noted by Richard Simpson: the creation by the privileged of new positions—for servants, footmen, courtesans, and the like, whose function is to serve as lackeys catering to the most trivial wants of their masters. Davis and Moore note the existence of reward for

"pure ownership," but add in a phrase with curious evolutionist overtones that it "becomes more subject to criticism as social development proceeds toward industrialization." [20]

It cannot be assumed, however, that a hereditary ruling class
always degenerates into a "decadent" leisure class in Veblen's sense.
Clearly, there have been hereditary aristocracies deeply imbued with
an ethos of honor, responsibility, and noblesse oblige serving to motivate conscientious role performance. Hereditary upper classes may
even exhibit a stronger sense of duty and accountability to society
than *arriviste* elites precisely because of their awareness that they are
the recipients of "unearned" privileges which can only be justified by
continuous effort. [21] C. Wright Mills has suggested that the way of
life of Veblen's leisure class is probably more characteristic of the
nouveau riche, specifically of the self-made millionaires whose antics
loomed so large on the American scene when Veblen was writing,
than of established hereditary aristocracies. [22] Which model—
Veblen's leisure class or responsible aristocracy—characterizes a hereditary class is a matter of the particular historical context.

Although American social scientists have stressed the "dysfunctions" for society of inequality of opportunity, they have also been
highly sensitive to the negative consequences for the individual of
vertical mobility, upward or downward. But they have been extraor-
dinarily remiss in exploring systematically the disintegrative effects for
society of high rates of mobility, as well as the dangers posed by full
equality of opportunity to other cherished values. Scores of books and
articles have been written attributing neurosis, criminality, and de-
moralization to the competitiveness allegedly inspired by intense mobility strivings in a society which holds out the promise of high
rewards to those who rise to the top. This was, in fact, a major
theme, if not *the* major theme, of the most widely read works of
American social science and social criticism in the 1930s and early
1940s. [23] Most writers failed to distinguish between the effects of competition per se and of competition under conditions where full equality of opportunity is manifestly absent. Merton, however, explicitly
attributes the "strain toward anomie" he finds in American life to the
"contradiction between cultural emphasis on pecuniary ambition and
the social bars to full opportunity," but it is far from certain that the

deviant and anomic responses he describes would disappear in an industrial society which successfully removed all major barriers to opportunity. In fact, the cultural emphasis on success might very well be enhanced under such circumstances.

One can cite few writings by Americans which deal directly with the negative consequences for the social structure of rapid mobility [24]— apart from Davis's argument, echoed by other functionalists, that the requirements for family solidarity set limits to complete equality of opportunity. However, a number of nonsociologists, many of them English, have concerned themselves with the question of just how much mobility and equality of opportunity a modern society can stand. [25] Will the trend toward the replacement of class hierarchies by ladder hierarchies in industrial societies eliminate the evils (or, if preferred, the "dysfunctions") which have been so widely attributed to inherited class privileges? Considering the charges of ideological bias which have been bandied about by both sides in the debate over the Davis-Moore theory, it is worth noting that in England staunch conservatives and confirmed socialists alike have raised this question. Both sociologists and nonsociologists have also considered the following questions: [26]

1. Might not a self-made elite owing its position to demonstrated merit alone be even more intolerant and self-righteous in its attitude toward the lower strata than an elite owing its position largely to birth?

George Orwell wrote in *1984*:

The Party is not a class in the old sense of the word. It does not aim at transmitting power to its own children, as such; and if there were no other way of keeping the ablest people at the top, it would be perfectly prepared to recruit an entire new generation from the ranks of the proletariat. In the crucial years, the fact that the Party was not a hereditary body did a great deal to neutralize opposition. The older kind of Socialist, who had been trained to fight against something called 'class privilege,' assumed that what is not hereditary cannot be permanent. He did not see that the continuity of an oligarchy need not be physical, nor did he pause to reflect that hereditary aristocracies have always been shortlived, whereas adoptive organizations such as the Catholic Church have sometimes lasted for hundreds or thousands of years. The essence of oligarchical rule is not father-to-son inheritance, but the persistence of a certain world-view and a certain way of life, imposed by the dead upon the living. A ruling group is a ruling group so long as it can nominate its successors. The Party is not concerned with perpetuating its blood but with perpetuating itself. Who wields power is not important, provided that the hierarchical structure remains always the same.[27]

Too many American sociologists resemble Orwell's "older kind of Socialist" in their views on stratification. Confusion of biological continuity with permanency of structure is particularly marked in Buckley's article.[28]

2. Would not those who failed to achieve high positions feel even more guilt-ridden, demoralized, and alienated than at present if their failure were truly owing to proven lack of objective ability rather than to "accidents of birth" or "not knowing the right people," excuses which can now be employed as rationalizations for failure?

3. Is it really desirable that the lower strata should consist only of those who are genuinely inferior, thus depriving their ranks of a leaven of able and aggressive individuals to lead and represent them in conflicts of interest with the more highly placed groups and to contribute variety and liveliness to their social experience?

Let us ignore the extreme case of a brutal centralized totalitarianism which, as George Orwell has suggested, may actually be more compatible with a social structure resembling a ladder hierarchy than with a regime of hereditary social classes. Whether rapid mobility and full equality of opportunity in a democratic industrial society have the effects described above depends on a number of conditions, of which the major ones probably are the cultural value placed on upward mobility, the range of inequality or what I have called "the scale of unequal rewards," and the rate of economic expansion and technical progress. These factors, of course, are only partially independent of one another.

If the price of failure to rise socially—or even of downward mobility—is not too great, if a definite floor and ceiling are institutionalized to confine inequalities within tolerable limits, and if the general standard of living is high, then upward mobility, as David Potter has suggested, may come to be viewed as "optional rather than obligatory" and equality of opportunity need not produce a monolithic elite ruling over an inert mass. A diversified value system which recognizes and honors human qualities other than functional intelligence and single-minded ambition will be more likely to flourish.

Potter, Davis Riesman, W. H. Whyte, and others have noted the decline of the Protestant ethic, the relaxation of the success-drive, and the new importance of leisure as opposed to work in American life. There are also signs, however, that the decline of strong aspirations to occupational mobility has coincided with an increase of status-seeking in leisure pursuits and consumption behavior.[29] Davis and Moore, and others who have theorized about the limits to equality in human societies, have been chiefly concerned with the relationship of unequal rewards and mobility to the functional division of labor; the newer forms of "status panic" raise questions of a cultural and psychological nature that fall outside the scope of theories that focus primarily on social structure.

Finally, if economic expansion and technical progress continue to change the shape of occupational stratification, producing "automatic" upward mobility by reducing the number of workers needed in low-status positions, the combination of hierarchy and equality of opportunity will be less likely to generate social tensions.[30]

All the dimensions of hierarchy—the range of inequality, the shape of the hierarchical structure, the amount of mobility, and the ways in which each of these is changing—are empirically interdependent and jointly produce particular social consequences, although they can and must be analytically distinguished. American sociologists, reflecting the values of their own society, have been preoccupied with the amount of mobility to the neglect of the other dimensions.

Conclusions

If the inducement of unequal rewards is required to encourage men to convert their talents into skills, exercise their skills conscientiously, and undertake difficult tasks, it is also the case that, having won their rewards, they will use their superior power, wealth, and prestige to further widen existing inequalities in their favor. And they are likely to do so even when their chances of passing on differential advantages to their children are strictly limited. Thus there may *never* be a correspondence between the existing scale of unequal rewards and the minimum scale required to maintain the social order—although democratic government and the organization of the lower strata to countervail the initial power superiority of the elite may stabilize or even narrow the existing scale. But conflicts between unequally rewarded groups and a sense of injustice on the part of the less privileged may be just as endemic in society as the necessity for unequal rewards itself. This of course is the central insight of the Marxist tradition. Sociologists pay lip service to the theoretical obligation to stress both the integrative and the divisive effects of social arrangements. The obligation applies with special force to discussions of stratification. Power, justice, and social necessity are perhaps ultimately incommensurable.

SEVEN
Social Inequality
without Social Stratification

ATTEMPTS TO DEFINE and redefine the concepts generally used to describe social stratification have been so common in recent years that one hesitates to undertake the task once again. In addition to the risk of achieving no more than a retracing of familiar ground, there is the danger of perpetuating the larger failure of so much contemporary sociological theory to overcome its purely definitional character, its tendency to produce a distinctive nomenclature rather than significant propositions about social reality. Conceptual analysis, however, need not be sterile if two conditions are met. First, the effort to clarify concepts should not be undertaken in a prescriptive spirit but should be guided by a sensitivity to the contextual uses of language in everyday and scholarly discourse. And second, instead of concentrating on the construction of static typologies and paradigms, conceptual analysis should lead directly into the elucidation of social processes and historical trends with which we are directly familiar.

We should not, therefore, feel dismay if we are required to constantly revise our concepts in the light of new historical realities, for *all* sociological concepts need to be continually refitted to our individual experience if they are truly to illuminate it.[1] And never is this more clearly the case than when we try to understand such large-scale societal phenomena as systems of social stratification, which are represented in history by not much more than a dozen examples. Moreover, our concepts should not only encompass past social realities but also enable us to grasp emerging possibilities suggested by the direction of social change. If sociology should not "shut the door on inquiry into alternative social arrangements," [2] it is even more in-cumbent on it to consider types of social structure that represent not merely hypothetically attainable utopias but genuine possibilities dis-cernible in the shape of contemporary society though still far from full concrete existence. Continuing changes provide a test of the rele-vance of our vocabulary for talking about the facts of inequality and stratification.

Recently several sociologists, notwithstanding the increased preoc-cupation of their colleagues with the subject, have argued that the concept of social class is becoming more and more irrelevant to the understanding of advanced industrial societies.[3] They have largely confined their remarks to the United States. Several European writers, however, have made similar suggestions with respect to the major countries of Western Europe, though rather more tentatively, since much that has already become a reality in America remains a trend on the other side of the Atlantic.[4] On the whole, the claim that social classes have disappeared or are disappearing has been rejected by the majority of American sociologists. For the most part their rejection has been based on little more than a preference for different definitions of class and has been offered good-humoredly, as if the matter were merely a trivial issue of terminology. Yet, as so often in sociology, definitions defended on pragmatic or operational grounds turn out on closer examination to obscure full recognition of the con-trast between past and present and of the new possibilities latent in contemporary social reality.

Those writers who maintain that social class is no longer a useful concept take what has been called a "realist" position regarding the existence of classes. They are committed, that is, to the view that social classes, in the words of one of them, "are groups possessed both of real and vital common economic interests and of a group-consciousness of their general position in the social scale." [5] Their contention that social classes are disappearing in industrial societies rests on the failure to locate such groups. The opposing "nominalist" point of view regards class as a useful classificatory concept, grouping together for purposes of analysis individuals who possess certain attri-butes in common, whether or not they feel any unity or are even aware of having something in common with their fellow class members. The sociologist, in effect, creates the "class structures" he describes, which are no more than a means of organizing his data on variations in human behavior within a society. He may find several different class systems or pyramids of stratification within a society, none of which are perceived or experienced as collective realities, as real social groups, by their members.

A denial of the existence of social classes as defined by the "realist" perspective in no way implies a trend toward general equality or social uniformity. Inequalities in the distribution of income, the invidious ranking of occupations with respect to prestige or status, and functional hierarchies of power and authority may remain solidly established in the absence of social classes. Individuals or social roles may be ranked with respect to varying income, status, or power, as is commonly done by sociological researchers, but the categories or percentiles into which individuals or roles are grouped are not social classes in the realist sense unless there is independent evidence that they are internally cohesive and that their members see themselves as a distinct collectivity with *common*, rather than merely *like*, goals, interests, and values.

The so-called realist-versus-nominalist dispute over the kind of objective reality that should be ascribed to social classes has long been a standard theoretical and methodological issue in discussions of social stratification. Yet it has not always been acknowledged that all the major nineteenth- and twentieth-century theorists of class were unmistakably on the realist side, regardless of whether they thought classes were based on economic interests, shared values, or common access to social power.

To Marx, a class was not fully formed until it had ceased to be a potential membership group (*Klasse an sich*) and had achieved a solidarity based on awareness of the common interests of its members in opposition to those of another class (*Klasse für sich*).

Joseph Schumpeter wrote: "Class is something more than an aggregation of class members. . . . A class is aware of its identity as a whole, sublimates itself as such, has its own peculiar life and characteristic 'spirit'." [6]

Max Weber is frequently cited by American sociologists in support of the contention that stratification in modern societies involves at least three partially independent hierarchies. He is also often invoked to justify the treatment of status rankings of occupations as synonymous with "class structure." Weber is the source of the "class-status-power" triad so favored by contemporary sociologists, but he was clearly concerned with identifying relatively cohesive groups differentiated with respect to these three bases of stratification and did not consider each as forming a continuous scale on which individuals or positions could be located. Thus, defining "class," like Marx, in strictly economic terms, he saw classes as "possible, and frequent, bases for communal action," although he was less certain than Marx that aggregates of people sharing like interests would become aware of their common interests and resort to "communal action" to advance them. Commonly regarded as the first modern social theorist to stress the importance of status, Weber was chiefly concerned to describe "status groups" or *Stände*—a term that clearly designates self-conscious collectivities. With reference to power, he used the less fortunate term "party," which nevertheless is unambiguous in connoting a collective entity rather than an attribute with respect to which individuals or roles vary continuously.

Finally, W. Lloyd Warner has always insisted that the six social classes he discovered in Newburyport were ultimately derived from "the way in which people in American communities actually classify themselves," although his critics have repeatedly challenged the validity of this claim after reanalyzing Warner's own data.

I doubt that any of these men would have devoted so much time and effort to the study of class had they thought it a matter of indifference whether classes "really" existed in the experience of their members or were no more than artifacts constructed by the sociologist as a means of ordering and summarizing his observations. The grouping together by the sociologist of individuals sharing a common position with respect to several distinct variables is a thoroughly legitimate and useful procedure in certain kinds of empirical research. But to call the resultant groupings "social classes" is to risk confusion with the quite different meaning of class in the writings of the leading theorists of stratification. Those researchers who use such terms as "socioeconomic group" or "level" at least implicitly recognize the distinction. But there are others who persist in referring to combined measures of occupation, income, or education as "indexes" of social class, although the entity these measures allegedly indicate appears to have no independent reality and "class" becomes no more than a shorthand expression for the ensemble of the same variables that have been combined to form the index.[7]

Critics of the realist conception of social classes have claimed that it necessarily implies that members of a society must be fully aware of the class system, and that its nature can therefore be determined by a simple opinion poll.[8] Surely, this is a specious argument. To assert that social controls and expectancies are present in the minds of the people whose conduct they influence is not to maintain that these people can readily put them into words. Even in the case of social norms in primary groups, which are clearly operative influences on behavior, those who conform to them are not always able to provide a coherent account of the codes that guide and restrain them in their day-to-day interactions with others.* The kind of awareness-in-behavior that frequently characterizes social class relations may involve still less self-consciousness, since classes (except in small isolated local communities) are not even potential primary groups; hence the frequent use of the term "quasi-group" to describe them.

The existence of classes, then, is a matter of degree, depending upon the extent to which their members are conscious of their unity and of the boundaries separating them from other classes.[9] But recognition of this does not invalidate the realist position. All the theorists previously mentioned, with the exception of the ahistorical Warner, dealt at length with what Schumpeter called "class formation" and saw it as a process that frequently did not result in fully developed classes. All of them attempted to specify the conditions under which aggregates of similarly situated individuals acquire cohesion and begin to behave as if they constitute at least a fictive membership group. Nor does the existence of individuals or families whose position is marginal within the class structure pose special theoretical dif-

---

* Many of the simplifications to which sociologists are prone in discussing the question of the degree to which people are aware of the determinants of their own behavior result from a failure to take into account Ryle's distinction between "knowing how" and "knowing that." See Gilbert Ryle, The Concept of Mind (New York: Barnes and Noble, 1949), pp. 25–61.

ficulties, for this is an inevitable result of interclass mobility, which is also a temporal process of uncertain outcome.

Finally, if the existence of a class system implies *some* stratification, it is also possible for particular classes to exist which do not fit into an orderly hierarchical system—most frequently new and rising classes.[10] Thus if we regard social stratification as a stratification of groups, classes may be formed in partial independence of stratification. But, more important, inequalities in the distribution of income, prestige, and power may exist in complete independence of it.

So far, my emphasis has been primarily definitional, and I have done no more than insist on a number of distinctions that are widely recognized in theory, although often ignored in research practice. Applied to contemporary industrial societies, however, these distinctions are acquiring new relevance, for modern societies are unmistakably moving in the direction of maintaining considerable institutionalized inequality in the absence of a class system, a condition that the Polish sociologist Stanislaw Ossowski has characterized as "nonegalitarian classlessness." [11] This condition has not yet been fully achieved even in the United States, much less in Western Europe. But the steady approach toward it increasingly transforms social classes into "ghost" communities preserving a fitful and wavering identity rooted in historical memories, similar to that ascribed by Nathan Glazer to the "ghost nations" of third-generation immigrants which continue to play a minor role in American politics.[12]

Since so many American sociologists have failed to see any significance in the disappearance of social classes in view of the survival of pronounced status inequalities, I shall briefly suggest several differences between societies where classes to some degree are present and societies where social inequality is relatively detached from stratification.

1. Income, educational, and status mobility are experienced differently in the two kinds of society. The person who moves upward (or downward) in a classless society does not encounter a class boundary in addition to the career obstacles he has to overcome in order to rise. Surely, it is the relative absence of classes in American society, whatever the historical causes for this absence, that accounts for the general belief that mobility is greater in the United States than in

Europe, a belief that Lipset and Bendix have shown to be unfounded.[13] Quite minor improvements in status or income are more readily perceived as mobility where no class boundary has to be crossed or confronted. There have been no real counterparts in the United States to the British "angry young men": persons of provincial and working-class origin who rise through educational or occupational attainment but become embittered on experiencing real or imagined exclusion when they try to cross a class line. The closest American equivalent is the experience or upwardly mobile blacks and members of ethnic or religious minorities. The fact that occupational status rankings are similar in America and Britain, and indeed in all advanced industrial societies,[14] merely underlines the difference between these rankings and a social class system.

2. More important, the distinction between stratification and social inequality aids us in understanding the political sociology of modern industrial societies. The distinction holds, it should be noted, regardless of whether economic interest or style of life is considered the basis of class. The latter—the "Marx vs. Warner" issue—is a separate definitional problem. However, last-ditch defenders of the relevance of the class concept, such as Rudolph Heberle,[15] fall back on the Marxist view of classes as interest groups divided by ownership or nonownership of the means of production. They plausibly argue that, although classes separated by sharp status and associational boundaries have been largely supplanted by a continuous hierarchy of status, conflicts of interest have by no means disappeared, and major groups continue to think and act in concert politically, at the very least in their voting behavior. The prediction of American Marxists in the 1930s that national cleavages of economic interest would increasingly supersede regional and ethnic divisions as the main basis of political alignment has on the whole been borne out.

But a second part of the prediction was that more tightly drawn class lines would result in an intensification of the political class struggle between Left and Right. The opposite has occurred: "class" has become a more important determinant of voting at the same time that the bitterness of class struggle has unmistakably abated.[16] While it may, therefore, be formally correct to insist that the term "class" in the Marxist sense is still applicable where society-wide conflicts of interest find political expression, it is surely more relevant to the understanding of modern politics to recognize that today economic interest groups and the political associations based on them do not, in T. H. Marshall's words, "permeate the whole lives of their members, as social classes do, nor are they always in action, and at times the constituent sub-groups may be more important than the largest aggregates." [17]

Ralf Dahrendorf attributes the obsolescence of the Marxist two-class system to what he aptly calls the "institutional isolation of industry" in modern society. But he tries to preserve the emphasis on conflict and change in Marxist class theory by redefining classes as the result of tension between power-holders and their subordinates, arguing that the division between owners and nonowners of property, and even conflicts of economic interest in general, are merely special cases of this more fundamental phenomenon. [18] Dahrendorf does not hesitate to conclude that there are as many class systems in a modern society as there are functional hiararchies of power and that a single individual may therefore simultaneously be a member of several different classes if he belongs to several associations each with its own structure of authority. In effect, Dahrendorf makes three main contentions: that social conflict is generated by differences in power; that classes are conflict groups; and that all conflict groups are classes. He may be right on the first two points (I am inclined to think that he is), but the third assertion surely represents the most quixotic effort to uphold the continuing usefulness of the concept of class in recent sociological writing. [19] Moreover, it would seem to be of no use at all in explaining the major political divisions in modern societies, although this has been precisely the most valuable feature of class theories that take their point of departure from Marx. Yet notwithstanding the inadequacies of his own class theory, Dahrendorf shows a far more acute grasp of the many differences between stratified and nonegalitarian classless societies than most American sociologists.

3. The absence of classes also helps account for the invisibility of poverty in the United States, to which several writers have recently called attention. The poor are composed of a number of categories of persons with particular demographic characteristics whose economic plight is no longer clearly linked to what Marx or Weber would con-

sider a "class situation." [20] Both in status and in economic terms, only black Americans come close to constituting a definable and cohesive deprived group, with the possible exception of tenant farmers and laborers in certain sectors of the agricultural economy. There is indeed some justification for calling blacks *the* American lower class. [21]

The emerging social structure of post-bourgeois industrial society can best be understood if, except for secondary purposes and for historical analysis, we abandon the concept of social class and redefine much of the work done under this label as a contribution to the sociology of equality and inequality. But American sociologists have been unwilling to make this necessary redefinition because of the influence of three biases, sometimes found together, sometimes apart, in the writings of different scholars.

First is a methodological bias. The procedures of multivariate analysis, particularly in survey research, have seemed to confirm the continuing relevance of "social class" by revealing correlations between summary measures of an individual's position on a number of socioeconomic variables and other aspects of his behavior.

Second is a theoretical bias. Structural-functional theorists consider societies to be coherent "systems" largely held together by a consensus on basic values. They are predisposed, therefore, to see social inequalities as the inevitable result of "differential evaluation" of roles and activities according to a shared value-system. They then equate the scale of invidious valuation with "social stratification" or the "social class system," frequently seeing the latter as identical empirically with status rankings of occupations such as the North-Hatt scale. [22] Given the theoretical commitment of structural-functionalists to the view that common values should be the main focus of sociological analysis, this practice has become so ingrained that alternative conceptions of stratification are regarded as eccentric and the whole issue is treated as one of terminology and conceptual nominalism, as if it made no empirical difference whether classes in the traditional sense existed or not. [23] Nevertheless, the debate over the so-called functional theory of stratification has done a great deal to clarify our understanding of the limits to human equality in societies with an elaborate division of labor. And one of the creators of the

most widely discussed version of that theory has recently acknowledged that it is a theory of inequality rather than of stratification and
that it "does not presuppose" the "conceptual category" of class.[24]

Finally, there is an ideological bias. Celebrations of the United
States have traditionally affirmed its "classlessness" and at the same
time extolled the equality of opportunity to attain the unequal rewards it allegedly provides. In challenging the reality of the latter,
sociologists have been unwilling to concede any truth to the claim of
classlessness lest they should appear to be denying the facts of inequality and barriers to opportunity. A spirit of liberal muckraking
still pervades much American sociological writing on stratification,
whether the writer's intent is to deplore or, like W. Lloyd Warner, to
counsel adjustment to the "brute facts" or inequality that are concealed or minimized by the official egalitarian ideology. The result
has been that sociologists have perpetuated the very confusion of
classlessness with equality that the official ideology makes.

American sociologists have failed to see that the absence of classes
may both in ideology and in social fact *more* effectively conceal existing inequalities than a social structure clearly divided into recogniz-
able classes. The invisibility of poverty in the United States, already
referred to, suggests such a conclusion, as does the fact that income
distribution has become more unequal in the past decade,[25] the very
decade of the "affluent society," which has witnessed so much individual and collective mobility, the mass diffusion of formerly restricted status symbols, and the breakdown of long-standing ethnic,
religious, and even racial barriers to opportunity.

In distinguishing conceptually between stratification and inequality
and noting some of the consequences of their increasing factual separation in contemporary society, I have avoided direct discussion of
mobility and equality of opportunity. Many writers who have insisted, as I have, that stratification involves a hierarchy of groups
rather than of positions or of individuals possessing unequal amounts
of income, prestige, and power, have gone on to argue that stratified
groups, or social classes, must necessarily be hereditary.[26] By transmitting the unequal privileges of one generation to the next through
the family, classes thus inevitably prevent the full institutionalization
of equality of opportunity.

The class systems of the past have undeniably been hereditary, though permitting sufficient mobility to justify distinguishing them from *caste* systems. But need this be so in the future? Historically, biological continuity has been the major means of preserving the internal solidarity and the distinctive ethos of classes from generation to generation, but is it necessarily the only possible means? Hereditary social classes may not be succeeded by nonegalitarian classlessness but by new classes whose members are not recruited by the intergenerational transmission of privileges through the family and whose cohesion does not depend on familial socialization.

Equality of opportunity could literally be achieved in full only by a method of allocating individuals to social positions that was strictly random, such as drawing lots. In contrasting equal opportunity with the inheritance of social position, however, sociologists obviously mean by the former the allocation of individuals to positions according to the single criterion of demonstrated ability to carry out the position's requirements. They have usually assumed that equality of opportunity thus defined not only is morally superior to any hereditary principle but also would prove to be more humanly tolerable, eliminating the social gulf that has divided hereditary social classes and removing the sense of injustice of low-status individuals who feel deprived of social rewards by the accident of birth.

There is some evidence that the absence of clear-cut class lines in the United States and the prevailing "democracy of manners" make it easier for low-status individuals to tolerate hereditary inequalities, provided they continue to believe that at least *some* opportunity to rise is available to them and their children.[27] But the most devastating attack on the belief that an inegalitarian order combined with full equal opportunity would reduce social conflict has been made by the English sociologist, Michael Young, in his brilliant sociological satire *The Rise of the Meritocracy: 1870–2033.*[28] This book has been completely ignored by American sociologists,[29] even by the journals, although it contributes vastly more to our theoretical understanding of class and inequality than the innumerable continuing studies of community class structures or of correlations between "class affiliation" and various kinds of behavior.

Young's book is cast in the form of historical interpretation written by a sociologist in the year 2033. His meritocratic social order is located in England, rather than "nowhere," and its evolution, under the pressure of social forces powerfully at work in today's world, is fully described. Although Young's purpose, like that of other anti-utopian writers, is to warn rather than to prophesy, the form he has chosen gives his book a sociological relevance greater than that of many similar efforts which do not succeed in becoming more than a kind of sociological science-fiction or satiric caricature of contemporary society.

Young's meritocracy is the result of three forces: the attack by socialists on all hereditary privileges; the pace of international economic competition requiring Britain to maintain high rates of economic growth; [30] and improvements in intelligence testing that have made it possible to reorganize the school system so that students can be segregated by intelligence at progressively earlier ages and trained for their eventual positions in the social order. Thus the testing centers and the school system have become the vehicles for selecting the ruling elite of meritocrats. Possessing a monopoly of ability, the meritocracy easily prevails in conflicts of interest with the lower strata, who are completely bereft of leadership, since all their potential leaders have been elevated into the meritocracy, and who must live with the knowledge that they have been scientifically proven to be inferior in ability to their rulers. The family, however, has survived in its present form and, echoing the functional theory of inequality, Young sees this as the Achilles heel of the regime. The meritocratic parents of inferior children and women, whose occupational skills suffer as a result of their withdrawal to bear and raise children, become infected with a discontent that eventually leads to revolution.

In Young's account the meritocracy clearly constitutes a unified ruling group, sharing common interests and a similar style of life, even though it is not recruited by heredity. And the same is true to a lesser degree of the "technicians"—the regime's euphemism for the industrial working class. Rather than defining class and stratification by the hereditary principle and calling the meritocracy a "classless" or unstratified society, it is surely more reasonable to see it as a new form of class society.

Yet one must raise some doubts about the general relevance of

Young's meritocracy to contemporary trends in advanced industrial societies. One might question, to begin with, his assumption that the family will remain cohesive and unchanged when so much else has been transformed. More important, the very plausibility of Young's account depends heavily on the roots of the meritocracy in English history with its characteristic "inevitability of gradualness." Thus Young sees the sharpness of class lines and the steepness of the status hierarchy that have existed in English society from feudalism to the present day as surviving even when birth has been entirely supplanted by merit as the basis of status. While the independence of stratification in general from the particular form of stratification by hereditary social classes is thus brilliantly suggested, one is forced to wonder whether a meritocracy would have the same consequences in an industrial society that lacked the pervasive continuities of English history—in, say, the United States.

I know of only one even sketchy account of a possible American meritocracy. It is provided, not by a sociologist, but by a lawyer and unsuccessful politician, Stimson Bullitt, in his perceptive little book *To Be a Politician*. [31] Bullitt envisages an American meritocratic order as being far more stable and less riven by class conflict than Young's Britain. He writes:

> The free flow up and down and the narrow range of variations in revealed ability among members of the great majority will make class differences less sharp. Also, the classes will be equally well fed and in most ways equally free; people on different levels of talent will be closer in many ways than were the social classes of the past. All people will have greater understanding, and therefore sympathy, for persons on other levels of talent than used to be the case between classes whose members lived like different species. [32]

While Bullitt attributes the absence of class tensions in a meritocratic United States in part to general prosperity and a high degree of material equality—conditions which are absent in Young's less economically self-sufficient England—the traditional classlessness of American society clearly leads him to anticipate an American meritocracy that would resemble a continuous hierarchy of unequal positions rather than Young's more stratified order.

Will the decline of hereditary social classes and the trend toward meritocracy eventuate in nonegalitarian classlessness or in a new class society allocating individuals by specialized abilities rather than by birth? What will be the peculiar discontents of each order? What form will the ancient dream of an egalitarian society, equally frustrated by both orders, take under these conditions? These are likely to be the questions, only dimly adumbrated in our present imperfectly affluent society, with which future sociologists of inequality will concern themselves. We are not likely to make much progress in answering them if we cling to a conceptual apparatus that does not distinguish between stratification and inequality, or between stratification in general and the particular form it has taken in the hereditary class societies of the past.

EIGHT

Jews, Gentiles, and the
New Establishment

MOST AMERICAN SOCIOLOGISTS believe in the ideal of an "open" society in which equality of opportunity generally prevails—and equality of opportunity means, of course, the opportunity to become unequal as a result of personal talent, effort, and achievement. The doctrine of leveling, that is, of a fraternal commonwealth in which all social differences are seen as secondary and even accidental, has not played much of a role in the ideology of American liberalism, although it has been central to British and European socialist thought.

American liberals, accordingly, have tended to concentrate their efforts on removing the barriers to mobility represented by hereditary class and racial or ethnic differences, and American sociologists have demonstrated the existence of these barriers with muckraking zeal. Such a standpoint has readily associated the inheritance of status through family membership with racial and ethnic discrimination, which denies the right of access to high social positions and rewards to certain minority groups on the ground that they are genetically unfitted. In *The Protestant Establishment*, [1] E. Digby Baltzell attempts to revise this perspective. Baltzell shares the liberal indignation over racial and ethnic discrimination—indeed his book is partly devoted to documenting and condemning the discrimination practiced against Jews since the 1880s by upper-class white Protestants. Baltzell does not, however, share the concomitant liberal opposition to an elite recruited primarily by birth. Instead, he argues the traditional conservative idea (rarely found among his fellow American sociologists) that a complex changing society needs a stable upper class based on familial continuity as a training ground for responsible political leadership.

Turning the tables on the liberal critics of hereditarian theories of human nature, Baltzell contends that aristocrats are made rather than born. For this very reason, he insists, we should value and preserve the upper-class institutions and agencies that make them: private schools, colleges, clubs, and elite suburbs. But access to these sanctuaries should be open to all who merit it. When men of talent or wealth are excluded solely on the grounds of race, national origin, or religion, the aristocratic principle is corrupted by the opposing principle of caste, which appeals to heredity rather than training and moral character to legitimate the superior position of the upper class. The men of talent and wealth who are rejected retaliate by rejecting the political leadership of the upper class; minority ethnic groups set themselves against the establishment; and even a section of the elite itself defects, accusing its peers of betraying their own best traditions of civic responsibility. Thus, in a democratic society, the upper-class elite eventually finds itself bypassed by politics and history, even though it retains its wealth and economic power as well as its control over the exclusive institutions that are its primary habitat. This, according to Baltzell, is largely what has happened to the Protestant establishment in America over the past three decades as a consequence of the long-standing conflict within it between the principles of aristocracy and caste.

What makes Baltzell's analysis of the evolution of the American elite superior to the accounts of earlier writers from Veblen to W. L. Warner, not to mention journalists like Cleveland Amory, is that he exposes the connections between high social status and political and economic power. In doing so, however, he leads one to question the relevance to contemporary America of his model of an aristocratic ruling class. Indeed, his description of the gradual loss of political power by the traditional Protestant upper class of the Eastern seaboard works to persuade us that the process is irreversible, despite the fact that this elite has produced leaders of the liberal wing of the Democratic Party such as Franklin Roosevelt, Averill Harriman, Joseph Clark, and others who emerge as the exemplars of his model. Writing before Dallas, Baltzell also reads too much long-range significance into the Eastern private school–Ivy League ambience of the Kennedy administration, which is the same error that C. Wright Mills—attacking what Baltzell wishes to defend—made in *The Power Elite* with regard to the Eisenhower administration.

Although Mills's "power elite" is not identical with Baltzell's "Protestant establishment," Mills attributed enormous importance to upper-class family bonds and old-school-tie loyalties. He was led to do so because he needed to find some plausible basis for the cohesiveness and community of interests he imputed to the small group of political, business, and military archons who, he claimed, directed American society. Baltzell knows better, and his book may be read as a refutation of at least this aspect of Mills's theory, for he rightly maintains that the upper class has lost political power, although his conviction that its decline is the result of caste barriers erected to preserve its ethnic and religious homogeneity is open to question.

Be that as it may, the forces in American society working against the restoration to political leadership of a traditional aristocracy—even a liberalized one—are far too powerful to be arrested by the belated removal of caste barriers. Among these forces is the movement westward of population and industry, already reflected in shifts in the political center of gravity in both political parties. The new men of the West and the Southwest are Protestant, and they certainly are not lacking in the crude caste impulses that Baltzell excoriates. No doubt these new men will mellow in time, but it is hard to believe that the mellowing agents will be the tradition-bearing institutions created by the old Eastern elite. There are not enough Grotons and Harvards, which is why it is the California system of state colleges and universities that represents the future.

Yet even if the American upper class had behaved like the nineteenth-century British aristocracy that Baltzell, following Tocqueville, so much admires, would the outcome have been so different? Modern history is the graveyard of aristocracies, both those that have bent with the gale of egalitarianism and those that have resisted it. The real value of Baltzell's book as social criticism, therefore, lies less in his argument for a stabilizing upper class and against the advocates of a dead-level egalitarianism, whom he labels "Marxists," than in the overall perspective which he summed up for a *Newsweek* reporter:

"I think it's a lousy situation in this country when the Protestants control business, the Catholics politics, and the Jews intellectual life." This is, of course, an oversimplification that applies mainly to the big cities of the East and Midwest. Even so, Baltzell's sense that there is a real trend in America toward ethnic-religious separatism is accurate, and it is this that makes his protest against continuing WASP exclusiveness more than merely another reminder that a few pockets of anti-Semitism and religious animosity still exist in American life.

One can also sympathize with Baltzell's insistence on the value of preserving the traditional upper-class schools and colleges. If it is quixotic to see them as nurseries of future statesmen, they are nevertheless indispensable as centers of resistance to the vocationalism, present-mindedness, and pallid middle-class conformism of a public education that is subject to all the bureaucratic and political pressures of our mass society. Edgar Z. Friedenberg has argued that the cause of educational diversity and cultural variety is served by maintaining schools and colleges created by the old elite, provided they are not discriminatory. And indeed, Baltzell's review of the changed admissions policies of these schools and his discussion of the extracurricular interests and political sympathies of Andover and Exeter students show that they have ceased to be caste institutions.

The heart of Baltzell's book, however, is his account of modern American history from the viewpoint of this struggle between aristocracy and caste within the Protestant elite. He tells of the coming of the immigrants and of the ideological response of those "Brahmin intellectuals" who embraced social Darwinist and racist theories; of the creation in the Gilded Age of exclusive suburbs, resorts, and schools; and of the solidification and extension of these caste barriers against Jews and other ethnic groups in the 1920s. This is, of course, a familiar tale, and Baltzell draws on the familiar historical, biographical, and literary sources—the opinions and careers of Henry Adams, John Jay Chapman, and A. Lawrence Lowell, the scholarship of Hofstadter, Handlin, and Schlesinger, Jr., and the literary evidence of Fitzgerald, Mencken, and Marquand.

The more interesting facet of Baltzell's narrative is that he counterpoints each chapter on the rise of caste barriers with one on the opposition to them by members of the Protestant upper class. Thus the anti-Semitic John Jay Chapman and the racist Madison Grant are contrasted with Charles Eliot (president of Harvard and foe of the Immigration League), Woodrow Wilson, and the two Roosevelts. Baltzell also emphasizes the contribution to the intellectual attack on racist doctrines by old-stock scholars like Dewey, Beard, and Charles Horton Cooley, and the important role of patricians who defected from the Republican Party in the Wilson, FDR, and Kennedy administrations, as well as of those who participated in the municipal reform movements of New York and Philadelphia. This reading of recent political and intellectual history is, to be sure, a highly selective one: the rise of ethnic minorities and organized labor as a major force in American life recedes into the background, while the New Deal, the debate over American entry into World War II, and McCarthyism are seen as episodes in the struggle for the soul of the old elite. But Baltzell does not pretend to be writing a comprehensive history; and his evidence that American liberalism, along with the environmentalist and antiracist perspectives of contemporary social science, is indebted to the Protestant patrician tradition provides a necessary corrective to interpretations which treat both American politics and American intellectual life exclusively in terms of conflict between classes and ethnic groups.

Baltzell goes on to show that if the aristocratic principle today is embodied in the old Eastern colleges and private schools, the caste principle remains entrenched in the suburban country clubs and the metropolitan men's clubs. "Country club anti-Semitism" has become something of a joke among Jews, now that they are so heavily, and to all appearances permanently, concentrated in the upper reaches of the occupational and income hierarchy. Perhaps Baltzell takes it a bit too seriously; but then he is concerned over anti-Semitism as a blot on the best traditions of the establishment rather than as a social problem or an actual hardship for Jews in its own right. His outrage also diverts him from any discussion of the tendency of Jews and other minorities to create parallel structures of ethnically homogeneous resorts and clubs, thus perpetuating the kind of separatism he deplores.

The metropolitan clubs, however, are another matter altogether.

Baltzell demonstrates that their denial of membership to Jews is closely related to the almost exclusively Anglo-Saxon composition of the top leadership of our largest corporations. His chief horrible example is the Duquesne Club of Pittsburgh, which is the informal meeting place for executives of the steel industry. Since the major corporations have not yet adapted to the ethnic diversity of the white population and to the economic and educational rise of the children of immigrants, it is small wonder that they have not made the slightest contribution to winning full civil rights and equal job opportunities for blacks. Baltzell quotes a Coca-Cola executive who, when asked about his company's stand on the racial issue, replied: "Our problem is to walk a very fine line and be friends with everybody. I've heard the phrase 'Stand Up and Be Counted' for so long from both sides that I'm sick of it. Sure we want to stand up and be counted, but on both sides of the fence. For God's sake, why don't they let us go on selling a delicious and refreshing beverage to anybody who's got a gullet he can pour it down." [2]

The genteel anti-Semitism of the metropolitan clubs frequented by executives is further reflected in the college recruiting policies of the corporations. In turn, the executives who enter politics give local Republican organizations their predominantly Anglo-Saxon cast, though after each GOP debacle at the polls Republican leaders fill the air with demands that the party "broaden its base" by attracting other ethnic groups. Baltzell wants the corporations to reform themselves: "Top managers must be 'uncommon men' and take the lead rather than wait to be pushed by FEPC legislation, the NAACP, the Anti-Defamation League, or the American Civil Liberties Union. Moreover, if management waits until the state takes the initiative, it will have the statism it deserves. The national corporation must now be seen as a moral community whose duty it is to set standards on a national scale." [3]

The trouble with this demand is that today's corporate elite overlaps but is not identical with the old Protestant establishment. There is little likelihood that the best civic traditions of the latter will spread throughout the business world. The aggressive and politically retrograde role of Western business communities in backing Goldwater and financing radical-right causes is no transitory phenomenon.

Even the radical right, to be sure, strives to avoid the appearance of anti-Semitism, but this is hardly reason to believe that it can provide responsible moral and political leadership on a national scale. Baltzell is surely right to treat anti-Semitism as evidence of caste irresponsibility; however, it does not follow that its disappearance will insure the flourishing of the aristocratic noblesse oblige he extols.

Baltzell is most illuminating when he confines himself to the Eastern elite, which he knows at first hand and whose Philadelphia branch he has previously studied. He has a particularly good eye for crucial generational differences. The Wilsons and the Roosevelts were patrician reformers who never quite overcame their upper-class reserve and distaste for members of the ethnic minority groups politically allied with them. The great divide separating them from the Kennedy generation, Baltzell suggests, was service in the armed forces during World War II. This experience most nearly realized "the American ideal of equality of opportunity and a hierarchically organized social structure. . . . It is hard to believe that down in Washington on the New Frontier the accidents of birth meant much to leaders of men who shared a common war experience, a common educational background and common ideals about our democracy." [4]

The "common educational background" to which Baltzell refers is, of course, the elite private schools and colleges. Both the faculties and the student bodies of our major universities have transformed themselves during the years since World War II into "ethnic aristocracies drawing on a truly national pool of talent." The kinds of contacts between Jews and non-Jews that now prevail in academic, professional, and intellectual circles may very well prefigure future relations in widening upper middle-class circles. Although the trend toward ethnic-religious separatism is a reality, there is also, as Baltzell notes, a countertrend toward greater employment of Jews in some of the newer industries (especially in technical positions), and toward increased participation by Jews in politics, civic groups, and community-wide voluntary associations. It is probably too early to say which trend is likely to predominate, although one may doubt whether the attitude of the patrician elite will be quite as decisive as Baltzell believes.

Yet even in university circles, relations between Jews and non-Jews are not as free of frictions and covert animosities as is suggested by the remark of a professor whom Baltzell quotes: "It is not that some of my best friends are Jews—as a matter of fact, most of my best friends are." [5] The old caste attitudes and stereotypes of the Jew as parvenu have little to do with these newer relations and the particular tensions they breed. Baltzell is so concerned with the residues of classic genteel anti-Semitism that he provides scant guidance on this score. For example, he cites numerous instances of social discrimination against prominent men of Jewish origin who have attended the best schools, married non-Jews, and have even converted, or had fathers who converted, to Christianity. (He even repeats a few stories of slights suffered by Barry Goldwater.) These incidents dramatically underline the irrationality of surviving caste barriers, but one wants to ask, What about men who haven't converted, who still value their Jewish heritage, whether in religious or secular terms? Are there not subtle differences in character and style between Jews and non-Jews that the former may wish to maintain? What about the whole issue of preserving Jewish identity in prosperous middle-class America?

This is not Baltzell's subject and it is perhaps unfair to tax him for ignoring it. The Protestant caste attitudes he examines have little to do with the kinds of relations between Jews and non-Jews that are now developing. Undoubtedly, the group images formed in present academic, professional, and intellectual circles reflect the subtle realities of ethnic differences more closely than the standard stereotypes of Jew and *goy* of an earlier period. More or less accurately, non-Jews in these circles are apt to attribute to Jews such traits as intellectuality, political liberalism, intense parental solicitude with close bonds between mothers and sons, strong attachment to the extended family, a liking for food and physical comforts in general, volubility and emotional expressiveness, fear of violence, and ironic humor. These traits obviously will be perceived only where there is considerable intimacy in informal social contexts. And they may be evaluated either positively or negatively—either "anti-Semitically" or "philo-Semitically," to use labels that are perhaps too strong in this connection.

Jews living in such environments, for their part, perceive certain distinctive WASP traits that also have little to do with formal religious affiliation or with traditional hostile stereotypes. Again more or less accurately, they often see Anglo-Saxons as emotionally reserved, prone to attach greater value to formally correct manners, inclined to resist contemporary fashions and innovations, loyal to institutional ties but less so to kin, less permissive in child-rearing, and touched with residual asceticism, if not puritanism. These traits, too, may be evaluated positively or negatively.

Thus each group tends to develop new stereotypes of the other as a result of closer contact. The new images, whether favorably or unfavorably evaluated are far more accurate than the older ones, which are long outdated and were always distorted by projective thinking. Such new contacts between Jews and Anglo-Saxon Protestants in upper-middle-class circles perhaps have little relevance to traditional anti-Semitism or to the character of the dominant elites in American society. Yet they may well be opening a new chapter in the relations between Jews and non-Jews in America.

NINE

How Important Is Social Class?

THE OLD QUESTION of why there has been no socialism in the United States has often been answered by referring to the racial, ethnic, and religious divisions within the ranks of labor, which are the result of successive waves of overseas immigration and the partial incorporation into the labor force of the rural blacks. Accordingly, the American Left has been impatient with the ethnic loyalties and animosities of American workers, seeing them as fossilized survivals that retard the growth of class consciousness. Radicals have charged the ruling classes with deliberately fomenting racial and religious prejudice as part of a divide-and-rule strategy. Yet liberal pluralists have argued that multiple loyalties to class and interest organizations, nationality groups, and churches have enabled the United States to maintain a stable yet flexible order, and to avoid those bitter conflicts in which class, ethnic, and religious divisions are superimposed upon one another. Both radicals and liberals have joined in deploring the race consciousness of American workers, who have so often excluded blacks, Orientals, and Chicanos from their organizations, thus subjecting these groups to relatively unrestrained exploitation.

These attitudes now have been modified by what Andrew Greeley has called "the legitimation of ethnic self-consciousness." New Left radicals and those liberals influenced by them have supported the growing ethnic solidarity of blacks, Chicanos, and American Indians. But they have looked with disfavor upon the revival of ethnic sentiments among whites—seeing them, not inaccurately, as a response to the new black militancy. Having written off the working class and its unions as a force for major change, the New Left is prone to dismiss the stirrings of ethnic awareness among blue-collar workers as no more than tokens of the incurable racism of the American society. Older socialists, though they have abandoned the millennial expectations of classical Marxism, have retained their attachment to the proletariat, accepting it as it is, "warts and all," as a force for peaceful democratic change. And many of them have, as a result, adopted a newly sympathetic attitude toward the American workers' ethnicities. Both ideological orientations have aroused new interest in the tangled web of class and ethnic identification in American society.

Less politically committed social analysts also have tended to minimize the role of ethnic groups in American society, seeing them as destined to disappear within a few generations. In the 1950s, religious identifications were thought to be acquiring new significance in an emerging "mass society" in which even objective class inequalities were believed to be diminishing. A religious revival was widely proclaimed, and some survey researchers claimed that "religious affiliation" was becoming the crucial variable, supplanting class, ethnicity, and rural-urban residence in accounting for surviving differences in behavior within an increasingly homogenized soeiety. Religious organizations were seen as replacing the old ethnic associations founded by immigrants in providing individuals with secure group membership and social and emotional support as a protection against the impersonality of the larger society. Will Herberg's *Protestant-Catholic-Jew* and Gerhard Lenski's *The Religious Factor* were the two most impressive books representing these tendencies. Lenski, however, has recently conceded that *"The Religious Factor* is, at best, a picture of an era that has ended." [1]

Sociologists and a host of popular social critics who exaggerated and oversimplified their conclusions called attention in the 1950s to new forms of community life in the expanding suburbs. Although it was recognized that economic and ethnic segregation was maintained and even increased in the suburbs, suburbia was seen primarily as a new and relatively classless way of life, supplanting the old ethnic urban neighborhoods. It was thought to represent the future to which surviving working-class, lower-class, and ethnic subcultures would eventually succumb under the impact of continuing prosperity. Most of the commentary on suburbia was derisive in tone, and by the early

1960s many sociologists were refuting negative stereotypes that had often originated in popularizations of earlier studies by their colleagues.[2]

Some stressed the persistence of class differences, even in suburbia itself, as against the view of a standardized suburban life-style embracing almost everyone. A smaller number argued that ethnic differences had far from disappeared. But even Nathan Glazer, who had insisted for years on the neglected and often subterranean influence of ethnic ties in American life, recently conceded in his introduction to a new edition of *Beyond the Melting Pot* that he and Daniel Patrick Moynihan had underestimated the durability of ethnicity in 1963, when they had concluded the first edition with the sentence "religion and race define the next stage in the evolution of the American peoples." [3]

In the early sixties, attention shifted from religion and suburbia back to the inner city and, to a lesser extent, to the rural and small-town South and the border-state region. The reason, of course, was the black revolution and the rediscovery of poverty. Racial discrimination and economic deprivation, victimizing a sizable minority of the total population, seemed more significant than the largely symbolic religious and intra-middle-class differences stressed in the previous decade. The gradualist view of poverty as confined to "pockets," destined to be wiped out in the course of continued economic growth, no longer seemed plausible. Nor did the comfortable liberal notion that the elimination of racial discrimination constituted the "unfinished business of American democracy," bound to be achieved painlessly within a few decades. By the end of the sixties the student and youth revolts and the emergence of a new feminist movement had added age, generation, and sex to the list of major group identifications seen as shaping values in America.

Clearly, the shifts in the attention of social analysts from class to religious, residential, race, sex, and generational divisions reflect real discontinuities in the recent development of American society. But the mass media, with their voracious appetite for novelty, pick up and publicize each new group that comes into focus, enhancing the impression of discontinuity and casting into outer darkness the "Other Americas" or "forgotten men" or "silent majorities," who then have to be "rediscovered" when the currently fashionable group has been overexposed.

Yet the most scrupulous, perceptive sociological studies of different segments of American society give rise to disagreements as to exactly *which* group memberships or cultural identities account for the attitudes and life-styles that even the critics of such studies concede they accurately describe. I shall give several illustrations of such controversies that arise out of the findings of some of the more influential recent sociological studies, stressing those bearing on class and ethnicity. Sociological research, to be sure, reveals the multiple affiliations and identities of its subjects; but sociologists, sometimes out of a polemical desire to refute prevailing scholarly or popular stereotypes, often stress the primacy of one set of social or cultural determinants over others. Even where this is avoided, the precise way in which age, generation, class, religion, ethnicity, race, and residence interact to produce a subcultural profile poses a difficult problem of analysis.

The sociologist Herbert Gans has insisted on the primacy of class, viewed as the resultant of income and educational and occupational opportunities, in shaping group values and behavior. Gans's first book was *The Urban Villagers*,[4] a study of an Italian community in the West End of Boston which was influential in mobilizing liberal intellectuals against urban renewal projects that destroyed cohesive neighborhoods. Gans insisted that his subjects' way of life reflected a generic working class rather than a specifically Italian American subculture, pointing to patterns of family structure, sex role and courtship practices, and other values that West Enders shared with a wide variety of ethnically different working-class communities, including the culturally homogeneous British working class. In a review of the book, Peter Rossi, one of the few leading American sociologists of Italian American origin, demurred. He invoked "memories of my childhood and adolescence in New York City during the twenties and thirties" to argue that "there is much more characteristically Italian (or perhaps more generally Latin) in the social organization of the West End than Gans would have the reader believe."[5]

In a later study of a planned suburban community in the Philadelphia area, *The Levittowners*,[6] Herbert Gans attacked the "myth of suburbia," arguing that the move to the suburbs had not fundamentally changed class-determined life-styles and that the major conflicts in the multiclass community he studied arose out of clashes of upper-middle-class with lower-middle and working-class values and interests. Gans has also been a major critic of the notion that there is an at least semiautonomous "culture of poverty," insisting that the behavior of the poor is essentially a response to economic deprivation and lack of opportunity.

Bennett Berger's *Working-Class Suburb* was an earlier study attacking the suburban myth. It described, unlike *The Levittowners*, a purely working-class planned development in San Jose, California. Like Gans in *The Urban Villagers*, Berger argued that his subjects embodied an "incipient native white working-class culture" destined to replace older ethnic cultures, although in contrast to Gans the main thrust of his argument was directed against the claims of suburban residence rather than of ethnicity as a shaper of life-styles. He wrote:

We have no clear images of *American* "working-class style" precisely because the lowest positions on our socioeconomic ladder were traditionally occupied by the most recent groups of European immigrants, each of which, as they arrived, pushed earlier groups of immigrants up. Our images of working-class life, consequently, are dominated by ethnic motifs. But the end of mass immigration from Europe may promote the development of an indigenous white working-class culture in the United States in the near future. . . . the blue-collar work force is likely to remain at between 20 and 25 million for some time to come, and it is extremely doubtful that Mexicans, Puerto Ricans, and Negroes will constitute the major part of this industrial labor force. Moreover, the facts of color, marginal occupations (largely not unionized), and ghetto residence are likely to sustain the ethnicity of these groups for the foreseeable future and isolate them from the native, white working-class culture apparently incipient in the San Jose suburb. [7]

Berger's interpretation of his own evidence did not pass unchallenged. In a review, Harold Wilensky argued that since Berger's community was only two years old at the time of the study, he had not given its residents sufficient time to develop such suburban middle-class patterns as the coffee klatsch among wives, joining voluntary associations, becoming active in the church and PTA, reading consumer-oriented magazines, and raising their aspirations for their children.[8] Wilensky also claimed that Berger's own evidence suggested that some of these patterns were beginning to appear, although they had not been present in the grimy industrial slum Berger's respondents had inhabited before moving to the suburb. Wilensky concluded of Berger's community that "it looks like a suburban variant of lower-middle class culture."

In a later publication, Wilensky forcefully generalized his viewpoint, maintaining that:

in the United States and in other rich countries, class consciousness among manual workers is a transitional phenomenon characterizing workers not yet accustomed to the modern metropolis and the modern work place; that a clearly defined working class no longer exists, if it ever did; that much behavior and many attitudes said to be rooted in class are instead a matter of race, religion, ethnic origin, education, age, and stage in the family life cycle.

Insofar as class categories remain at all useful, the line that divides stably employed, well-educated, well-paid workers from the lower class is becoming more important than the split between upper working class and lower middle class.[9]

The Gans-Rossi difference was over the relative importance of class as against ethnicity, but Berger and Wilensky disagreed over whether there are distinct lower-middle and working-class subcultures, although Wilensky was evidently inclined to attach more importance than either Gans or Berger to suburban residence as producing at least a "variant" of lower-middle-class culture. Wilensky's later statement, however, downgrades the significance of class as such. But he fails to distinguish between politically militant class consciousness in the Marxist sense and the more common emphasis in American sociology on class as the shaper of life-styles and the source of a diffuse "consciousness of kind" that is hardly the same thing as Marxist class consciousness.

The concept of class has been used with reference to American life in three distinct ways. First, there is the Marxist model of classes as rival groups organized and mobilized for conflict arising out of clashing economic interests. Wilensky correctly questions the importance of this kind of "class consciousness" in the United States today and even in the past. Except perhaps for a few brief moments in the 1930s and in particular regions or industries, the American working class has not conformed to the Marxist model. There has never developed here a network of working-class interest associations and trade-union- or party-created institutions sufficiently far-flung and powerful to constitute a distinctive subculture resembling the "nation within a nation" formed around the SPD in imperial Germany.[10] The distinctive working-class way of life and "we-them" consciousness described by such English writers as Richard Hoggart, Raymond Williams, and E. P. Thompson has scarcely even been present in America.

Most American sociologists have favored a noneconomic conception of "social class," defining classes as aggregates of persons or families differing in values and behavior and forming a rank order of status levels. Most research on class in American communities has employed, at least implicitly, this view of classes as ranked subcultures. The studies of W. L. Warner and his associates in the 1930s and 1940s were pioneering examples. The much-criticized idea of a "culture of poverty" doubtless initially caught on so quickly because it was consistent with this approach.

However, when such sociologists as Herbert Gans and Bennett Berger insist on the importance of class in American life, they suggest a third conception. Essentially, they stress the role of economic inequalities in shaping people's aspirations and outlooks. Classes in this view are neither solidary groups mobilized for social conflict nor more diffuse groups sharing a common life-style and status pride. Rather, classes are groups whose members' aspirations and opportunities, beliefs and life-styles, far from reflecting a coherent self-sustaining culture or subculture, are basically shaped by their market position in the national economy, and, to use a formulation of Max Weber's, by their differential "life-chances" in the commodity, credit, and labor markets.

Neither the alternative subcultural nor the unequal life-chance views conceive of classes as sharply defined groups inspiring intense loyalties and becoming the focus of self-consciously affirmed identities. True, such analysts as Veblen, the Lynds, Mills, and, more recently, G. William Domhoff have imputed at least a modified form of Marxist class consciousness to American upper or "ruling" classes.* And some versions of the subcultural model have pictured classes as membership groups creating strong identifications, at least at the local community level. But these partial exceptions either exclude the vast majority of Americans or confine, in Stanislaw Ossowski's phrase, "class structure in the social consciousness" to the local community.[11]

This is significant because it means that class fails to lend itself to the interpretation most favored by American sociologists to account for both changing and constant group loyalties and the process of identity-formation in America: what might be called the "protection-against-anomie" theory. Sociologists have contended that strong social bonds and identities based on religion, ethnicity, locality, and occupation have persisted or developed in America because they provide emotional security and a sense of community in face of the impersonality and rapid social change of the large society. The fierce peer-group loyalties—often affirmed as "generational" solidarity—of the young, the appeal of communes, and the new popularity of encounter and sensitivity-training groups, all are recent phenomena readily explained in these terms. The "quest for community" as a reaction to the forces promoting anomie—whether these forces are primarily identified with capitalist market relations, industrialization, urbanization, bureaucratization, or all of these together—has long been a major theme of sociological thought going back to nineteenth-century thinkers, in particular to Durkheim and Tönnies.

But the influence of class on conduct in America cannot be understood in terms of this theory, for neither classes nor associations based explicitly on class bonds and interest have been recognized objects of loyalty, or membership groups with which people could proudly identify. Frank Tannenbaum's *A Philosophy of Labor* [12] is one of the very few efforts by an American to present trade unions as *Gemeinschaften*, protecting their members against the impersonal forces of industrial society rather than as limited economic-interest organiza-

---

* However hard-headed corporate elites may have been in protecting and advancing their own interests, even in the 1930s the claim by upper-class conservatives that FDR was "a traitor to his class" had a forced, anachronistic ring.

tions. But even Tannenbaum was suggesting a potential role rather than describing an actual one. Milton Gordon in his *Assimilation in American Life* [13] argues that the combination of ethnic origin and class position has produced a group he calls an "ethclass," and that this is the largest "reference group" with which Americans feel a positive sense of identification. People define themselves, Gordon maintains, primarily as upper middle-class Jews, working-class Poles, or lower-class blacks rather than by class or ethnic origin alone.

Tocqueville was the first to suggest that the leveling of class distinctions in the United States created the risk of an atomized, anonymous society threatened by the "tyranny of the majority," and he saw the American predilection for forming voluntary associations as a response to this situation. Nearly a century later, European theorists of "mass society" such as Emil Lederer and Hannah Arendt held that the decline and breakup of social classes under the impact of war, inflation, and depression had produced a spiritual homelessness conducive to the rise of totalitarian movements that adopted slogans promising the restoration of brotherhood and community. But in America groups other than classes have played an intermediate role between the family and the total society, protecting the individual from anomie.

Sociologists have used the protection-against-anomie theory to account for everything from rises in the birth rate to the appeal of fanatical ideological movements, so it hardly suffices to explain why particular groups become major carriers of identity. "Why," Andrew Greeley asks,

was not social class the membership around which American city dwellers could rally, as it was in England? Why have the trade unions rarely, if ever, played quite the fraternal role in American society that they have in many continental societies? Granted that urban man needed something to provide him with some sort of identification between his family and the impersonal metropolis, why did he stick with the ethnic group when there were other groupings to which he could make a strong emotional commitment? [14]

Why, moreover, do different groups—churches, suburban communities, ethnic groups—appear to succeed one another as centers of "belongingness"? To a degree this is, as I have already noted, a matter of appearance encouraged by fashions in sociological theorizing and the nervous faddishness of the media. As Greeley observes,

The relevant issue for social research is not whether one [means of self-definition] replaces the other or even whether these factors are being replaced by yet another means of self-definition. The important question is, rather, under what sets of circumstances, which kinds of people find what sources of self-definition pertinent. When, for example, do I choose, explicitly or implicity, to define myself as Irish, when as Catholic, when as Irish Catholic, when as an academic, when a Chicagoan, when as an American? [15]

But what, then, of the current "resurgence of ethnicity," noted by such sociologists as Greeley himself, Glazer and Moynihan, and increasingly publicized by the media? Obviously, the new assertiveness of blacks and the adoption of separatist slogans by some black militants have provided the occasion for a newly self-conscious and unapologetic ethnicity among whites. Yet this cannot be dismissed, as it so often is, as a mere cover for racism. Glazer and Moynihan suggest that

ethnic identities have taken over some of the task in self-definition and in definition by others that occupational identities, particularly working-class identities, have generally played. The status of the worker has been downgraded; as a result, apparently, the status of being an ethnic, a member of an ethnic group, has been upgraded. . . . Today, it may be better to be an Italian than a worker. Twenty years ago, it was the other way around. [16]

Such an emphasis on ethnicity rather than class or occupation reflects a general shift away from work identities and the workplace, which now has been noted in a variety of contexts for two decades. Even New Left radicals have argued that "the community" (the inner-city community, or ghetto) rather than the factory is now the major locus of social conflict. "Member of the community" and "community control" have acquired in much radical rhetoric the aura that once attached to "worker" and "workers' control." Christopher Lasch, a spokesman for this outlook, has advocated "building socialism" in the ghetto, although in his critique of black nationalism he asks, "Would self-determination for the ghetto threaten General Motors?" And he answers in the negative—which should be sufficient to dispose of "socialism in one community" as a primary objective in itself. [17]

Recently, the assertion of a "generation gap," in which age and generation are regarded as crucial bases of identity and group allegiance, has been subjected to criticism that in many ways resembles the earlier debunking of the suburban myth. [18] Both critiques emphasized the persistence of class differences within, respectively, the younger generation and suburbia. College youth may have been attracted to the New Left and the counterculture but, it is pointed out, George Wallace also drew disproportionate support in 1968 from working-class and lower-middle-class youth. These polar outlooks attract, nevertheless, minorities: most young people continue to divide on political and social issues along the same economic and educational lines as their parents.

The restless hunger of many young people for new ideals and new forms of group life has obviously been influential out of proportion to the numbers involved. As if in response, the erosion of familiar moral landmarks has evoked self-conscious reaffirmations of traditional ethnic, religious, and territorial ties; this, of course, has happened often in the troubled course of modern history. Yet much as it has contributed to our understanding of the stresses of contemporary life, the emphasis of the sociological perspective on anomie and "alienation," "the quest for community," "identity crisis," and "the need for participation" tends to lead to a relative neglect of the importance of the *economic*, of inequality in income and opportunity, as major determinants of the fate of individuals and groups. It has been the special merit of such sociologists as Herbert Gans and S. M. Miller to remind us of the continuing, pervasive influence of economic forces at the national level.

One may readily agree with Andrew Greeley that ethnic groups are not merely a cover for white racism, that they provide emotional support and prideful identities to their members, are a valuable source of diversity within American society, and that their legitimation need not result in the kind of divisiveness that prevents multiethnic coalitions in support of broad social goals. I also share Greeley's distaste for rootless "technological man" and for Warren Bennis's "temporary society," as well as for Robert Jay Lifton's "protean man"—and, more recently, for the ambivalent account by Greeley's fellow Irishman, William Irwin Thompson, of the "Los Angelization of America." [19]

It remains all too possible that the new positive valuation of ethnicity could become a matter of purely symbolic concessions, diverting attention away from the need for egalitarian economic reforms. This danger has often been pointed out in connection with black studies programs, courses in Swahili, and plans to encourage "black capitalism" in the ghettos. Why should it be any less of a danger where the group pride of working-class "white ethnics" is involved? The likelihood of purely symbolic gains and "tokenism" seems somewhat greater than that white ethnic feelings will take an ugly racist turn and provide the basis for a fascist movement, although that possibility cannot be dismissed should American society face acute disaster.

One negative corollary of close-knit group ties, and the support they provide for the individual, has been the stifling of impulses to freedom, self-determination, and striking out on new paths. If ethnic groups have often, as Greeley acknowledges, been a "mobility trap" for their members, may not heightened ethnic solidarity lead to an even greater sense of imprisonment for working-class boys and, especially, girls, who have become aware in recent years of new options in life-styles and career patterns and a more permissive hedonist ethos? The life-styles of ghetto blacks living on welfare in matrifocal families have often enough been held up by white liberals as models for emulation, and critics of the violence, family instability, lack of achievement orientation, and the many physical and mental pathologies prevalent in the black underclass have been accused of being "hung up on middle-class values." Such anthropological romanticism is unlikely to promote the kind of social change needed to eliminate ghettos, poverty, and racial discrimination. Are we to extend it to white ethnic groups, celebrate the cultural diversity of American society—and ignore its persisting economic injustices and the continuing arbitrary authority to which workers, both black and white, are subject on the job?

Despite the familiar claim that the ethnic diversity of the American labor force was a barrier to the birth of a powerful socialist movement, it is worth recalling that immigrant groups constituted the bulk

of the membership of the newly created Communist Party—or parties—after World War I.[20] Even 53 percent of the membership of the
indigenous Socialist Party was foreign-born by 1920.[21] The core of
the New Deal coalition is usually described as consisting of labor and
the urban minorities, although, to a considerable degree, these two
groups contained the same people. If the Church of England, as the
old saw has it, is the Tory Party at prayer, it has been almost as true
that America's white ethnic groups have been the Democratic Party
and the union movement at home. Today "white ethnics" and "blue-
collar workers"—when not the invidious "hard hats"—are terms
often used interchangeably, each serving as a euphemism for the
other in different contexts.

The revival of ethnic sentiments, therefore, need not be an obstacle to a coalition politics working through the Democratic Party for
reforms. One does not have to choose between extolling the new ethnicity, on the one hand, and ignoring or even deploring it, on the
other. But recognition of the reality and the value of ethnic groups is
no substitute for improving the school systems, reforming the tax
structure, providing better housing, cleaning up the cities, and, in
general, redistributing the good things of life in a way that will both
increase the opportunities for individuals to escape from their ethnic
communities, if they so wish, and improve the levels and quality of
living in the ethnic communities themselves.

PART THREE
Power and Politics

Introduction

THIS SECTION is considerably more heterogeneous in subject and theme than the two previous ones. Several of the essays in it have little in common other than that they touch in some way on power or politics.

The first three essays have not previously been published. They are drawn from a work in progress on the concept of power in social theory. The first and longest, however, incorporates large parts of "Some Problems in Defining Power," *American Journal of Sociology*, 73 (May 1968), 673–81. The third essay, "Competent Authority: Reality and Legitimating Model," was presented at a plenary session on "the expert society" at the 1975 American Sociological Association annual meetings held in San Francisco. It will also be included in a volume of selected papers presented at the plenary sessions to be edited by Lewis A. Coser and Otto N. Larsen and published by The Free Press.

"Economic Development and Democracy" was written in 1967 at the request of the editors of *Dissent* as a critique of an article by Robert L. Heilbroner that appeared in *Commentary*. [1] Heilbroner was invited to reply to me in *Dissent*, and I wrote a counterrebuttal, the whole exchange, with the exception of his original article, appearing in the same issue. [2] Both Heilbroner and I felt that our debate had raised real issues and avoided personal and ideological polemics. So little was he offended at having been singled out for criticism that he himself joined the editorial board of *Dissent* shortly afterward.

Heilbroner ended his reply to me with the suggestion "let us wait 10 or 20 years and see which of us is right." [3] Eight years have passed, but it can hardly be said that events have unambiguously confirmed either of our positions. Communist regimes have come to power in South Vietnam and Cambodia, in the former as a result of conventional military conquest from the north rather than by successful internal revolution, the once-powerful Viet Cong having played little part in the final collapse of the Saigon government in the spring of 1975. In Cambodia a locally based movement, the Khmer Rouge, triumphed mostly because of the opportunity given it when the United States installed the flimsy Lon Nol puppet government. Far from proposing ambitious programs of economic development, the new Cambodian government appears to have opted for a deurbanized, deindustrialized agrarian communism isolated from any foreign influences, carrying even further the downgrading of economic development in Mao's statements at the time of the "Cultural Revolution."

Robert Heilbroner has become much more pessimistic about the possibilities of the Third World's *ever* achieving what he once called the "great ascent" to economic development and the end of mass poverty. Moreover, he now doubts not only the likelihood of democracy's promoting development in the Third World but even the capacity of long-established democratic governments in the advanced countries to avert increasing civil strife under conditions where economic growth must be sharply curtailed to avoid ecological disaster. [4] The continuing population explosion, a new awareness of ecological limits to economic growth and the energy expenditure such growth requires, the threat of nuclear war in a world divided between rich and poor nations, all have led Heilbroner to generalize the views expressed in his earlier article, so that he now sees authoritarian governments as the agencies most able and most likely to overcome these threatening tendencies throughout the world. In short, where he once saw totalitarianism as a requisite for Third World economic development, he now sees it as a necessity almost everywhere to avert economic deterioration, or as the inevitable heir of economic and political collapse. He has, accordingly, won much celebrity as a Cassandra of our time. This is not the place to comment on Heilbroner's dark view of the human prospect, although my criticisms of "futurology" in the last essay in this section are perhaps not totally irrelevant to it.

My own qualified hopes for democracy in the Third World have been severely jolted by India's turn toward dictatorship under Indira Gandhi and the abandonment or overthrow of democratic government in Chile, Uruguay, Bangladesh, and the Philippines. The trend toward military regimes, whether leftist or rightist in outlook, has become even more marked since 1967. I now think that I was mistaken even to have tentatively endorsed Donald Bogue's optimism about the imminent end of the population explosion. I should have known better: Kingsley Davis, under whose direction I had written my doctoral dissertation in demography at Columbia, published in that same year what became a highly influential article questioning the efficacy of birth-control programs in the underdeveloped nations on both demographic and sociological grounds. [5]

"The Rhythm of Democratic Politics" is one of my own two or three favorite essays. Having failed to find anything very original to say on the topic I had been asked to write about, I finally prepared it for publication in a *Dissent* series that was eventually to become a book, [6] although I had been teaching its central ideas for some years and had written them down in several drafts for presentation as guest lectures at a number of universities. The *Dissent* book was intended as a critical analysis of the "new conservatism" of some intellectuals disillusioned by the limited success of social policies in the 1960s and by the demagogy of the New Left. This context accounts for my stressing at various points in the article my own overall identification with the political Left. However, I do not disagree with Nathan Glazer's judgment in a review of the book that I "seem rather cool about the entire conflict and see both sides as in effect cooperating (objectively) in making a good society." [7] As a matter of fact, I had at one time considered preparing the "rhythm" thesis for submission to *The Public Interest,* of which Glazer is now an editor and which was a target of attack by some of the contributors to the *Dissent* volume.

"Max Weber: The Scholar as Hero," previously unpublished, was originally written at the request of the *New York Times Magazine* and is the only essay in the book that might conceivably be regarded as a popularization. Not a very successful one, however, for the *Times* rejected it as "too advanced" for their readers. I revised and considerably expanded it for publication as a pamphlet in a series intended for classroom use, but the publisher went out of business before it went to press. I have borrowed the title from that of a much earlier and shorter article of mine on Max Weber.[8] Martin Green's bold, challenging, and altogether enthralling treatment of Max Weber in *The von Richthofen Sisters* appeared too late to be discussed in this essay, although I undoubtedly owe something to a memorable (to me, at least) conversation with Green at the time when he was engaged in writing the book.[9]

"Ends and Means in Politics" is adapted in slightly revised form from a long introduction I wrote to an anthology of readings about Max Weber.[10] The essay's point of departure is Weber's distinction between two political ethics, but it ranges fairly widely into more general questions about the modalities of political faith in relation to practice in the contemporary world. I am surprised that debate over the meaning of Weber's typology continues, for I remain convinced that my interpretation is the correct one and shall have more to say on this subject in the future.

"On Thinking about the Future" has little connection with the other essays in this section, and it is only located here because it seemed to fit even less well into the two previous sections. It was originally a contribution to a debate on "The Future of America" at the University of North Carolina, Charlotte, in 1973. It might be regarded as an example of the sociologist as "mocker" referred to in the prologue, though the mockery is largely directed at the presumptions of his fellow sociologists. I do believe that the last paragraphs on the inevitable tension between theory and practice contain the germ of an important argument that I hope to elaborate more fully in the future.

TEN

Problems in Defining Power

THE MOST GENERAL USE of the word "power" in English is as a synonym for capacity, skill, or talent. This use encompasses the capacity to engage in certain kinds of performance, or "skill" in the strict sense, the capacity to produce an effect of some sort on the external world, and the physical or psychological energies underlying any and all human performances—the "power to act" itself, as it were. Sometimes the word is used in the plural to denote the total capacities and energies—or "faculties"—of a human being, as in reference to the increasing or failing "powers" of a person. When power refers to the energies released by human actions, it merges into the physical concept of energy as the capacity to do work or to move matter, as in steam or electrical power. Applied in this sense to human energies, power is equated with *potency*, or an actor's general ability to produce successful performances.

The notion of controlling or acting on resistant materials is implicit in the idea of power as skill or capacity. Some writers have equated power in this general sense with *mastery*, or with the ability "to produce observed modifications in the external world." [1] In the case of complex physical or mental skills, the recalcitrant materials to be mastered are the actor's own body and mind rather than objects in the external environment. The actor exercises a power over himself that we usually call "self-discipline" or "self-control." Freudian writers, beginning with Freud himself, habitually employ political metaphors to describe intrapsychic processes: the "tyrannical" superego, the "imperious" id, the "bargaining" or "compromising" ego.

Power as potency and, though less unambiguously, as mastery is unmistakably a "dispositional" term in Gilbert Ryle's sense, referring not to an actual performance but to the capacity, latent in the actor even when not being exercised, to produce a particular kind of performance.[2] When we are concerned with power as a social relation between actors, it is important, as I shall argue in more detail below, to retain the dispositional sense of the term, although the sociological concept of power must not imply that it is an attribute of an actor rather than a relation between actors, whether individuals or groups.

Two famous British philosophers, separated by nearly three centuries, defined power similarly. Thomas Hobbes defined it as "man's present means to any future apparent good,"[3] while to Bertrand Russell, power was "the production of intended effects."[4] Hobbes's definition is clearly a dispositional one, for a man may obviously possess the means to attain a future good even when he is not engaged in employing them to that end. Russell's definition, however, lends itself to being understood as "episodic"[5] rather than dispositional, unless one adds the phrase "the capacity for" in front of "the production of intended effects."

But both definitions identify power with potency or mastery and are therefore too general if one's interest is in power as a social relationship, for both cover power over the self and over nature as well as the power of men over other men. Self-mastery is, of course, a major subject for psychology, especially for psychoanalysis, but it is distinguishable from social and political power relations among individuals and groups. The relation between power over nature and power over men is also a highly important subject on which Russell made a number of acute observations over thirty years ago, before the advent of computers and nuclear weapons.[6] Nowadays it is a fashionable topic among left-wing intellectuals alarmed by the possibility that the new technical and scientific intelligentsia constitutes a technocratic elite menacing human freedom.[7] However, political and social theory requires a more restricted definition to differentiate power over nature from power over men.

Although there are hundreds, perhaps thousands, of more recent definitions of social power, or of the power of men over other men, in the literature of social science, I see no reason why we should not make do with older, simpler definitions so long as they are intellectually adequate. I shall therefore adopt a modified version of Russell's definition: *Power is the capacity of some men to produce intended effects on other men.*[8] The terms in this definition require detailed analysis to show how they cope with major problems and confusions in the conceptual analysis of power. There are five such problems. First, there is the issue of the *intentionality* of power, and secondly, of its *effectiveness*. The *latency* of power, its dispositional nature to which I have already alluded, is a third problem. The unilateral or asymmetrical nature of power relations implied by the claim that some men have an effect on others without a parallel claim that the reverse may also be the case is a fourth issue, to be discussed below as the problem of *asymmetry and balance* in power relations. A final question is that of *the nature of the effects produced* by power: must they be overt and behavioral, or do purely subjective, internal effects count also?

The Intentionality of Power

People exercise mutual influence and control over one another's conduct in all social interaction—in fact, that is what we mean by social interaction. It is essential, therefore, to distinguish between the exercise of power and social control in general—otherwise there would be no point in employing power as a separate concept or in identifying power relations as a distinct kind of social relation. That social control is inherent in all social interaction—at least, in all recurrent or "patterned" social interaction—has been clearly recognized by contemporary sociologists, though some of them have minimized the degree to which resistance to the demands and expectations of others also pervades human social life. Even if it is often overemphasized, however, the influence of group norms in shaping individual conduct is a basic assumption of modern social science. If norms are the prevailing rules of conduct in a group, and are enforced by positive or negative sanctions, then does not all normatively regulated social behavior involve power exercised by the group over the individual? Individuals, to be sure, undergo a process of socialization in the course of which they internalize many group norms. When social controls have been internalized, the concept of power as a social relation is clearly inapplicable, but to assume that most conformity to norms is the result of internalization is to adopt what I have called an "over-socialized conception of man." [9] Moreover, the power of the parent over the child precedes the child's internalization of parental rules; the child's superego is formed by his identification with the parents, whose commands the child eventually issues to himself without reference to their original external source. Submission to power is thus the earliest and most formative experience in human life. As R. G. Collingwood (no Freudian, to the best of my knowledge) put it: "A man is born a red and wrinkled lump of flesh having no will of its own at all, absolutely at the mercy of the parents by whose conspiracy he has been brought into existence. That is what no science of human community . . . must ever forget." [10]

But if to collapse the concept of power into that of social control is to vitiate all need for a separate concept of power, it then becomes necessary to distinguish the diffuse controls exercised by the group over socialized individuals from direct, intentional efforts by a specific person or group to affect another's conduct. Power is identical with *intended* and effective influence. It is one of two subcategories of *influence,* the other, empirically larger subcategory consisting of acts of *unintended* influence. In contrast to several recent writers, I do not see how we can avoid restricting the term power to intentional and effective acts of influence by some men on other men. It may be readily acknowledged that intentional efforts to influence others often produced unintended as well as intended effects on their behavior—a dominating and overprotective mother does not intend to femininize the character of her son. But all social interaction produces such unintended effects—a boss does not mean to plunge an employee into despair by greeting him somewhat distractedly in the morning, nor does a woman mean to arouse a man's sexual interest by paying polite attention to his conversation at a cocktail party. The effects others have on us, unintended by and even unknown to them, may influence us more profoundly and permanently than direct efforts to control our our sentiments and behavior. Dahl and Lindblom call such unintended influence "spontaneous field control" and sharply distinguish it from forms of deliberate control. [11]

The distinction between intentional and unintentional effects on others may seem to be hairsplitting. Does not the elephant who dances with the chickens exercise a power of life and death over them even though he has no wish to trample them underfoot? Do not the acts of governments today shape and destroy the lives of millions even though these outcomes in no way were intended or even foreseen by shortsighted statemen? Yet rather than equate power with all forms of influence, unintended as well as intended, it seems preferable to stress the fact that the intentional control of others is likely to create a relationship in which the power-holder exercises unintended influence over the power subject that goes far beyond what he may have wished or envisaged at the outset.

To revert to a previous example: it is only because a mother exercises socially approved power over her children that she may unintentionally shape their personalities along lines that are repugnant to her and defeat her most cherished hopes. So to confine the term "power" to the exercise of intentional control is not to make power less important or less pervasive in history and society. The study of the unintended consequences of social action may well be one of the major tasks of the social sciences,[12] but this does not preclude the necessity of carefully distinguishing between outcomes that are intended and those that are not.

The Effectiveness of Power

When attempts to exercise power over others are unsuccessful, when the intended effects of the aspiring power-wielder are not in fact produced, we are confronted with an absence or a failure of power. We do not ascribe power over heavenly bodies to Chanticleer the cock, who believed that his crowing caused the sun to rise; this was merely a delusion of power on his part. When in *Henry IV, Part I* Owen Glendower boasts "I can call spirits from the vasty deep" and Hotspur replies skeptically "Why, so can I, or so can any man; But will they come when you do call for them?" Hotspur is questioning the reality of Glendower's power over the spirits, or perhaps, the very existence of a spirit world. When an attempted exercise of power fails, although similar attempts may have been successful in the past, we witness the breakdown of the power relation. The effectiveness of power would seem to be so obvious a criterion for its presence as to preclude any need for further discussion.

The Latency of Power, or the
Actual/Potential Problem

Power is often defined as a capacity to control or influence others. I have already briefly referred to some of the implications of so defining it: the capacity to perform acts of control and their actual performance are clearly not the same thing—power when thought of as a capacity is a dispositional concept. What Gilbert Ryle says about "knowing" and "aspiring" also applies to power conceived of as a capacity to control others: "To say that a person knows something, is not to say that he is at a particular moment in process of doing or undergoing anything, but that he is able to do certain things, when the need arises, or that he is prone to do and feel certain things in situations of certain sorts." [13] Ryle calls verbs such as "to know," "to aspire," and "to possess" dispositional words that refer to recurrent tendencies of human beings to behave in certain ways, in contrast to the episodic words we employ to refer to specific behavioral events. The distinction between "having power" and "exercising power" reflects the difference between viewing power as a dispositional and as an episodic concept. [14] Unfortunately, power lacks a common verb form, which in part accounts for the frequent tendency to see it as a mysterious property or agency resident in the person or group to whom it is attributed. The use of such terms as "influence" and "control," which are both nouns and verbs, as virtual synonyms for power, represents an effort (not necessarily fully conscious) to avoid the suggestion that power is a property rather than a relation. [15]

The evidence that a person or group possesses the capacity to control others may be the frequency with which successful acts of control have been carried out in the past. Thus it makes perfect sense to say that the king or president still "has" power even when he is asleep in his bed (though not if there has been a successful insurrection since he retired, and armed rebels are guarding the door to his bedroom). Or power may be imputed to an actor when the probability of his intending to achieve and effectively achieving control over another actor is rated high, even though he may not have previously exercised such control.

However, this sense in which power is latent or dispositional is sometimes confused with another, or at least the distinction between them is blurred. Power is sometimes said to be potential rather than actual, to be "possessed" without being "exercised," when others carry out the wishes or intentions of the power-holder without his ever actually having issued a command to them or even having interacted with them at all to communicate his aims. Carl Friedrich has called such cases "the rule of anticipated reactions." [16] Obviously they differ from a situation in which there may be a considerable time lag between the issuance of a command and compliance with it; to my knowledge, no one has ever regarded such a situation as anything other than an instance of actual, exercised power, in view of man's "time-binding" capacities enabling him to orient himself simultaneously to past, present, and future events.

The ruler may be asleep in bed while his subjects are not merely engaged in carrying out directives he gave them before retiring but making decisions and taking actions based on their anticipations of what he would wish them to do in the relevant circumstances. It is this that is often called "latent" or "potential" power, as distinct from "manifest" or "actual" power, where observable communications are transmitted and acted upon. Clearly, more is involved in such cases than the previously described situation where the ruler may be said to "have" power while asleep in the sense that he has an unimpaired capacity to issue commands in the expectation that they will be obeyed. Both cases, however, seem to me to indicate essential attributes of all power relationships. In this sense Robert Bierstedt is entirely correct in maintaining that "it may seem redundant to say so, but power is always potential." [17]

But imputations of power based on the "anticipated reactions" of the power subject confront a number of difficulties. For A's power over B to be real when it is not actually exercised, B must be convinced of A's capacity to control him and must modify his behavior accordingly. Thus a mother has power over her child when the child refrains from doing something in anticipation of her displeasure even when the mother is not present to issue a specific prohibition. Similarly, the president has power over Congress when congressional leaders decide to shelve a bill in anticipation of a presidential veto. The consciousness of the power subject is a crucial consideration in imputations of power on the basis of anticipated reactions. Max Weber's conception of power as "the probability that one actor in a social relationship will . . . carry out his own will" [18] must be interpreted as attributing the estimate of probability to the judgment of the power subject and not merely to that of the observer, say a social scientist. Otherwise, only overt acts of control or the subsequent imposition of a sanction after the performance of an act would validate an imputation of power made by an observer, and the distinction between latent and manifest power disappears.

When power is regarded as a capacity, therefore, and when it is understood to include B's acts based on his anticipations of A's reaction to them, the distinction between latent and manifest, or potential and actual, power is implicit in the very definition of power. Yet even when empirical students of power define it as a capacity, they frequently ignore the implications of such a definition in practice by treating power as identical with its actual exercise and confining themselves to its manifestations in directly observable act-response sequences. [19] Other writers define power in such a way as to require the overt performance of an act by an imputed power-holder that precedes the response of the power subject, thus excluding B's anticipatory responses from the realm of power relations. Actual participation in decision-making or observed "initiation of interaction for others" become the criterion of power. Power is thus seen as a type of social behavior that can be directly observed and unambiguously identified. (Frequently, of course, acts of power may have to be retrospectively reconstructed: the observer, at least where institutionalized power relations between groups are involved, is rarely right at the elbow of the decision-maker.)

Those who prefer to equate power with its exercise in a social relationship fear the subjectivity that appears to be implicit in the view that actors may "have" power without exercising it so long as belief in the probability of their exercising it limits the choices of others. As I have already indicated, treating power as a capacity runs the initial risk of seeing it as vested too exclusively in the power-holder "from where it radiates to others." [20] But once we correct this possible overemphasis by insisting that power is always a relation between two actors, do we not then risk going to the opposite extreme of making it dependent entirely on what is in the mind of the power subject? Are we not in effect saying that someone's belief that someone else has power actually confers power on the latter? [21] Advocates of the so-called decisional method of studying community power structures have leveled this accusation at researchers who have used the reputational method. [22] Defenders of the reputational method have replied that the attribution of power to someone may indeed confer it on him. However, if this were always the case, popular beliefs about the distribution of power would never be false. Since it is doubtful that the users of the reputational method would themselves make so extreme a claim, it is obviously necessary to study the actual exercise of power to confirm or disprove the reputations for power revealed by opinion surveys. Supporters of the decisional method, however, have often recoiled so vigorously from the suggestion that reputation for power is equivalent to having power that they have fallen back on narrowly behavioristic definitions, equating power with its observable exercise.

Yet to avoid such a suggestion, one need only repeat the line of reasoning followed in correcting the opposite inference that power is a kind of force emanating from the power-holder. If an actor is believed to be powerful, if he knows that others hold such a belief, and if he encourages it and resolves to make use of it by intervening in or punishing actions by others who do not comply with his wishes, then he truly has power and his power has indeed been conferred upon him by the attributions, perhaps initially without foundation, of others. But if he is unaware that others believe him powerful, or if he does not take their belief seriously in planning his own projects, then he has no power and the belief that he has is mistaken, a misperception of reality. We would not say that the residents of a street had power over a man with paranoid delusions who refused to leave his house because he feared attack by his neighbors. Nor would we say that the American Communist Party actually has great power because a certain segment of the public, influenced by right-wing ideologists, believes this to be the case and acts accordingly.

Raymond Aron has pointed out that the English and German languages employ the same terms, power and *Macht*, respectively, to refer both to the capacity to do something and to the actual exercise of the capacity.[23] In French, however, there are two distinct words: *puissance*, indicating potential or capacity, and *pouvoir*, indicating the act. While the prevailing usage of both terms, according to Aron, has tended to blur this distinction between them and to create new, less meaningful distinctions, Aron argues that *puissance* should be regarded as the more general concept of which *pouvoir* is a particular form. Unfortunately, this terminological distinction does not exist in English, but the idea of "potential" should be regarded as implicit in all nonbehavioristic definitions that treat power as in some sense a capacity distinguishable from its overt exercise.

Asymmetry and Balance in Power Relations

Power relations are asymmetrical in that the power-holder exercises greater control over the behavior of the power subject than the reverse, but reciprocity of influence—the defining criterion of the social relation itself—is never entirely destroyed except in those forms of physical violence which, although directed against a human being, treat him as no more than a physical object.[24]

The asymmetry of power relations, however, is often stressed to a degree that would make it logically contradictory to speak of "bilateral" power relations or of "equality of power" in bargaining or conflict. Thus Gerth and Mills write: "When everyone is equal there is no politics, for politics involves subordinates and superiors." [25] And Peter Blau maintains that "interdependence and mutual influence of equal strength indicate lack of power." [26] Such assertions risk going too far in severing power relations from their roots in social interaction in its generic form, for the asymmetry of power relations is at least immanent in the give and take of dyadic interaction between equals, in which the control of one actor over the other's behavior is reciprocated by a responsive act of control by the other. Asymmetry exists in each individual act-response sequence, but the actors continually alternate the roles of power-holder and power subject in the course of their interaction. In a stable social relation (where there is recurrent interaction between the parties rather than interaction confined to a single occasion) a pattern may emerge in which one actor controls the other with respect to particular situations and spheres of conduct—or "scopes," as they have often been called—while the other actor is regularly dominant in other areas of activity. Thus a wife may rule in the kitchen, while her husband controls the disposition of the family income. Or a labor union, as in the unions of seamen and longshoremen, controls hiring, while the employer dictates the time and place of work.

Thus if we treat power relations as exclusively hierarchical and unilateral, we overlook an entire class of relations between persons or groups in which the control of one person or group over the other with reference to a particular scope is balanced by the control of the other in a different scope. The division of scopes between the parties is often the result of a bargaining process which may or may not have followed an open struggle for power—a separation in a marriage, a strike against an employer, a lawsuit in commercial rivalry, a war between nations.

The term "intercursive power" has been suggested for relations characterized by a balance of power and a division of scopes between the parties.[27] It is contrasted with "integral power," in which decision-making and initiatives to action are centralized and monopolized by one party. Intercursive power exists where the power of each party in a relationship is countervailed by that of the other, with procedures for bargaining or joint decision-making governing their relations when matters affecting the goals and interests of both are involved. Riesman's notion of a balance of veto groups, each able to prevent the others from acts threatening its interests, constitutes a negative system of intercursive power relations.[28] The various conceptions of "pluralism" in contemporary sociology and political science are models of systems of intercursive power relations.

Integral power always raises the question *quis custodiet ipsos custodies?*—or who rules the rulers, guards the guardians, oversees the overseers? The assumption behind the query is that the rulers' power to decide at their own discretion cannot be entirely eliminated in human societies. "Power cannot be dissolved into law," as Franz Neumann observed,[29] and the liberal slogan, "a government of laws, not of men," is, if taken literally, mere ideology expressing a mistrust of political power. Thus where integral power is established and recognized as unavoidable in at least some situations (or scopes), as in the case of the power of the state in modern times, attempts to limit it take a form other than that of transforming integral power into an intercursive power system. Integral power may be restricted without either reducing the decision-making autonomy of the power-holder or countervailing it by giving others power over him with reference to particular scopes. Measures designed to limit integral power include periodic reviews of the acts of the power-holder (legislative and judicial review), periodic reaffirmations of his power-holding status or his removal and replacement (rules of tenure and succession), the setting of limits to the scopes he can control or to the range of options available to him within each scope ("civil liberties"), and rights of appeal and petition concerning grievances.

If such measures are to be truly effective and not just window dressing, like the impressive constitutions created by so many absolute dictatorships in recent history, there must be sources of power independent of the integral power-holder that can be mobilized to enforce them. The law must be a web that catches the lawmaker as well as his subjects. Conditions making this a reality may include the separation of executive, legislative, and judicial powers within the government, the creation of different and independent levels of government as in federative states, divided rather than unified elites within society at large, and, ultimately, strong support for constitutional guarantees or traditional "unwritten" rights and liberties on the part of the power subjects. In other words, there must be real countervailing power centers able to enforce limits on the power of the integral power-holder, and, insofar as this is required, the distinction between intercursive and integral power is not an absolute one. The checks on integral power, however, are largely negative. To quote Neumann again: "All traditional legal conceptions are negative ones. They limit activities but do not shape them. It is this very character of law which grants to the citizen a minimum of protection." [30]

There are four broad ways in which power subjects may attempt to combat or resist the power of an integral-power holder: (1) they may strive to exercise countervailing power over him in order to transform his integral power into a system of intercursive power; (2) they may set limits to the extensiveness (the number of power subjects), comprehensiveness (the number of scopes), and intensity (the range of options within particular scopes) of his power; (3) they may destroy his integral power altogether, leaving the acts he formerly controlled open to free and self-determined choice; (4) they may seek to supplant him by acquiring and exercising his integral power themselves.

With reference to the integral power of modern states within their territorial jurisdictions, the first three alternatives correspond roughly to, respectively, efforts to establish democratic government, efforts to establish constitutional government, and the elimination of all government, or anarchy. The first two, of course, have frequently been combined as a political objective. The fourth alternative obviously corresponds to the different forms of political succession, such as putsch, revolution, or the legally regulated competition of electoral contests.

Such devices as the initiative, the referendum, and impeachment by ballot, as well as the conception of elections as popular mandates, are established ways in which subjects exercise countervailing power over their rulers. The transformation of integral power into intercursive power, however, can never be complete in the case of modern states, insofar as there is an irreducibly integral element in political power that cannot be eliminated altogether.[31] Bills of rights, constitutional guarantees, jurisdictional restrictions, and statutory limits on the options available to the political decision-maker are ways of checking the integral power of the state without eliminating it altogether by depriving the ruler of any scopes in which he can decide and act according to his own discretion. The removal of certain substantive areas of choice by power subjects from any control by the state—such as the "basic" freedoms of speech, religion, assembly, residence, etc.—has the effect of eliminating the integral power of the state in these areas, though the total elimination of state power—the third alternative above—has never been permanently realized in any civilized society. (It has, of course, been the goal of anarchism as a political movement.)

It is misleading, therefore, to contend that "all politics is a struggle for power." The subjects or victims of power may seek to replace the power-holder because they envy him and wish to use his power in the service of their own goals and interests, or because they are vengeful and wish to punish him as he may have punished them. But alternatively they may wish to free themselves from his control over them by limiting or abolishing his power and enlarging their own range of free choice. Politics includes both a struggle *for* power and a struggle to limit, resist, and escape *from* power.

The Nature of the Effects Produced by Power

This issue does not strike me as an especially thorny one, so I shall discuss it very briefly. If A produces no change in B's actual behavior but only a change in his feelings, attitudes, or beliefs, are we justified in imputing power to A? [32] The answer is implicit in the definition of power as the capacity of some person or persons to produce intended effects on other persons. If A's intention is to affect or alter B's attitudes rather than his behavior and he succeeds in doing so in the desired direction, then he clearly has power over B to this extent in the relevant scope to which the attitudes refer. If, however, his intention is to produce a particular act by B and he fails to do so, his attempt to exercise power eliciting only an inner disposition on the part of B to comply that is not acted on, or a feeling of guilt, then he has not exercised power over B but rather unintended influence. The same would be true if he evoked B's bitter hostility and strong determination to resist compliance. Surely, in this latter case we would not wish to impute power to A at all but rather to speak of the failure of his effort to control B, though he may indeed have influenced B by arousing his antagonism. In many actual situations, A is likely to aim at influencing both B's sentiments and his behavior. If he succeeds only in the former, then he has exercised power that is limited in comprehensiveness and intensity while failing in his more ambitious effort to control B's behavior. But there are many situations where the aim of the power-holder is no more than to maintain or strengthen an existing attitude or belief system of the power subject, an attitude or belief system, for example, that sustains inaction or "non-decisions" in Bachrach and Baratz's sense. [33] One thinks of propaganda to reinforce uncritical loyalty to a political regime, or to rekindle the fires of hostility toward foreign enemies or domestic dissenters. Clearly, the controllers of the mass media often aim at this sort of power, whether they are an arm of the government or represent "private" organizations engaged in "public relations" or "institutional advertising."

Three Attributes of Power Relations

Bertrand de Jouvenel has distinguished three variable attributes of all power relations, which, when specified, greatly facilitate the comparison of different types of power relations and structures.

"Power or authority," as de Jouvenel states, "has three dimensions: it is *extensive* if the complying B's (the power subjects) are many; it is *comprehensive* if the variety of actions to which A (the power holder) can move the B's is considerable; finally it is *intensive* if the bidding of A can be pushed far without loss of compliance." [34]

The *extensiveness* of a power relation may be narrow or broad. The former is illustrated by an isolated dyadic relation in which a single person exercises power over a single other, the latter by political regimes in which one man rules over millions of subjects. De Jouvenel mentions only the number of subjects, but the power-holder may of course also be plural—there may be many A's as well as many B's. The Aristotelian classification of forms of government is primarily based on whether sovereignty is "in the hands of one, or the few, or of the many." [35] Under kingship and tyranny, one man rules over many; under aristocracy and oligarchy, a few men rule over the many; and under polity and democracy, the majority of the community rule themselves. The direct democracy of the Athenian polis can be regarded as a differentiated, asymmetrical power structure with regard to the imposition of majority decisions on minorities and non-citizens (slaves and women). Much of classical and modern political theory, as well as a large literature in the fields of public administration and organization theory on the "span of control," deals with the extensiveness of power relations. One might define extensiveness as the ratio of the number of persons who hold power to the number of the powerless. The major (and perhaps the only?) significant contention of the Italian neo-Machiavellian or elitist school to political theory (Pareto, Mosca, Michels) was to insist that in large societies or associations a minority of men inevitably come to wield power over the majority, or "the masses."

A serious limitation in the writings of the neo-Machiavellians is their readiness to assume that power wielded by a minority is likely to be unlimited, ideologies and rituals implying the contrary notwithstanding, and the more so the smaller the minority.[36] They failed to give independent consideration to the *comprehensiveness* of power: the number of scopes in which the power-holder(s) controls the activities of the power subject(s). Robert Dahl employs the term "scope" to refer chiefly to different institutional activities or "issue-areas," such as education, political nominations, urban planning, and the like.[37] As a political scientist, he is primarily concerned with governmental decision-making. For a more general analysis of power relations, one may conceive of scopes as the different areas of choice and activity of the power subject. The comprehensiveness of a power relation, therefore, refers to the number of scopes over which the power-holder holds power, or to the proportion or range of the power subject's total conduct and life-activity that is subject to control. At one extreme there is the power of a parent over an infant or young child, which is very nearly total in its comprehensiveness, extending to virtually everything the child does. At the other extreme, there is the very limited and specific power of the incumbents of highly specialized "situated roles," [38] such as those of a taxi dispatcher or a high-school student appointed to traffic safety patrol.

A third generic attribute of power relations is the *intensity* of the relation. If I understand correctly de Jouvenel's brief discussion of this attribute, he has in mind the range of effective options open to the power-holder *within* each and every scope of the power subject's conduct over which he wields power. What limits are there to the actions which the power-holder can influence the power subject to perform? Will the power subject commit suicide or murder under the power-holder's influence? What intended effects sought by the power-holder will be resisted, producing, at least initially, a breakdown of the power relation? Justice Holmes once wrote: "I heard the original Agassiz (Louis) say that in some part of Germany there would be a revolution if you added a farthing to the cost of a glass of beer. If that was true, the current price was one of the rights of man at that place." [39] Or, in the language employed here, the intensity of the power of tavern-owners to set the price of a glass of beer was severely limited, with the prevailing price setting the upper limit.

I have previously noted that formal statutory guarantees of "the rights of man," or civil liberties, set limits both to the comprehensiveness and the intensity of power. In the former case, certain scopes are specifically excluded from the control of power-holders, such as the freedoms of speech, assembly, religious worship, travel, and so on. Statutory limits on the intensity of power curtail the range of options available to the power-holder within those scopes where he does have control. Thus the courts may possess the power to impose punishments on lawbreakers, but not "cruel and unusual punishments"; a trade union certified as a collective bargaining agent may require a union shop, but not, under the Taft-Hartley Act, a closed shop. These examples refer to formal legal limitations on the intensity of a power relation within a given scope, but obviously, as the remark of Justice Holmes reflecting his famous legal positivism suggests, de facto limits are likely to be present in even the most informal, interpersonal power relations. At the pole of maximum intensity one might locate the relationship between a lover and a loved one where the former declares "your wish is my command"—and means it. At the opposite pole stands the "decision-maker" whose choices are confined to a very narrow range: a tax assessor, for example, who by statute can raise or lower tax rates by no more than a few percentage points. The tendency in some social science writing to identify "decision-making" with the exercise of power can be misleading if the intensity of the decision-maker's power to decide is not taken into account.

What interrelationships are there among these three attributes? The most total and unlimited power, power that is greatest in comprehensiveness and intensity, is likely to be least extensive: namely, dyadic relations in which one person has power over a single other. As far back as Aristotle, the power of a master over a household slave has often served as the standard example of virtually unrestricted power. The power of a parent over a small child—the *fons et origo* of the human character structure—is another obvious example. The power of the loved one over the lover in a passionate, "romantic" love relationship represents the most narrowly extensive and highly individualized form of power relation, since the relation is based entirely on the uniqueness of the particular individuals involved. As Philip Slater has argued, an exclusive love relationship constitutes what he calls a "dyadic withdrawal" from society and its obligations, in its most extreme form the *Liebestod*, and has been subjected by all societies to normative controls.[40] A love relationship, however, is often a relatively balanced, or bilateral, power relation between two individuals. A relationship between a sadist and a masochist best exemplifies a narrowly extensive but highly comprehensive and intensive interpersonal power relation.

A patriarch in the family, a tribal leader, or a village despot may also wield highly comprehensive and intensive power over a relatively small number of subjects. The limited extensiveness of his power enables him to dispense with intermediaries to whom power is delegated and who as subordinate power-holders may become potential rivals and competitors. Where the power subjects are few in number, less power has to be delegated from the top, and levels of power in a pyramidal or scalar power structure are less likely to emerge. This is a special case of the well-known "generalization of organization" theory that the larger the group and the more differentiated the activities of its members the greater the number of supervisory levels required if it is successfully to achieve its goals.

The term "totalitarianism" has come into use to describe tyrannical or oligarchical (in the Aristotelian sense) political regimes that wield more extensive, comprehensive, and intensive power than any of the monarchies, tyrannies, or oligarchies of the past. Totalitarian regimes exercise more extensive power in that they have flourished in large and populous nation-states rather than in small city-states or agrarian communities. Some writers indeed have argued that full totalitarian rule is possible *only* in large and populous societies.[41] Modern technology, especially new media of communications, permits more highly centralized bureaucratic control over the lives of the subjects, thus concentrating decision making in fewer hands even though the power structure includes more intermediate levels between top and bottom. Yet the power of a totalitarian dictator over his subjects is scarcely as comprehensive as that of a parent over a child or a master over a slave. The difficulty of maintaining the *visibility* at all times of the behavior of all the subjects sets limits to the comprehensiveness of totalitarian power. A Nazi once boasted that "the only free man in Germany is a man who is asleep," but even in Nazi Germany at the time this was a considerable exaggeration. Negative utopian visions, such as those of Orwell and Zamiatin, which describe societies even more totally controlled by small elites than the historical examples of totalitarianism in the present century, depend to a considerable extent on science-fiction solutions to the visibility problem, Orwell's two-way television screens being the best-known example.

In her great book, *The Origins of Totalitarianism,* Hannah Arendt regards the concentration camp as the ultimate and most significant expression of totalitarian rule. She calls the Nazi camps "experiments in total domination." [42] But the camps were, of course, smaller communities than the wider totalitarian society in which they existed; so the total power their rulers exercised over the inmates does not invalidate the general rule that the comprehensiveness and intensity of power tends to vary inversely with its extensiveness.

New media of communication, techniques of observation and persuasion, and instruments of violence have also, it has often been argued, increased the intensity of power in totalitarian states. Propaganda over centrally controlled mass media and psychological methods of "thought reform" have allegedly enabled totalitarian power-holders to indoctrinate their subjects more thoroughly with passionate and unconditional loyalties to the regime. At the same time deviance and noncompliance, let alone active resistance, have become more difficult with the use of new techniques of surveillance and extracting information, and new means of coercion. Even in the democracies, enormous anxieties have been aroused in recent years by electronic "bugging" and wiretapping devices, subliminal advertising, and so-called "brainwashing." Events in Eastern Europe since 1945, and even in the Soviet Union and China, have somewhat reduced the plausibility of the assumption that control of the new technology has made totalitarian regimes virtually invulnerable to internal dissent and opposition. Political will and organization and the legitimacy of the regime in the eyes of its subjects remain, as in the past, crucial factors determining the efficacy of opposition, and these factors are by no means entirely subject to control by the ruling elite. Even though the new technology permits more centralized control and speedier response to incipient threats, it also requires the disciplined and dedicated cooperation of a larger number of men trained to wield its complex instruments, and this dilutes the total power of the ruling elite.

In summary, there are three main reasons why the greater extensiveness of a power relation sets limits to its comprehensiveness and intensity. First, the greater the number of power subjects, the greater the difficulty of supervising all of their activities. Second, the greater the number of power subjects, the more extended and differentiated the chain of command necessary to control them, creating new subordinate centers of power that can be played off against each other and that may themselves become foci of opposition to the integral power-holder. Third, the greater the number of subjects, the greater the likelihood of wide variation in their attitudes toward the power-holder. The power-holder will not be able to wield power with equal comprehensiveness and intensity over all of his subjects. A few may be eager and pliant servants of his will, others will "go along" less enthusiastically, still others will require constant supervision and threats to keep their performances in line, and there will be some against whom force must be used even to the extent of eliminating them from the ranks of the living.

ELEVEN

Force and the Threat of Force as Distinct Forms of Power

FORCE REFERS most commonly to physical or biological force: the creation of physical obstacles restricting the freedom of another, the infliction of bodily pain or injury including the destruction of life itself, and the frustration of basic biological needs which must be satisfied if the capacity for voluntary choice and action is to remain unimpaired. Force involves treating a human subject as if he were no more than a physical object, or at most a biological organism vulnerable to pain and the impairment of its life-processes. The ultimate form of force is violence: direct assault upon the body of another in order to inflict pain, injury, or death. But the methods of nonviolence adopted by some recent social movements, which proved so successful against the British in India and, more recently, against racial segregation laws in the American South, also exemplify force as a form of power. In nonviolence, people use their own bodies as physical objects to prevent or restrict actions by others rather than acting directly on the bodies of others. By "sitting in" in a building or public place they make it impossible for the activities usually carried on there to take place. By lying down on railroads or highways they confront the drivers of trains or cars with the choice of either stopping or running them over. Conversely, by declining to appear at a workplace or other site of customary cooperative activities, nonviolent activists remove themselves from exposure to the commands, threats, or appeals of the resident authorities and bring about a stoppage of the customary activities. The deprivation of basic biological needs is also a form of physical force. Obvious examples are the denial of food and of rest, as in the forcing of prisoners to stand for hours with lights flashing in their eyes, or the long hours of exhausting physical labor in the German and Russian concentration camps. All destruction of valued property or imposition of economic sanctions amount to physical force in milder forms. Where the property destroyed or the economic benefits withheld are not necessary for subsistence or survival in the biological sense, one cannot say that the victim of force is being treated solely as a physical or biological object, since his social and psychological needs are being taken into account. Yet the act of destruction or withholding need not be a social act involving any interaction between two subjects.

The relation between the use of force and its threatened use is obviously an intimate one, but a forceful act is distinguishable from a threat to use force. A punch on the jaw is not the same thing as shaking a fist; a shot from a gun is distinct from pointing a gun and shouting "Hands up!" or "Your money or your life!" The crucial difference is that the latter examples are clearly social relations in which the threatener engages in communication with the other at the symbolic level; he does not, in short, treat the other as something less than a human being capable of understanding and choice. To be sure, he wishes to narrow drastically the range of the other's choices. Few have expressed the difference as well as Georg Simmel, who is worth quoting at length:

Even in the most oppressive and cruel cases of subordination, there is still a considerable measure of personal freedom. We merely do not become aware of it, because its manifestation would entail sacrifices which we usually never think of taking upon ourselves. Actually, the "absolute" coercion which even the most cruel tyrant imposes upon us is always distinctly relative. Its condition is our desire to escape from the threatened punishment or from other consequences of our disobedience. More precise analysis shows that the super-subordination relationship destroys the subordinate's freedom only in the case of direct physical violation. In every other case, this relationship only demands a price for the relization of freedom—a price, to be sure, which we are not willing to pay. It can narrow down more and more the sphere of external conditions under which freedom is clearly realized, but, except for physical force, never to the point of the complete disappearance of freedom.[1]

The threat and the actual application of force are often collapsed together conceptually and labeled "coercion," but the implications of the preceding analysis necessitate drawing a sharp distinction between them. Failure to distinguish between force and the threat of force, as I shall argue more fully below, leads to a tendency to minimize the role of coercion, defined as the threat of force, in human affairs. It is often stated that so-called "naked power" (which invariably means power based on force) is inherently unstable and limited in what it can achieve. Such statements underplay the elements of coercion present in nearly all concrete power relations. They derive much of their plausibility from the fact that the intended effects on others which the actual use of force is capable of producing are strictly limited. Recognition of the large range of effects that can be achieved by the threat of force and the fear it arouses in the subject is therefore blurred.

It is also frequently stated that the use of force or violence, far from being the fundamental manifestation of power, is evidence of the breakdown of power. Hannah Arendt, for example, writes: "Power and violence are opposites; where the one rules absolutely, the other is absent. Violence appears where power is in jeopardy, but left to its own course it ends in power's disappearance." [2] Such assertions are elliptical. When an effort to exercise power by other means fails, force may be applied as the "final persuader." Or it may be applied as punishment for previous noncompliance. In both cases the resort to force is indeed the result of the prior failure of power, although its successful use as a last resort represents the exercise of a new form of power insofar as it restricts the subject's freedom with respect to certain acts in accordance with the intention of the wielder of force. The use of force as punishment may also succeed in reestablishing the preexisting power relation, whether it was based on the threat and fear of force, duty, self-interest, or some combination of these.

It should now be obvious that force as a form of power has reality only in its manifest form. Latent force is a separate form of power, social rather than physical. Someone who bases his conduct on the anticipation that force will be applied to him unless he performs, or refrains from performing, certain requisite actions is not subject to force but rather to the threat of force. David Easton is one of the few political scientists who has fully recognized the necessity of making this distinction conceptually:

I distinguish here between force and the threat of force. In the latter case we have an example of the exercise of authority. There is a significant difference between actually eliminating a person from the political system by jailing him and merely threatening him with incarceration. When only threats are made, the individual may be inclined to obey, thereby participating in an authority relationship, whereas in the case of pure force the individual continues to refuse to obey but is nevertheless compelled to conform to the decision of the authorities.[3]

Force is more effective in preventing or restricting people from acting than in causing them to act in a given way. "The one thing you cannot do with bayonets is to sit on them," as Talleyrand observed. Force can eliminate a man's freedom to act at all by killing him, starving him, or maiming him, confining him within four walls or otherwise removing him from the scene, or placing physical obstacles in his path. Force can achieve negative effects: the destruction, prevention, or limitation of the possibility of action by others. But one cannot forcefully manipulate the limbs and bodies of others in order to achieve complex positive results: the fabrication or construction of something, the operation of a machine, the performance of a physical skill. Force, however, is often employed not just to eliminate someone's capacity to act, but to establish in the mind of the power subject the future credibility of the power-holder's willingness and capability to use force, or, in effect, to create, or recreate, a power relation based not in force but on the threat and fear of force.

It is tempting to confine the use of the term force to *physical* force, as so many writers have done, including myself in the preceding discussion. But there is a form of conduct, often described as psychic, psychological, or moral force or violence, which does not fit readily under the rubrics of any of the other forms of power. If physical violence involves inflicting damage on the body of a person, how is one to classify the deliberate effort to affect adversely a person's emotions or his feelings and ideas about himself by verbally, or in other symbolic ways, insulting or degrading him? If power includes the production of purely mental or emotional effects and is not confined to the eliciting of overt acts, then the psychic assault of, say, a nagging, browbeating spouse or parent, the defamation of the character of a political foe or even of an entire social group, constitute exercises of power. There are, moreover, institutionalized forms of psychic violence: ritual degradation ceremonies, the practice of black magic or sorcery, the pronouncement of a curse.[4] Damage to the psyche is surely as real as damage to the body. But the former requires, as the latter does not, recognition of the human capacity of the subject to understand and respond, of his orientation to symbols. It is plainly not true that "sticks and stones may break my bones but names can never hurt me." Psychic violence, in which the intended effect of the perpetrator is to inflict mental or emotional harm, is continuous with physical violence and does not clearly fall under any of the other classifications of forms of power: manipulation, persuasion, or authority.

A great many sociologists, of whom Parsons is the most prominent, have defined "authority" as compliance based on the consent of the power subject and have contrasted it with "naked power," or power based on force.[5] This dichotomy is misleadingly simple. In the first place, it fails to distinguish between force and the threat of force, or coercion, and thus biases the issue of the relative importance of coercion and consent in human society in favor of the latter because the effects obtainable by the actual application of force are obviously restricted and largely negative. Moreover, in equating authority with the subordinate's acceptance of an obligation to obey, it unduly directs attention to the motivation and consciousness of the subordinate rather than emphasizing the nature of the communicative relation—that of commanding and obeying—between superior and subordinate.

It scarcely clarifies matters when authority is regarded as a special case of power, namely legitimate or institutionalized power characterized by the voluntary submission of the subject, and power itself is defined to include the capacity to impose sanctions or deprivations. Harold Lasswell and Abraham Kaplan, Robert Bierstedt, and Hans Gerth and C. Wright Mills are among the writers taking this line, as is Weber insofar as the reference to resistance in his definition of power * implies a similar view.[6] Now there is a genuine paradox, analyzed by Bierstedt and Peter Blau,[7] in the fact that submission to legitimate authority is voluntary and yet at the same time is experienced as mandatory or compulsory. But since power and authority are relations between actors, definitions that focus on the nature of the relation itself rather than on only one side of it, whether the resources of the power-holder or the motivations of the power subject, are preferable and are more likely to avoid endless polemics on the coercion versus consent issue. To define authority as resting on consent and power on coercion necessitates probing the tangled, often obscure, and "overdetermined" motivations of the power subject. "Authority" is more simply and usefully defined as *any* command-obedience relationship, or successful ordering and forbidding, regardless of the motivational grounds for obedience on the part of the power subject. As David Easton maintains: "Anyone who is regularly obeyed is an authority."[8] Any and all command-obedience relations between men, including those that are coercive, constitute instances of authority.

But definitions are largely matters of convenience. If someone wishes for whatever reason to stress the contrast between obedience motivated by fear of punishment or the desire for reward, on the one hand, and voluntary submission because of imputed "intrinsic" social or psychological qualities of the giver of commands, on the other, he or she is at liberty to reserve the word "authority," which has long possessed consensual overtones, for the latter, and to treat *coercion* and *inducement* (obedience exacted by threats and by the promise of rewards, respectively) as separate forms of power. I prefer instead to stress the common features of command-obedience relationships as such by subsuming them under the generic term "authority" and then distinguishing subtypes, including coercive authority, on the basis of varying motivations for obeying.

For A to obtain B's compliance by threatening him with force, B

---

* Weber's well-known definition is: "Power is the probability that one actor within a social relationship will be in a position to carry out his own will despite resistance. . . ."

must be convinced both of A's *capability* and of his *willingness*
to use force against him. A may have succeeded in convincing B of
both by advertising and displaying the means and instruments of
force that he controls. States stage elaborate military reviews, or publicized tests of nuclear weapons, to impress foreign diplomats as well
as their own citizens. Policemen flourish nightsticks and wear highly
visible revolvers on their hips. New political movements of the Right,
and often of the Left as well, may adopt paramilitary forms of organization even when, as in the case of the S.A. before Hitler's coming to
power, their arsenals are empty or virtually nonexistent. Large prop-
erty-owners electrify the fences surrounding their property and post
signs stating that it is patrolled by armed guards. Small property-
owners put up "beware of the dog" notices on their lawns. Would-be
"tough guys" develop a swaggering walk and cultivate bulging biceps.

When such methods are unsuccessful in cowing others into compliance, an actual test of force may be necessary to establish in the
mind of the power subject the credibility of the power-holder's ability
and readiness to apply force successfully. Force is often employed
simply to eliminate people from the scene or to prevent them from
acting at all, but it is more often used to establish credibility and thus
to create a future power relation based on the threat of force that
precludes the necessity of overt resort to it. Men are subjected to
physical and psychic punishments to deter them from future repeti-
tions of proscribed acts. Rebellions are brutally suppressed to discour-
age their surviving supporters from future attempts at rebellion. Prisoners are tortured to induce them to cooperate with their captors by
providing desired information as a condition of avoiding further torture. Offenders may be removed by death or confinement to set an
example to others—*pour encourager les autres*—and thus to reinforce
a coercive relation between a power-holder and power subjects who
have yet to test his strength. In all these cases force is used less for the
immediate effects on its victims than to establish and maintain a relation of coercive authority in the future between its wielder and either
victims or others who witness its use.

But a coercer may succeed without possessing either the capability
or the intention of using force so long as the power subject believes
he possesses both. Men have robbed banks by brandishing water pis-

tols or even by cocking their fingers to resemble a hand-gun in their pockets. The rhetoric of violence sometimes succeeds even where the capacity to use it is lacking. On the other hand, superior force may be overcome where its possessor hesitates to use it. Grandhi's use of non-violent force against the British in India was successful because the British lacked the ruthlessness to massacre his followers, but, as has often been pointed out, it is doubtful that he would have prevailed against Nazis, Communists, or even the prewar Japanese.

What is unique about the introduction of nuclear weapons into world power politics is that no power dares use them against another nuclear power in the absence of certainty that their use will destroy the enemy's nuclear arsenal, so immense are the destructive capacities of the weapons. Whether the nuclear "balance of terror" might have been arrived at had atomic bombs not been used by the United States against Japan at the end of World War II is still subject to bitter debate. But with the balance of terror ruling out an actual test of the credibility of a nuclear power's force, such a power could, in theory at least, destroy its stockpile of bombs without altering the balance so long as its rivals continued to believe that it still possessed a formidable nuclear arsenal.

At least in the short run, coercive authority is undoubtedly the most effective form of power in extensiveness, comprehensiveness, and intensity: "Out of the barrel of a gun grows the most effective command, resulting in the most instant and perfect obedience." [9] With the exception of the actual use of force, coercion is potentially the most extensive form of power of all because it requires a bare minimum of communication and mutual understanding between the power-holder and power subject to compel the latter's obedience. The brandishing of a weapon is easily understood by men of utterly diverse cultural backgrounds. The military conquest and subsequent rule of alien peoples make up a large part of the historical record. Many past civilizations have based their economies on the forced labor of slaves. Since most men value life and health, more often than not they prefer submission even to the point of slavery to the injury, starvation, or death risked by forceful resistance to a stronger adversary.

Because of its potential universal effectiveness and the wide range of conduct it can dictate and control, coercion is, with legitimate authority, one of the two major forms of political power—that is, of the most extensive kind of power of all, power that rules over a constituency larger and more inclusive than those subject to the social controls of families, local communities, churches, voluntary associations, and the many other groups composing the social order. Political institutions are, in fact, most clearly differentiated from other institutions by virtue of their monopolistic control of the means of coercion. A leading tradition in Western political and social thought that goes back at least to the Greeks and includes Machiavelli and Hobbes, the Social Darwinists of the nineteenth century, and the Italian neo-Machiavellian school of the early part of the present century, has regarded coercion as both the ultimate and the only "real" form of power, seeing it as the foundation of social order itself in all but the smallest communities.[10]

William J. Goode has cogently criticized the tendency of sociologists to minimize the role of force in human societies in terms that often come close to my argument here.[11] But while earlier sociologists have blurred the distinction between force and the threat of force in order to underplay the effectiveness of the latter by emphasizing the obvious limitations of the former, Goode is partially guilty of the opposite tendency. He correctly stresses the pervasiveness and efficacy of the threat and fear of force in influencing much human conduct, but he does not sufficiently distinguish the actual application of force from what he calls "force-threat," often lumping both together under the labels of "force" or "coercion." He explicitly states, in fact, that by "use of force" he means "both force-threat and overt force."[12] Goode is understandably concerned with correcting the overemphasis of sociologists on "values and value-consensus," but failure to distinguish sharply between the application of force and the threat of force can also support a too crude Thrasymachean (in Dahrendorf's phrase), neo-Machiavellian, or *Realpolitische* view of power and social control against which the sociologists themselves were originally and quite rightly reacting.

The rival tradition in Western thought stresses the primacy of *consensus*, the bond of shared values uniting ruler and ruled which enjoins the latter's submission. The consensualist view lays stress on the limitations of coercive authority. Coercion, in the first place, requires costly expenditures of material and human resources on the instruments of coercion and the social organization needed to wield them, even when the threat of force is rarely put to a test. Moreover, usually, as Kenneth Boulding observes, "the credibility of threats depreciates with time if threats are not carried out. Hence threats occasionally need to be carried out in order to reestablish the credibility. Another reason is that threat capability declines if threats are not occasionally carried out, particularly where this capability is enshrined in complex social organizations and in apparatus such as armed forces." [13]

Coercion also has to face the visibility problem in especially acute form: if rebels and deviants are restrained primarily by the fear of punishment, the power-holder must be constantly vigilant in overseeing and keeping informed about their activities. Otherwise, "when the cat is away, the mice will play." Students of crime have long argued that it is not so much the severity of punishment that deters potential criminals—when indeed they *are* deterred by fear of the law—but the degree of *certainty* of punishment, or the probability of being caught and punished. The reliability of anticipated reactions is low for the coercive power-holder unless the power subject is convinced that he is under constant surveillance. Thus efficient information gathering and espionage organizations must be added to the power-holder's investment in the means of violence and the social organization trained in their use.

Finally, power based on coercion both presupposes and creates a conflict of interest between power-holder and power subject and ensuing hostility and antagonism on the part of the latter which requires over time ever-greater vigilance and investment in the means of coercion by the power-holder. For these reasons, Boulding argues, "the unilateral threat system, or the threat-submission system, which may be fairly successful for a time, almost inevitably degenerates into the bi-lateral threat system, or deterrence." [14] Or, in other words, the integral power of a coercive-power holder is successfully countervailed and transformed into a system of intercursive power.

Another common objection to the alleged overemphasis on the

role of force in human societies is the "praetorian guard" argument.[15] Since both the actual use of force and the display of its instruments for purposes of threat require a social organization, it is argued that the wielders of force themselves must submit to the direction of their own leaders out of motives other than the fear of force even if they succeed in cowing the rest of the population. Material rewards or belief in the legitimacy of their collective task must be the basis of their compliance, for they cannot reasonably be afraid of themselves. Thus even under the most ruthless military dictatorships or police states, the army or the police are not coerced by their own leaders but obey them for reasons other than fear.

This argument is generally a valid and compelling one, but Michael Polanyi, with the last years of Stalin's rule in mind, has suggested an exception to it:

It is commonly assumed that power cannot be exercised without some voluntary support, as for example by a faithful praetorian guard. I do not think this is true, for it seems that some dictators were feared by everybody; for example, towards the end of his rule everyone feared Stalin. It is, in fact, easy to see that a single individual might well exercise command over a multitude of men without appreciable voluntary support on the part of any of them. If in a group of men each believes that all the others will obey the commands of a person claiming to be their common superior, all will obey this person as their superior. For each will fear that if he disobeyed him, the others would punish his disobedience at the superior's command, and so all are forced to obey by the mere supposition of the others' continued obedience, without any voluntary support being given to the superior by any member of the group. Each member of the group would even feel compelled to report any signs of dissatisfaction among his comrades, for he would fear that any complaint made in his presence might be a test applied to him by an *agent provocateur* and that he would be punished if he failed to report such subversive utterances. Thus the members of the group might be kept so distrustful of each other, that they would express even in private only sentiments of loyalty towards a superior whom they all hated in secret. The stability of such naked power increases with the size of the group under its control, for a disaffected nucleus which might be formed locally by a lucky crystallization of mutual trust among a small number of personal associates, would be overawed and paralysed by the vast surrounding masses of people whom they would assume to be still loyal to the director. Hence it is easier to keep control of a vast country than of the crew of a single ship in mid-ocean. [16]

Polanyi's example depends on the widespread existence of what social psychologists have called "pluralistic ignorance": each individual member of the group fails to communicate his real feelings and perceptions to the others in the belief that they are not shared and that he would be punished for expressing them. Yet in fact there is a consensus within the group, although it is unknown and concealed. Thus all group members may share a secret hatred for their leader. By requiring frequent public manifestations of deference, ritual flattery, head-bowing and foot-scraping, and the equivalent of *Heil Hitler* salutes, the ruler may help create this situation and exploit it to his advantage. His insistence on compulsory displays of obeisance therefore has a function in helping to maintain his power in addition to that of merely feeding his vanity. Yet well aware of his power to compel the *appearance* of deference and willing compliance, the ruler can never be certain that genuine loyalty motivates the obedience of his followers rather than fear or calculated self-interest. Hence the frequent paranoia of absolute rulers—why, in Shakespeare's words, "uneasy lies the head that wears the crown."

An incident that occurred at the famous Twentieth Congress of the Communist Party of the Soviet Union, when Khrushchev delivered his "secret speech" denouncing Stalin, is consistent with Polanyi's argument. As Khrushchev was describing the indignities to which Stalin forced even his closest associates to submit, someone in the audience shouted out "Why didn't you kill him?" After a stunned pause, Khrushchev bellowed back "Who said that?" but no one answered. The silence was itself an answer to the original question, for the veteran delegates in the audience were well aware that they were being addressed by a man who had not only been one of Stalin's confederates but who had recently emerged as his successor.

In actual power relations, the subject himself may scarcely know, let alone be able to verbalize truthfully, the motive or motives that underlie his compliance. He may claim to obey out of profound moral conviction when in fact he fears the authority's power to punish him, or, conversely, he may insist that he is coerced or concerned only with material rewards when actually complying out of a sense of obligation—like men who pretend that they work hard only to provide for their families though really driven by an intense achievement motive.

All human motivation is overdetermined in the psychoanalytic sense. If it is easy to identify the actual use of force to "produce an intended effect," it is by no means easy to isolate the part played by the threat and fear of force in much human conduct. Certainly, threatened force is ubiquitous and the fear of it pervasive and often inextricably intertwined with the desire for prestige, material acquisitiveness, duty, and love as human motives. In real life it is never easy to disentangle voluntary consent from subjection to "naked power." Or, one might say that power rarely is naked, but usually comes clothed in garments of legitimacy.

TWELVE

Competent Authority:
Reality and Legitimating Model

BOTH PLATO AND ARISTOTLE compared the relation of a ruler to his subjects to that of a helmsman to the crew of a ship and a physician to the human body. Hannah Arendt observes of Plato's political philosophy: "Here the concept of the expert enters the realm of political action for the first time, and the statesman is understood to be competent to deal with human affairs in the same sense as the carpenter is competent to make furniture or the physician to heal the sick." [1] Plato in *The Republic* and Aristotle in *Politics* saw as a defining trait of the authority exercised by the helmsman, the physician, and "the arts in general" that, in Aristotle's words, it "is exercised in the first instance for the good of the governed or for the common good of both parties, but essentially for the good of the governed." [2] Socrates, addressing Thrasymachus in the first book of *The Republic*, concluded that "there is no one in any rule who, in so far as he is a ruler, considers or enjoins what is for his own interest, but always what is for the interest of his subject or suitable to his art." [3]

For the moment let us beg the question of the validity of the comparison between the authority of the pilot or physician and political rule, which I shall consider later on. In their descriptions of the former, Plato and Aristotle clearly had in mind what I shall call *"competent authority."* They were also well aware that it was far from being the only type of authority in human society. Aristotle specifically distinguished it from the master-slave relationship in which "the rule of a master . . . is . . . exercised primarily with a view to the interest of the master." [4]

Competent authority is a power relation in which the subject obeys the directives of the authority out of belief in the authority's superior competence to decide which actions will best serve the subject's interests and goals. The phrase "competent authority," however, is often used to refer to authority that is exercised in accordance with public or private statutory law. Such a usage makes it merely a special case of legitimate authority, notably Weber's rational-legal type. But, as Talcott Parsons has pointed out, "competent authority" in this sense is not at all the same thing as authority based on "technical" competence, that is, on knowledge or expertise. In Parsons's example, the treasurer of a corporation authorized to sign checks is not necessarily a better check signer than the secretaries and clerks who work in his office.[5] "Competent authority" in the sense I mean rests solely on the subject's belief in the superior knowledge or skill of the exerciser rather than on position in a hierarchy. It is the authority of the "expert."

"Doctor's orders" may be taken as the prototype of competent authority. The doctor who says "stop drinking or you'll be dead within a year" is not threatening to kill the patient should the patient refuse to comply; the doctor's authority does not rest on the ability to impose any coercive sanctions. Nor is he appealing to a duty or moral obligation to obey that is incumbent upon the patient; he may greet the patient's refusal with a shrugged "Do what you want, it's your life." Legitimate authority therefore is not at issue. Competent authority resembles persuasion, which is why it has been seen since the time of the Greeks as the most benign and desirable form of authority.

In common speech the term "authority" is used as a synonym for possessor of special knowledge or expertise, as when we describe someone as an authority on tax law or on the philosophy of Hegel. Such a usage does not refer to a social relationship at all, let alone a power relation, although it at least implies that we are disposed to act on the advice of such authorities in practical matters, recognizing that their directives possess, in Carl Friedrich's phrase, the "potentiality of reasoned elaboration."[6] But there is nothing mandatory about such authority, which is why it appears to be close to, if not identical with, persuasion. Yet we are not speaking loosely when we refer to doctor's "orders" rather than "suggestions" or "arguments." Successful persuasion involves acceptance by the persuaded of the *content* of the persuader's communications on the basis of an independent assessment of them, whereas authority involves the subject's compliance with a directive because of its *source* rather than its content. The subject's belief in the superior competence of another provides, therefore, a basis for authority that is not simply a special case of persuasion. The patient may understand nothing of the rationale for the doctor's directives; he complies with them out of trust in the doctor's superior competence to judge what will cure him of his ailment. The doctor may even become annoyed if the patient presses for a detailed explanation of the connection between the symptoms and the proposed cure, thereby attempting to convert a relationship of competent authority into one of persuasion. As Freidson has argued, when competence has been granted professional status, "[What] is desired— even demanded—by the profession is that the client obeys because he has faith in the competence of the consultant without evaluating the grounds of the consultant's advice." [7]

Despite the apparent specificity of competent authority, it tends to shade into legitimate authority when it is vested in professional roles. Freidson's paper from which the above quotation is taken is entitled "The Impurity of Professional Authority," and his major conclusion is that "the authority of the professional is . . . in everyday practice, more like that of an officeholder than conventional characterizations would have us believe." [8] The professional practitioner possesses no sanctions over the client, but he has achieved through state recognition a virtual monopoly of the service he supplies. His formal credentials function like insignia of office in permitting him to avoid the burden of having to persuade the client to follow his advice. The client, moreover, as Freidson points out, is not free to prescribe drugs for himself, or to decide which academic courses should entitle him to a degree. In addition, a large part of professional work does not consist of applied technical and objective knowledge but of moral judgments and often self-serving occupational customs. In a later work, Freidson concludes that "the professional has gained a status which protects him more than other experts from outside scrutiny and criticisms and which grants him extraordinary autonomy in controlling both the definition of the problem he works on and the way he performs his work." [9]

Organizations of experts providing a service to the public strive to prescribe the technical and ethical standards of practice, required training, and certification procedures. Their success in winning state recognition of their exclusive control over these defines an occupation as a full-fledged profession. Professional associations, therefore, depend upon and, in a sense, exercise political power, a power that supports the competent authority of the individual practitioner dealing with a client. The power of the collective organization of experts and ultimately of the state play a significant role in establishing the competent authority of the expert.

If competent authorities sometimes take on some of the attributes of legitimate and even coercive authorities, it is also true that the latter may lay claim to certifiable competence in leadership and administration. This is typically the case in modern bureaucratic organization, as was recognized by Max Weber. "Bureaucratic administration," he wrote in a famous statement, "means fundamentally the exercise of control on the basis of knowledge. . . . The decisive reason for the advance of bureaucratic organization has always been its purely technical superiority over any other form of organization." [10] Weber's stress on the *expertise* of the bureaucrat, an expertise based not only on administrative experience but on educational certification as well, has been insufficiently recognized, according to Charles Perrow, by contemporary sociologists, who have exaggerated the difference between professionals and administrators, or between "staff" and "line" positions within formal organizations. [11] Increasingly, administrators present themselves as experts in management and exhibit graduate degrees from schools of business or public administration. Perrow, however, overlooks that these very fields of applied knowledge, or would-be "professions," presuppose that the practitioner has the power to impose sanctions and to enjoin compliance as a duty. His control over both coercive and normative resources, in Etzioni's terminology, [12] derives from his incumbency in office. The bureaucratic manager may lay claim to special competence in management, and the possession of educational credentials may even be a requirement for holding office. But in contrast to the expert or professional whose authority rests primarily on his certified competence, the manager has other resources at his disposal to obtain compliance, and these are clearly the chief basis of his authority. His claim to superior competence in administration amounts to an additional legitimating argument invoked to buttress the authority of his office, although his academic knowledge may indeed help him to exercise authority more efficiently.

In summary, the professional, who possesses power based on knowledge, also possesses, according to Freidson, some of the attributes of power based on legally ratified status, and this status depends on the power of the collective organization of his fellow experts. The bureaucrat with degrees in management has acquired knowledge that supplements the authority of office and the sanctions and resources it controls. Both, though not to the same degree, represent adulterations of an ideal-typically "pure" competent authority.

Plato and Aristotle did not consider the comparison between the authority of the helmsman or physician and that of the statesman to be no more than a metaphor, or even to be a lofty ideal rarely if ever achieved in practice (though Plato's conception was closer to this than Aristotle's). The Greek philosophers believed in the reality of "wisdom" or knowledge of "the Good" and regarded their application in ethics and politics as in no way different in kind from the application of knowledge of the winds and tides in navigation or of the workings of the human body in medicine. We owe such common expressions as the "ship of state" and the "body politic" to these Platonic analogies.[13] * Later thinkers, however, have viewed the possibility of a rational political authority comparable to that of the skilled crafts-

---

*In contemporary China, Mao is regularly described as "The Great Helmsman." I do not know whether the metaphor was borrowed from Western Marxism and thus ultimately may derive from Plato, or whether it is also indigenous to traditional Chinese culture. Stalin, from whom Mao imitated what Stalin's heirs later anathematized as "the cult of personality," used to prefer more modern, industrial metaphors such as "the Great Driver of the Locomotive of History." Incidentally, Richard Nixon, after his visit to China in early 1972, was frequently described in 1972 campaign literature as "the helmsman of the American ship of state," so there may have been a three-step West to East and back again diffusion of this ancient metaphor.

man or professional with skepticism. Bertrand Russell remarked that belief in a generalized gift of "wisdom" the possession of which "is supposed to make a man capable of governing wisely" is a view that "to us . . . seems remote from reality." [14]

Although Plato and Aristotle were well acquainted with tyranny in the experience of the Greek city-states, later thinkers have not only doubted the existence of political "wisdom" as a special ability to govern and dispense justice, but have expressed a deep suspicion and mistrust of *all* political power, not merely of that wielded by the "wrong people," that is, by tyrants and demagogues. This attitude, of course, is deeply rooted in Christianity and persisted among leading thinkers of the Enlightenment. Immanuel Kant wrote: "That kings should philosophize or philosophers become kings is not to be expected, nor is it to be wished, since the possession of power inevitably corrupts the untrammeled judgment of reason." [15] In doubting that political power can exemplify the rule of disinterested reason, we are disposed to interpret the physician-statesman comparison as a "mere" metaphor, one, moreover, which serves the interests of the powerful as a spurious legitimating argument or ideological rationale justifying their rule.

The birth of modern science led to a revival of the Platonic dream of the union of knowledge and power. In the early nineteenth century, the "prophets of Paris," Fourier, Saint-Simon, and Comte, foresaw and advocated a new society directed by social scientists who had acquired basic knowledge of the laws of social stability and change by applying to the study of human affairs the methods which had proved so successful in the study of nature. Living in an age in which science has become the ultimate cognitive authority, the vision of a society designed and controlled by "social engineers" survives to the present day as the core of "technocratic" theories and ideologies. But such conceptions have scarcely escaped corrosive doubt and criticism. The metaphor of the policy-maker as a social engineer has been debunked and unmasked as ideology with the same arguments employed against Plato's prescientific and preindustrial analogies between the statesman and the skilled craftsman. Few of us may share William F. Buckley's political views, but most of us are likely to respond with an initial twitch of amused sympathy to his remark that he would rather be ruled by the first one hundred names in the Boston telephone directory than by the faculty of Harvard College.

Freidson has argued that because of the extraordinary prestige and high degree of organization of professionals, "expertise is more and more in danger of being used as a mask for privilege and power rather than, as it claims, as a mode of advancing the public interest." [16] Freidson is referring primarily to the autonomy won by professionals to control the conditions under which they supply a vital service to the public. Professional organizations also engage in collective bargaining and political lobbying to advance the economic interests of their members in ways that do not differ from those of trade unions and other occupational associations. Although the halo of their professional status may for a time result in their demands being granted greater legitimacy than those of most groups, they are increasingly perceived as not essentially different in kind from other special-interest associations competing in the political and economic arenas. One is surprised to discover that in the early 1920s Thorstein Veblen believed that so prosaic an organization as the American Society of Mechanical Engineers could become a "class-conscious" political force promoting the "Soviet of Technicians" that he favored as an alternative to proletarian revolution. [17] (One of Veblen's admirers at this time was Howard Scott, a self-described engineer who later popularized the term "technocracy" as the founder of the movement by that name which flourished for a few years in the early 1930s.)

This brings us to the numerous "new class" theories that have cast experts or men of knowledge, variously defined, in the role of builders of a new rationally designed social order. Such theories, most notably that of Saint-Simon, actually antedated Marx's baptism of the proletariat as the revolutionary class, although since Marx they have usually, like Veblen's theory, been put forward as alternatives to the predicted ascendancy of the working class. Saint-Simon's "producers," Comte's priests of "positivism," Waclaw Machajski's "intellectual workers," Veblen's "engineers," James Burnham's "managers," J. K. Galbraith's "techno-structure," George Lichtheim's "scientific and technical intelligentsia," Robert Heilbroner's "scientific elites," Alain Touraine's "technocrats," Richard Flacks's "young intelligentsia in revolt"—all have been designated in the course of a century and a half as carriers of a movement toward a planned society in which social rationality prevails. Discussions of their role are central to the current debate over the nature of the "postindustrial," "knowledgeable," or "expert" society.

Some new class theorists have favored the groups and tendencies they discerned and predicted. Others have opposed them, treating technocratic visions of the future as ideologies making universalistic claims while actually, like all ideologies, promoting the particular interests of a limited group. If technicians and experts have often been welcomed as heirs to the failed mission of the proletariat, they have also been assailed as an actual or prospective new ruling class frustrating the dream of a classless society. Some writers have assigned to the "new class" the parts of both the bourgeoisie and the proletariat in the Marxist drama, seeing it as an outgrowth of the "old middle class" that is nevertheless destined to be the carrier of an anticapitalist ethos stemming from its antagonism to the planlessness and waste of the market and the vulgarities of commercialism. New-class theorists include writers who can be loosely classified as on the Left as well as on the Right, but even among those who identify themselves as leftists one finds diametrically opposed views: some, particularly those sympathetic to the so-called counterculture, see professionals and technocrats as a new class enemy, whereas others, buoyed by the student revolt of the late sixties, have regarded the university as the seedbed of a vastly expanded and radicalized intelligentsia equipped with skills that are functionally indispensable to modern society and therefore capable of transforming it.

The empirical and conceptual issues raised by new class theories are well known. There is, first of all, the ambiguity with which the alleged new class is defined. Does it include only technical and professional occupations in the strict sense, or does it also embrace administrators who wield an institutionalized bureaucratic authority that is based neither on property ownership nor solely on expertise? Are "pure" scientists who "do not have clients" [18] included, or is the new class confined to applied scientists and professionals claiming to exercise competent authority over a lay public? Failure to delimit clearly the boundaries of the group in question raises a second major issue: to what extent can social cohesion, a common ethos, and at

least nascent political aims be attributed to it? Is it, at least potentially, a full-fledged class with a distinctive class consciousness, or is
it no more than a stratum, scarcely even a *Klasse an sich* in Marx's
sense? Or is it an elite rather than a class or stratum, or merely a
congerie of different "strategic elites" [19] possessing little or no unity
of outlook?

These unsettled empirical and definitional problems lead to the
central issue of whether the knowledgeable have become, or merged
inseparably with, the powerful, or whether the powerful have enlisted
more and more of the knowledgeable in their service in the face of
the growing technical complexity of advanced industrial societies,
while retaining an individual and collective identity distinct from that
of their servants. In short, do "the knowledgeable have power," or is
it rather that increasingly "the powerful have knowledge," that is,
access to the services of a growing number of trained experts? [20]

There is by now a huge literature, much of it ideologically motivated, debating these issues. It is not my purpose here to make another contribution to it. I merely want to note that in all technocratic
theories the ultimate legitimation of the power of the technocrats is
seen as resting on the model of competent authority. The attrac-
tiveness to some of a society run by experts and the fears of others
that technocratic visions possess a special seductiveness that could
mask the self-interested elitism of a new intelligentsia both stem from
a recognition of the apparently benign character of competent authority. As Habermas has remarked, "technocratic consciousness is
. . . 'less ideological' than all previous ideologies" and yet at the
same time "more irresistible and farther-reaching than ideologies of
the old type." [21] Moreover, the group invoking and destined to bene-
fit from technocratic legitimations of power contains professionals
and consulting experts who are used to exercising competent authority in their relations with clients.

Describing the views of Saint-Simon, the first "technocratic visionary," Daniel Bell writes: "in a technocratic society politics would disappear since all problems would be decided by the expert. One would
obey the competence of a superior just as one obeys the instructions
of a doctor or an orchestra conductor or a ship's captain." [22] We encounter once again awareness of the legitimating use of the ancient

Platonic analogies. Lewis Coser has similarly observed of Comte's utopia that "freedom of conscience would no longer play a progressive part because it would be absurd to oppose a scientifically managed society, just as it would be absurd to oppose a scientifically established law of nature." [23] The equation of subjection to scientifically established laws of nature with obedience to scientist-rulers nicely demonstrates how a technocratic ideology obscures the difference between the cognitive authority of science and legitimation of the authority of rulers who claim to be social and political experts. Competent authority, linked today to theoretical science insofar as it is "knowledge based," may appear to be the ideal and minimally necessary form of authority in human society. However, as critics of Plato's philosopher-kings have long argued, people may be ready to accept the competent authority of the engineer or physician in their restricted spheres, but they are unlikely to acknowledge unanimously the superior competence of political and institutional leaders, with the result that manipulation, exoteric appeals to "miracle, mystery, and authority," in the words of Dostoyevsky's Grand Inquisitor, and ultimately coercion are required to buttress the esoteric legitimations accepted by the leaders themselves. Plato recognized this, which is why, since he abhorred the direct use of force, his utopian republic relies so heavily on manipulation and intensive educational indoctrination. [24]

The new class and postindustrial theorists, whatever the differences among them, regard technocratic consciousness as the distinctive ethos of scientific and professional workers. But there have been a number of ideological movements in the past century that have capitalized on the prestige of science without seeking their primary social base in the technical and scientific intelligentsia itself: Social Darwinism, various racist creeds, and most notably Marxism, a doctrine that has proved to be as protean in the adaptability of its appeals to diverse groups as an oriental religion. In the 1930s, a Marxism with a technocratic accent was attractive to many Western scientists, who thought of the Soviet Union as a "great experiment" and persuaded themselves that Communism gave scientific experts a free hand at social planning unrestrained by base political and commercial considerations. [25] Yet Marxism, even when claiming to be itself a science, has usually directed its appeals to groups other than experts and professionals.

Political ideologies such as Social Darwinsim, racism, and Marxism are characterized by what Hannah Arendt has called "scientificality." [26] "Scientificality" stands in roughly the same relation to science as an institution as "religiosity" stands to religious institutions. Far from expressing a technocratic consciousness, such creeds have usually been opposed by scientists and professionals, attracting primarily the charlatans, quacks, and failures within their ranks. They have by and large appealed to a half-educated public by claiming privileged insight into the laws of nature from which laws of history and politics can be inferred just as religious prophets claimed unique access to the will of God.

Arendt attributed scientificality to creeds reflecting the apparent victory of science over traditional religion, which evolved into the totalitarian ideologies of the twentieth century. More recently, scientificality *and* religiosity have been combined in the doctrines of a variety of movements, some of them defining themselves as religious rather than political, others advertising themselves as psychotherapies, and a few sharing aspects of all three. Maoism and Taoism, Marxist jargon and charismatic hero cults, "scientologies" appealing both to laws of nature and to occult spiritual forces, therapies starting with a medical model and ending in the celebration of mystical rituals of group communion, chemical knowledge of drugs and magical practices—syncretistic permutations and combinations of all of these have become common features of a host of cults and sects that have flourished in the past decade. Each of the polarities exists in pure strains as well, pitting Establishment against counterculture, science against gnosis, computer analysts and behavior controllers against swamis and gurus, technocrats against humanists. The blends may indeed reflect a healthy impulse, lurid and ludicrous though they presently appear. Not only do they bridge conflict between polarized outlooks, but they reduce the likelihood of static symbiosis between them, of a world in which, as Max Weber foresaw, "specialists without vision and sensualists without heart" might peacefully coexist with an oligarchy of highly trained technicians ruling a drugged and satiated mass of "proles."

We have come a long way from the simple model of competent authority with which I started. I have moved along a continuum from cases of actual competent authority to analogical generalizations from them put forward in order to legitimate the exercise of power in contexts where it is far from obvious that the superior knowledge of some and the self-interested need of others unite to create a distinctive, noncoercive power relation. The use of competent authority as a model for political rule had its beginnings in Western thought with Plato. The birth of modern science and its increasing application to human needs has since widened the gap between the knowledge and skill of experts and the innocence and ignorance of laymen. The vesting of competent authority in institutionalized professions, however, has led to its adulteration as a result of the collective power wielded by professional associations with the support of the state over the conditions of their work.

Still further along the continuum, technocratic theories and ideologies treat the habits of mind of professionals and technicians as applicable to the organization of society as a whole. Such theories have regarded the scientific and technical intelligentsia as the agency par excellence aiming at institutional innovation and planned social change. Ideologies that are still further removed from the actual exercise of competent authority in expert-client relationships have drawn on the popular cognitive authority of science to make totalistic claims to the understanding of reality which have sometimes served to legitimate actual totalitarian rule. More recently, curious blends of scientific and religio-magical beliefs have formed the basis of a variety of new movements.

It would be as great an error to deny the reality of the competent authority of the expert within his sphere as it is to make analogical use of it to legitimate power that inevitably and necessarily rests on the control of resources other than expert knowledge. Populist mistrust of the inherent "elitism" of all competent authority, giving rise to what might be called "technophobia," distorts reality as much as the most "nonreflexive" technocratic consciousness. It is an illusion to suppose that we can do away with experts by becoming jacks-of-all-trades, that we can "hunt in the morning, fish in the afternoon, rear cattle in the evening, criticize after dinner, just as [we] have in mind, without ever becoming hunter, fisherman, shepherd, or critic." As has often been pointed out, Marx and Engels actually here describe the occupational activities of an agrarian, preindustrial society rather than those of a developed technological order.[27] Yet however great our inescapable dependence on experts, the late George Lichtheim was surely correct in maintaining that "in the end the technocrats themselves may discover to their surprise that they cannot function unless someone tells them what the whole expenditure of energy is supposed to be *for*. And that someone won't be another technocrat." [28]

THIRTEEN
Economic Development and Democracy

ROBERT HEILBRONER'S ESSAY, "Counterrevolutionary America," is the most intelligent and forceful statement of a point of view that is widely held by writers on economic development in the Third World.[1] Although Heilbroner is an economist, his conclusions rest only to a minor degree on economic expertise. Both in the article and in his earlier book-length essay, *The Great Ascent*,[2] he fully recognizes that economic development necessarily involves massive social and political changes in addition to the changes in the techniques and the organization of production that the term connotes in its narrow sense. Heilbroner's argument, anticipated in his earlier book but stated far more strongly and without qualification in the more recent article, is that the obstacles posed to rapid economic development by traditional values and old established ruling elites are so great that only a revolution bringing to power a Communist-type totalitarian dictatorship can be expected to overcome them and proceed with the urgent task of modernizing backward societies.

It is worth reviewing step by step the reasoning by which Heilbroner reaches this conclusion. The essentials of his position are shared by many other writers—indeed, some of them have become virtually commonplace in discussions of economic development. If the argument is summarized as schematically as possible, and shorn of Heilbroner's considerable eloquence and richness of allusion, it should be possible to see its main structure and to separate the truths from the assumptions and hypotheses contained in it.

1. Only the starting point of the argument involves an economic proposition: namely, that the task of initial capital accumulation in

underdeveloped countries requires the holding down for a time of the living standards of the peasants, who constitute the mass of the population; not until the "infrastructure" of a modern economy has been built will it be possible for the resulting gains in productivity to be widely distributed.

But strictly economic considerations are transcended as soon as we ask what groups and agencies in contemporary underdeveloped countries are capable of organizing and directing the economic task of drawing a portion of the peasantry off the land to build capital, and of collecting part of the agricultural produce of the remaining peasants to feed this new nonagricultural labor force. The absence of rising commercial and entrepreneurial classes resembling the European bourgeoisie, or of any group imbued with an ethos, like the Protestant ethic, favoring hard work and the sacrifice of present material gains for the future, means that the state alone can play the necessary role in today's backward countries. Most experts on economic development concede (in the large view at least) that the state must assume the entrepreneurial function in the majority of the nations of the Third World and that these nations are therefore likely to adopt some form of collectivism or "state socialism." Only a handful of neoclassical economists disagree. The state must be a strong state if it is to initiate successful programs of economic development. That is, it must, in the first instance, possess the power and the will to coerce or buy off traditional elites that resist modernizing measures. But more important, it must command the allegiance of a significant portion of the population.

2. There is little in this analysis so far that is likely to arouse much disagreement. The next step in Heilbroner's argument, however, goes beyond the general consensus. In order to win the support of the masses, the argument runs, the state must promote a new ideological creed that will penetrate their minds and hearts, win them away from traditional habits, beliefs, and loyalties—"reach and rally them," as he puts it—and induce them to acquiesce in the sacrifices of the period of capital accumulation. Such a creed is bound to be intolerant of all dissent and is likely to contain a strong negative component, branding foreigners, in particular the West, as carriers of evil and as actual or potential supporters of oppositionists at home.

Clearly, this description is matched most closely by a revolutionary regime that has seized power after mobilizing a sizable segment of the population against the old order or foreign imperialists—or, most probably, a combination of both. Only a militant revolutionary state can make the sharp break with the past and impose the strict totalitarian discipline on a sprawling agrarian society that are needed to begin "the Great Ascent" to the heights of modernization.

Heilbroner's rejection of the belief or hope that democratic constitutional governments, preserving and fostering the political liberties of the individual citizen, are capable of achieving economic development is presented in less detail than his reasons for thinking that some form of totalitarian collectivism can do the job. But his case against democratic government is implicit in much of his argument and has been more fully stated by other writers who share his general outlook. I shall draw on some of them to flesh out his thesis.[3]

Most of the states in the Third World are far from being genuine nations. Democratic institutions and practices, it is held, can only delay the task of nation-building by encouraging all the diverse ethnic, religious, tribal, and linguistic groups that make up the populations of the new states to articulate their distinctive values and interests. The new states must create an overriding sense of national purpose and national identity transcending parochial group loyalties if they are to carry out effective economic development programs. A democratic, multiparty system will perpetuate and even accentuate the fragmentation of their populations. This argument has been applied most widely in defense of one-party dictatorships in Africa. It makes a specifically political case against democracy in the Third World, seeing nation-building as the prime requisite for the strong state that is in turn a prime requisite for economic development.

Unlike Africa, most Asian and Latin American nations do not confront the immediate necessity of welding together collections of tribal peoples who have often been traditional enemies and have never acknowledged any central political authority. The case against democracy in Asia and Latin America rests less on the alleged requirements of nation-building than on the contention that democratic governments cannot succeed in breaking the resistance to far-reaching social reform offered by old classes and elites—parasitic landlords, village moneylenders, compradore merchants, corrupt military and bureaucratic cliques, hoary priestly oligarchies. Democracy is likely to be no more than a facade behind which these groups retain full power, occasionally lulling the masses with token reforms.

A more general argument against democracy in the Third World, one that is more closely linked to the initial prerequisites for economic development, holds that the masses are likely to vote themselves welfare-state benefits, opting for immediate improvements in their standard of living rather than for capital investment and thus defeating long-range development programs. Argentina under Peron and particularly the persistence of Peronist sympathies among the industrial workers long after the dictator's fall from power are frequently cited as the standard horrible example.[4] There is an obvious contradiction between the assertion that democracy in the Third World is doomed to be a facade manipulated by the traditional ruling classes and the expressed fear that it will result in the mass electorate voting for immediate, "uneconomic" gains in income; but we shall let this pass for the moment.

This, in broad outline, is Heilbroner's thesis, omitting only his observations on the probable attitude of the United States to revolutionary regimes in the Third World, which I shall discuss very briefly later. The thesis, both in Heilbroner's and other versions, has evoked vigorous objections from liberals and democrats unwilling to accept the inevitability of the totalitarian trend it postulates. Their reactions, however, have usually failed to go beyond ringing reaffirmation of democratic and humanitarian values and expressions of moral outrage at the apparent readiness of so many Western writers to regard violence and repressive government as the unavoidable price of modernization. Heilbroner is entitled to reply to such protests—indeed, he has already so replied[5]—"don't blame me for being the bearer of bad news. To refute me you must first show that the news is not as bad as I've reported, that my analysis is mistaken, and this you have failed to do."

3. The Heilbroner thesis outlines certain social prerequisites for economic development and maintains that democratic institutions are bound to present obstacles to fulfilling them. Since democracy runs the risk of promoting anarchic factionalism, permitting privi-

leged classes to retain covert control over the government, and encouraging all groups to seek to use the state to advance their material interests, the thesis possesses an immediate plausibility. The plausibility carries over to the next step in the argument, where it is asserted that a government lacking democratic features will be able to avoid the problems of democracy and meet the requirements of modernization. But what if we start by asking, What are the difficulties that a totalitarian revolutionary regime is likely to face in carrying out development programs? These difficulties are conceded in passing by Heilbroner, but they fail to receive the attention they deserve because of the initial critical focus on the difficulties apt to be encountered by "mild," democratic governments.

To begin with, inflammatory nationalism, xenophobia, and the exaltation of the state—which are, according to Heilbroner, invariable ingredients of the "mobilizing appeal" of revolutionary elites—lead to the investment of considerable resources in armaments and the maintenance of large standing armies. Such expenditures are, of course, an utter waste from the standpoint of economic development. If demonstration steel mills and airlines are to be regarded as economically irrational national status symbols, how much more so are jet planes, tanks, and well-drilled armies? True, the desire for national strength and military glory may indeed motivate a nation to modernize its capital equipment and thus lay the foundation for eventual increases in productivity that will wipe out mass poverty and improve every citizen's material lot. A nation that can send sputniks into outer space is presumably capable of mass-producing shoes and automobiles, although the Soviet Union has yet to confirm this. However, underdeveloped nations are more likely to purchase the sinews of war from the advanced nations by intensifying their production of staple raw materials—the very condition that is part of the whole syndrome of their economic backwardness. Moreover, the trouble with large defense expenditures is that they tend to become self-perpetuating, not merely because they create vested interests, but because they persuade insecure neighbors to arm themselves, thus justifying the claim that a large military establishment is necessary for national security. Surely, those nations that have most closely followed Heilbroner's prescription—Russia, China, Egypt, Sukarno's Indonesia—have diverted enormous human and material resources from peaceful economic development to military uses.

In addition, the enhanced importance of the army makes a military takeover more probable should the revolutionary regime falter. If any "wave of the future" is discernible in the Third World at the present moment, it is in the direction of military dictatorships rather than Communist revolutions. Since 1960 revolutionary national socialist or left-nationalist reformist regimes have been overthrown in Argentina, Brazil, Bolivia, Algeria, Ghana, and Indonesia, and have been discredited—to put it mildly—in Egypt and Syria. It is still altogether possible that in China, Mao's "Cultural Revolution" will be terminated by an army takeover. Military dictatorships have also replaced shaky democratic civilian governments in Nigeria, the Congo, Greece, and a number of smaller African nations. A few of these new regimes are national socialist and even pro-Communist in ideological orientation (e.g., Algeria); a larger number are right-wing, strongly anti-Communist, or even protofascist (e.g., Argentina, Brazil, Greece, Indonesia).

Finally, aggressive nationalism and militarism may induce nations to seek territorial expansion, causing wars that risk spreading to engulf entire subcontinents, if not the world. Barrington Moore, Jr., observes that military defeat in World War II was part of the price paid by Japan for following a conservative-fascist path to modernization.[6] In other words, the dead of Hiroshima and Nagasaki, the Tokyo firebomb raids, and the Pacific islands campaigns must be cast into the balance against the "preventable deaths" from starvation and injustice under the old regime in toting up the costs of Japanese modernization.[7] Should not the Soviet Union's enormous losses in World War II be assessed, along with the victims of Stalin's purges and enforced collectivizations, as part of the price of totalitarian Communist modernization? Stalin's army purges, his opportunistic foreign policy toward Germany, and his unpopularity with the peasants who first hailed the Nazi invaders as liberators, all stemmed from his totalitarian rule and contributed to Russian military defeats in the early stages of the war.

Some Western nations also went through a military-expansionist phase in the course of their modernization. But in the present century technology has made even "conventional" warfare far more destructive than in the past. If, Heilbroner argues, greater population growth and density make economic development more urgent in the Third World today than in the West in the last century, then the changed scale of warfare and a more unstable international environment should also be taken into account if militaristic regimes are to be recommended as arch-modernizers.

What countries have achieved economic development to date as a result of nationalist-Communist revolutions? Let us concede the case of the Soviet Union, although the entire issue of whether the Bolshevik October revolution as distinct from the February revolution, let alone Stalin's totalitarian rule, was necessary for Russian economic development remains highly debatable among economists and historians. Heilbroner tells us that for himself he would rather be "an anonymous peasant" in China or Cuba than in India, Peru, or Ecuador.[8] But by his own admission "it may well be that Cuba has suffered a considerable economic decline" since Castro took power, and "we may not know for many years whether the Chinese peasant is better or worse off than before the revolution."[9] He praises Cuba for its educational effort, and China for having freed its youth from the bondage of the traditional family system. However, these achievements—assuming their reality—at most facilitate economic development rather than constituting development itself. Heilbroner might also reflect that the peasants of India and Peru evidently do not share his view of their prospects, having rejected in large numbers the opportunity to vote for Communist parties in free elections. In short, with the ambiguous exception of the Soviet Union, the Communist promise of rapid industrialization remains no more than a promise.

4. Heilbroner's case for the necessity of totalitarian ruthlessness to achieve modernization rests ultimately on his conviction of the enormous urgency of the problems of the backward countries. These countries cannot proceed according to the more leisurely timetable of past Western industrialization; they must take a giant step forward within the next three or four decades, or mass famine and internal chaos are sure to be their fare. Essentially, Heilbroner sees the continuing population explosion as imposing the need for an all-out attack on backwardness which must have priority over other values and

objectives. Not the entire Third World, but "primarily the crowded land masses and archipelagos of Southeast Asia and the impoverished areas of Central and South America" must look to revolutions led by modernizing elites to rescue them from deepening poverty. The extent to which Heilbroner's argument rests on the population explosion is striking, considering that, although there are many exceptions, economists as a rule are more optimistic than demographers in their estimates of the prospects for economic development in backward countries. Economists perceive the economic job to be done and are impressed by the ample technical resources—including their own counsel—available to do it; while demographers, horrified by the floods of additional people indicated by extrapolated population growth rates, insist that without birth control any development program must founder.

But are Communist countries likely to check population growth? Heilbroner refers patronizingly to India's failure to control the birth rate, but there is not the slightest evidence that China has had any greater success. Indeed, China's leaders lag behind India's in their awareness of the need for an antinatalist population policy. The relatively sparsely settled Soviet Union never faced a population explosion comparable to that of Southeast Asia—a further reason, incidentally, for questioning the necessity of totalitarianism for Russian economic development. The doctrinal anti-Malthusianism of Communist ideology imposes a special handicap on Communist countries with regard to birth control. Nor do non-Communist revolutionary elites imbued with aggressive nationalism and anti-Western fervor seem likely to assign high priority to diffusing family planning over building steel mills and armies.

But what if birth rates should turn downward before the "takeoff" point in economic development has been reached? In an article in *The Public Interest*, [10] Donald Bogue, the University of Chicago demographer, departed from the conventional pessimism of his colleagues[11] to predict the imminent end of the population explosion in the Third World. There is good reason to believe, he insists, that by the end of the present decade the efforts of government and private agencies promoting family planning will at last pay off and birth rates in India and several other Asian countries will begin unmistakably to decline. Bogue is unable to present decisive evidence supporting his forecast—he claims that the "catching on" of new birth-control methods in peasant populations is still too recent to have been statistically recorded. His main tangible evidence is based on studies in several countries, the most impressive of which was conducted in South Korea, showing that peasant women in surprising numbers have adopted in an exceedingly short space of time such recently developed contraceptive methods as intrauterine devices and even the pills. Maybe Bogue will turn out to be a false prophet, but it is worth recalling that sharp reversals of demographic trends have happened simultaneously before in a number of quite different countries, so there is no reason why sudden mass adoption of family planning resulting in lower birth rates might not occur in large areas of the Third World. Writing about Latin America, another demographer, J. Mayone Stycos of Cornell, also expresses cautious optimism in a book reporting his research in Peru and several Caribbean nations.[12]

5. I have argued that, although the difficulties faced by democratic governments in carrying out economic development are indeed real, totalitarian revolutionary regimes also face difficulties peculiar to them which Heilbroner and others tend to slight. Military dictatorships, a third and at present the most common type of regime in the Third World, have not been motoriously successful modernizers either.[13] One might conclude in an even more pessimistic vein than Heilbroner that neither democracy, revolutionary collectivism, nor military rule are capable of achieving modernization, and that it is therefore unlikely to take place at all. Yet such a conclusion would clearly be unjustified. In the past there have been a variety of paths to modernization: it has been achieved by essentially conservative regimes in Germany and Japan, by postrevolutionary bourgeois democracies in England and France, under a pure bourgeois democracy in the United States, and by Communist dictatorship in Russia; even a few military regimes have made considerable progress, as in Turkey and Mexico. There is apparently no intrinsic connection at all between economic progress and formal political institutions. The pace of economic development has also varied greatly, particularly among smaller nations free from the tensions of international rivalry.

Democratic institutions such as parliamentary government, ele-

mentary civil liberties, and the rule of law, though not—except in
the United States—universal suffrage, preceded economic development in the Western bourgeois democracies. Why should it be so
widely assumed that democracy can only emerge in the Third World
after modernization has been carried out by authoritarian governments? Those who argue this confuse the strong state that is indeed
required for economic development with a monolithic, authoritarian
state. The skeptics about democracy, with all their talk of avoiding
ethnocentric evaluations of the institutions of non-Western people,
often project the experience of Western democracies into the different social context of backward societies. And so these skeptics contend that Asian and African electorates will use the ballot to advance
their short-term interests like voters in the West accustomed to government whose rationalized welfare and service functions have succeeded, as Michael Walzer has argued, in demystifying the idea of
the state. Actually, the demands of the masses in underdeveloped
areas are likely to be too modest rather than excessive from the standpoint of stimulating development.[14] Democracy, moreover, may take
many different forms: ancient village communal bodies, such as the
old Russian mir and the Indian panchayats, can serve as two-way
communication channels between modernizing elites and the base of
the social structure, giving rise to a kind of "democratic centralism"
that is a reality rather than a facade for unilateral rule by the leadership. Also, even after universal suffrage was in effect in the Western
democracies, the political organization and mobilization of the lower
classes was a long, slow process. The masses in the Third World are
not going to leap at once into the political arena to make shortsighted and selfish immediate group demands. There is no reason
why they cannot be trusted to accept the guidance of enlightened
modernizing elites that truly consult them and give them a sense of
participation in the process. It is precisely such a sense of participation that Heilbroner sees as the forte of Communist revolutionaries, but there is no inherent reason why they alone should be
capable of instilling it.

6. What about American policy toward the Third World? Although
a secondary issue, this was ostensibly the main subject of Heilbroner's
essay. Heilbroner's denial notwithstanding, the United States has not

been consistently antirevolutionary, nor indeed consistently anything except opposed to states that have directly aligned themselves politically and militarily with the Soviet Union or China. The United States has given aid to Communist Yugoslavia, to nationalist, pro-Communist, and anti-American states such as Ghana under Nkrumah, and Algeria and Egypt, as well as to non-Communist revolutionary regimes such as Bolivia in the 1950s. Admittedly, the bulk of American aid has gone to "client states" ruled by conservative dictatorships, such as South Korea, Taiwan, and South Vietnam. But American policy on the whole has been shortsightedly opportunistic rather than ideologically consistent, willing to support almost any government, Left or Right, that is not a direct dependency of Russia or China. When Heilbroner suggests that the United States is unlikely to allow any nations in the Third World to remain neutral in the cold war,[15] he seems to be taking seriously Dulles's rhetoric of the 1950s, although even then the rhetoric did not correspond to American practice. More probably, he has in mind the war in Vietnam; but the flimsy American justification for the war rests on the assumption that China is the "real" enemy, not the Viet Cong or Hanoi. The United States accepted, after all, a neutral government in Laos.

Latin America, however, is obviously the area where Heilbroner's label "Counterrevolutionary America" is most applicable. Not only do the pocketbook interests of American businessmen have a greater influence on government policy there than elsewhere in the world, but the fall-out in effects on domestic policies of victories by Communist or proto-Communist revolutionaries is bound to be far greater. The Dominican tragedy reveals the panic that may strike an American administration if it persuades itself that there is even the slightest possibility of a repetition of the Cuban experience. It is indeed hard to imagine the United States passively tolerating any anti-American, revolutionary government in this hemisphere.

Finally, let us suppose that American policy-makers accept Heilbroner's analysis and become convinced that modernization of the Third World is possible only under Communist or authoritarian left-nationalist auspices. The results may be curious indeed. The *New Republic* of July 8, 1967, reports that a privately distributed newsletter subscribed to by Wall Street insiders suggests that it may very well be in the American national interest to allow the Third World to go Communist. The United States will save money in economic aid as the new Communist regimes seek development by sweating their own peasantries, whose labor will have to carry the whole burden of capital accumulation. If they fail, the United States cannot be blamed. If they succeed, they will in a decade or two become moderate and "bourgeois" in spirit like the Russians, and not only can we live in peace with them but we can engage them in mutually profitable trade. Such a view may well spread among those whom C. Wright Mills once called "sophisticated conservatives," and it may become more influential than the anger and frustration at the failure of American capitalism to convert the world that Heilbroner imputes to our leaders. And, as is so often the case in politics, the diagnosis may become self-confirming if America reduces instead of expanding its aid to the Third World in expectation of a wave of totalitarian revolutions. The Heilbroner thesis might thus ironically help bring about the conditions it claims to deplore in counseling us to resign ourselves to their inevitability.

A Reply to Heilbroner

I AM GLAD Robert Heilbroner finds that I have correctly understood and presented his views. He has done as well with mine, and I hope that the absence of rhetoric and polemical flourishes in our exchange will clarify the issues between us.

Heilbroner reiterates his conviction that left-authoritarian or Communist movements "offer the best chance for a breakthrough in the backward areas." Whether he is right or wrong in this belief, he fails fully to confront the prior question of how likely such movements are to come to power at all in the near future and win the chance to show what they can do. Far from foreseeing any upsurge of democratic modernizing forces in the Third World, I argued that the present trend was toward the overthrow of both democratic governments and left-authoritarian regimes by the armed forces. Heilbroner is more hopeful—given his assumptions—than I am that there will be successful Communist revolutions; I am more hopeful than he that some modernization will take place under a variety of political regimes. He apparently regards such recent events as China's declining prestige in the Third World, the turmoil inside China, the overthrow of left-nationalist "strong men" in Indonesia, Algeria, and Ghana, the misadventures of "Arab socialism," and the repeated failures and defeats of Cuban-sponsored guerrillas in Latin America as mere eddies in a broad historical current favoring revolutionary authoritarian regimes and movements. I, on the contrary, think that the Viet Cong may be the leaders of the last Communist-directed "war of national liberation" rather than the forerunners of a new revolutionary wave.

But if Heilbroner is right and Communist revolutions do take place in much of the Third World, can they achieve modernization? Communists have won power primarily by their own efforts in only five countries: Russia, Yugoslavia, China, North Vietnam, and Cuba. None of the three conditions Heilbroner adduces * for doubting the relevance of past Western experience to the contemporary underdeveloped world was fully present in Russia or Yugoslavia, so their record is scarcely more pertinent to the argument than the successful modernization achieved under democratic auspices by England and the United States. As to China, I agree with Heilbroner—Who knows? China may indeed have been "profoundly and irreversibly changed," but such change may or may not in the end facilitate the particular kind of "profound and irreversible change" we call modernization. In its exaltation of an ascetic, chiliastic revolutionary brotherhood, Mao's "cultural revolution" appears to be directed against assigning high priority to economic development and the materialism it inevitably brings rather than the reverse. North Vietnam has been involved in wars for over a decade. Cuba, a partially modernized country before Castro, has at most established some of the prerequisites for balanced modernization (e.g., mass literacy) while undergoing actual economic decline. I agree that promises are better than nothing, but Communists are not the only people in the Third World promising modernization.

The very polycentrism of the Communist world that makes nonsense out of the anti-Communist slogans invoked by Washington to justify the Vietnam war reduces the likelihood that future national Communist regimes will be the ruthless modernizers Heilbroner expects them to be. Would Egyptian national communism differ in any important way from Nasser's regime? Would an Algerian revolution create a state markedly different from the Ben Bella and Boumedienne dictatorships? Revolutions led by hard-bitten, Moscow-trained Stalinist orgmen might have a chance of successfully using totalitar-

---

* Heilbroner's three conditions are: the more acute population crisis, the absence of Europe's "three centuries of commercialization," and the "deformations of imperialism." See "Robert Heilbroner Replies," *Dissent* 14 (November–December 1967), 735.

ian methods to impose the drastic surgery of modernization on a recalcitrant peasantry. So might revolutions led by men like Mao's original cadres. So might revolutions led by orthodox Marxist-Leninists like most of the national Communists of Eastern Europe. But post-Stalinist Moscow no longer tightly controls the Communist parties in the Third World (or, indeed, anywhere), and Maoism today has little in common with traditional Marxist-Leninist doctrine. Revolutionary movements in the Third World are likely to be shaped by national character traits to a greater extent than was the case in past Communist revolutions, and such traits have usually been an obstacle—though by no means the only one—to modernization. The degree to which Communist parties in the Third World base themselves on dissatisfied ethnic, religious, and caste minority groups in their struggle against existing governments has been documented by Donald Zagoria.[16] Can we really expect such parties, should they win power, to be as relentlessly future-minded as the puritanical, iron-willed Bolsheviks who are the prototypes for our model of totalitarian modernization?

If Heilbroner is right that Communist revolutions offer the only hope for modernization, and I am right in doubting that there will be many successful revolutions in the near future, then the obvious conclusion is that there may be little or no modernization and that economic deterioration and political fragmentation are likely results. I agree that this is an entirely possible outcome for the next generation. It seems to me much more probable that disciplined, authoritarian revolutionaries will be able to seize power under conditions of mass famine and chaos than that they will succeed in overthrowing present governments which are maintaining some degree of order and economic progress, painfully slow though the latter may be. After all, in four of the five countries where indigenous Communist movements have triumphed (Cuba is the one exception), the Communist seizure of power occurred during or immediately after devastating wars and foreign invasions that had disrupted agricultural life and destroyed the control of previous governments over much of their territories. In such circumstances, determined revolutionary movements have their best chance of succeeding. But this possibility is not what

Heilbroner has in mind: he sees Communist revolutions as a way of averting political and economic collapse rather than as an eventual consequence of collapse.

The issue of the timetable for modernization is really the crucial one. I agree that none of the existing regimes in the Third World, neither the formal democracies, the collectivist one-party states, nor the military dictatorships, has achieved full modernization. But "when we look at the positive side of our ledger sheet, we perceive an astonishing fact. Against all the obstacles to development that we have described, economic progress has in fact been taking place, and at a pace which by comparison with the past amazes us with its rapidity." So writes Robert Heilbroner on page 89 of his book *The Great Ascent*. He immediately observes that both the gains already achieved and future gains risk "being washed out by population growth."

Now I am indeed not fully convinced that Donald Bogue is right in predicting the imminent end of the population explosion. Who can have complete confidence in any forecast of something that has never happened before, such as the mass adoption of birth control by peasant populations within a decade or two? But the probability of this happening seems to me somewhat greater than the probability of a wave of Communist revolutions in the Third World followed by the rapid achievement of modernization by the revolutionary regimes. The populations of the advanced countries, including Japan, have altered their childbearing habits in very short periods of time and without having been exposed to large-scale, state-directed campaigns urging them to do so. Since I wrote my original article, another leading American demographer, Frank Notestein, president of the Population Council, expressed qualified optimism over the prospect of new birth-control methods' spreading in the underdeveloped world and reducing current rates of population growth before the end of the century. [17] If this does happen, it will not remove entirely the urgency of the need for rapid modernization in the larger, more densely populated areas, for even a rate of growth that is half the present one (and this Notestein considers possible) will still be an economic burden. But slower population growth will certainly make it easier for any regime committed to modernization to make some progress and will allow a wider margin for retrievable error.

I am aware that Heilbroner is making a forecast rather than advocating a course of action. But forecasts can become self-fulfilling if those who possess power are persuaded by and act on them. I too would prefer a Communist Third World and an isolationist United States to a succession of Vietnams; but is Heilbroner really prepared to give up all hope that the United States and the West in general can have any constructive influence on the economic development of the backward areas? Did the author of *The Future as History* mean by that phrase that it is as futile in the end to reflect on what still might be as it is to mourn over what might have been?

FOURTEEN

The Rhythm of Democratic Politics

DEMOCRATIC SOCIETIES with universal suffrage and competing political parties experience a cyclical alternation of periods dominated by protest from the Left and retrenchment by the Right. The notion that politics conform to such cycles is scarcely a new one; it is implicit in the most commonplace language of political journalism, which regularly uses such metaphors as "swing of the pendulum," "rising and ebbing tides," or "waxing and waning" forces to describe events.

The conception of a Left/Right continuum along which parties, movements, regimes, and ideologies can be located has often been justly criticized,[1] yet some such conception seems indispensable and invariably creeps back in hidden guise when the conventional categories are repudiated. I shall use "Left" to refer to programmatic demands for planned or enacted social change toward a more equal distribution of economic benefits, social status, and power; or, in unpropitious times, to the defense of an existing, achieved degree of equality against advocates of increased inequality. The classic Left demand is to realize for all men "liberté, egalité, fraternité." Since the Left as a permanent political tendency came into being at the time of the French Revolution, the "Right" is best defined residually as resistance, on whatever grounds, to any further movement toward equality in the distribution of material satisfactions, status, and/or power, or as the demand for restoration of a (usually idealized) status quo ante in which greater inequality prevailed.

Obviously, these sparse definitions raise all sorts of problems if they are applied to the rich diversity of past and present political movements. Yet they embody the most common, minimal understanding of the Left/Right distinction. In emphasizing the broad *content* of political demands, they avoid the difficulties raised by classifying political groups as Left or Right according to their social base—whether they are supported by or direct their appeals to the victims or the beneficiaries of the existing distribution of rewards and privileges. Thus Peronism in the 1940s and 1950s was not necessarily a leftist movement because its main following was among industrial workers; nor must New Left student movements of the 1960s be considered "really" rightist because their members were disproportionately drawn from upper-middle-class backgrounds.

Nor need the structure of a party or regime determine its classification as Left or Right: parties of the Left may be led and controlled by tiny, self-perpetuating elites, while parties of the Right may be organized in a loose, decentralized, "populistic" manner. Communist dictatorships appeal, at least outside their borders, to supporters of the demands of the Left, although, since my primary concern is with the politics of democracies, the problem of how to classify nondemocratic regimes that claim legitimacy through an identification with the Left can be safely put aside.

Before the Enlightenment, a "Left" in the modern sense of a vision of a more egalitarian society to be created by organized political effort did not exist. Nor was there an identifiable "Right": conservative ideologies and organizations emerged only in response to the challenge of the Left. Citing Hegel's famous "owl of Minerva" metaphor, Karl Mannheim defined conservatism as traditionalism become conscious of itself, and wrote: "Goaded on by opposing theories, conservative mentality discovers its *idea* only *ex post facto*." [2] Since most societies through most of history have been traditionalist, claiming their legitimacy from continuity with the past rather than from a vision of the future, classical conservatives, viewing the world *sub specie aeternitatas*, have dismissed the outlook of the Left as the expression of Enlightenment naïveté over the perfectibility of man, as presumptuous intervention in the workings of "providential forces" (Burke), or as an attempt, necessarily tyrannical in its outcome, to destroy "organically" evolved societies and rebuild them according to an imposed design.

The more subtle conservative thinkers, from Burke to Michael

Oakeshott, have repudiated efforts to construct a conservative ideology, recognizing that the strength of conservatism lies in the emotional attachment of mortal men to the world as they have known it, in an only apparently irrational conviction that "what is, is right," which actually implies the unspoken major premise that it is right *because it is.* All men, including men of the Left, cannot help forming emotional attachments to what has the inestimable advantage and power of actually existing. Even prisoners have learned to love their bars, and most of us feel nostalgic about the places and people of our childhood no matter how unhappy it may have been. This is the existential root of conservatism—of the "eternal Right." Its strength, even within the Left's own constituency of the deprived and oppressed, has been habitually underestimated by the Left; the naturalness of conservative emotions is too often facilely dismissed as indoctrination by the ruling class (these days as "brainwashing by the mass media"), or, more pretentiously, as "false consciousness," a term that carries a heavy burden of responsibility not merely for ideological delusions but also for actual political crimes.

Contemporary technocrats, of course, are committed to the planned application of scientific knowledge. Their anti-ideological animus seems remote indeed from classical conservatism with its religious piety and preference for faith over reason, its aura of knights and ladies and agrarian life—and, for that matter, remote too from the free market of nineteenth-century capitalism. But there is a curious continuity between a technocratic outlook favoring a "pragmatic" politics engaged in by the representatives of established organizations and the implicit pragmatism of such conservatives as Oakeshott, who fear rational abstractions and universal principles and affirm instead their trust in the implicit truths of "experience."

But there is an "eternal Left" too, as deeply rooted in the human condition as the eternal Right, even if it only became a conscious political tendency after the Enlightenment. The vision of the Left derives from the Vichean insight that man makes his own history, or "socially constructs his reality," in today's fashionable sociological parlance. Once this insight enters general awareness, the social world is demystified and classical conservative veneration of a fixed social order sanctified by the past loses meaning. Men feel "alienated" precisely because they know that theirs is a man-made world of arbitrary, makeshift social arrangements which they can readily imagine quite otherwise. We have learned only too well that men may respond to this alienation with frenzied efforts to remystify the world, to press the genie back into the bottle, rather than by embracing the challenge to try to create the now possible free and egalitarian community envisioned by the Left.

Political democracy makes actual the eternal Left in time and history. By giving a voice to the voiceless, mobilizing the apathetic, and organizing the unorganized it introduces planned and directed social change as a principle of historical movement. The voice of the people need not be sanctified as the voice of God, but democracy requires that it at least be heard and taken into account. Democratic politics legitimizes demands for reform and, introduced into societies that remain highly unequal and create new inequalities in the course of their growth, is therefore incurably ideological. The end of ideology would mean the end of the Left as a political force and the end of democracy itself—either by the restoration or creation of an authoritarian or totalitarian regime, or by the achievement of utopia.

The institutionalization of the Left in democratic politics initiates a long-term movement toward realization of the goals of the Left, a movement inherent in the workings of political democracy. However, all firmly established groups, including parties of the Left, become committed defensively to their own continued survival within a system that has permitted them to develop and even flourish. Michels called this the "iron law of oligarchy"; it has recently been described more accurately and renamed the "iron law of decadence" by Theodore Lowi. As organized groups become frozen in defense of their own internal structure, the stasis of Lowi's "interest-group pluralism" threatens; the spirit of the Left seeks to reactivate not only itself but the very power of majoritarian democracy through those nascent groups we call "social movements." [3] But the resistance offered by the Right—as organized minority power, as inarticulate mass sentiment, as metaphysical reflection of the human condition—produces the oscillating pattern I have called the rhythm of democratic politics. How does this rhythm manifest itself, and what is its source?

The periodicity of Left and Right in democratic political life is not necessarily equivalent to an alternation of parties in power, nor of governments actually pursuing more or less egalitarian or conservative policies. Political leaders, in office or out, frequently talk one way and act another, or follow inconsistent policies whatever their rhetoric. The achievements of politics are often symbolic ones—which is not to minimize their significance. The rhythm or cycle is rather one of the *kinds of issues* that dominate political debate, and often intellectual and cultural life as well. Nor is this rhythm the sole, or even always the major, substance of democratic politics. If the division between Left and Right is the most enduring focus of political conflict, it is nevertheless often obscured by ethnic, religious, and racial cleavages within particular polities. In the past, Marxists in particular have been predisposed to deny the autonomy of such "subcultural" cleavages, although their domination of the political life of a large number of countries is by now fully clear. One can nevertheless abstract out of the welter of the democratic political experience a discernible rhythm, or dialectic, of Left/right conflict, which represents at least *one* major theme of their politics. Perhaps there is also a rhythm in the development over time of ethnic or religious struggles, a rhythm intersecting or superimposed upon that of Left/Right conflict. But my concern here is solely with the latter.

The cyclical rhythm is not the effect of a mysterious cosmic law; it rather reflects a pattern of change that is inherent in the workings of a democratic political system in a class-divided society. Political democracy based on universal suffrage was itself originally a demand of the Left introduced into previously authoritarian and hierarchical social orders. In European countries, though not in the United States, it was the central issue around which new working-class and socialist parties organized in the closing decades of the nineteenth century. For the formal, i.e., the legal and constitutional, redistribution of power achieved by universal suffrage to have any consequences in reducing social inequalities, a long period of political mobilization of the lower classes had to take place, a process that is scarcely complete even today in many countries, including the United States. Once, however, parties of the Left have been organized, or the lower classes have been successfully mobilized by older parties, some crisis such as an economic depression, defeat in war, or a split in the ranks of the Right is bound to give the parties of the Left the opportunity to win office, whether on their own or as part of a co-alition. They are then able to carry out reforms that constitute at least their minimum program. But the crisis passes or is resolved; the Right regroups, while conflicts between moderates and radicals on the Left become more acute; and the discontent of the Left's electoral constituency is temporarily appeased by the limited gains, actual or symbolic, that have been won. The Right then returns to office after successfully persuading a sizable segment of the Left's regular follow-ing that a conservative government will not wipe out these gains.

Although American political history has often been regarded as uniquely "consensual" and free of ideological conflict, it fits rather neatly into a pattern of oscillation between periods in which demands from the Left dominate and periods given over to reaction. In any case, whatever truth there may have been in the past to the view that American politics reflected the historical peculiarities of American origins and destiny—the doctrine of American "exceptionalism" as it has sometimes been called—the idea has increasingly lost plausibil-ity. Richard Rovere, one of the more astute observers of American politics, remarked in 1970 that "the Europeanization of American politics proceeds . . . apace."

The periodization of American politics into successive Left and Right eras was presented at length by Arthur Schlesinger, Sr., in a 1939 article, "Tides of American Politics," revised and expanded in his 1949 book *Paths to the Present*,[4] which attracted a good deal of attention at the time. His son, Arthur Schlesinger, Jr., revived and updated his father's thesis in the late 1950s to argue that the 1960s were destined to be a period of reform and innovation favorable to the liberal wing of the Democratic Party, in which he himself was an active figure.

The elder Schlesinger divided American history into 11 periods of alternating Right and Left ascendancy—he used the labels "conserva-tive" and "liberal"—from 1765 to 1947, each one averaging 16.5 years with very slight deviations around the mean, except in the period from the Civil War to the end of the nineteenth century. Schlesinger's inferences or "predictions" for the years ahead have been borne out to a surprising degree.

If we carry Schlesinger's periodization up to the present and modify it very slightly, in this century there are five distinct periods. The Progressive era is usually seen as beginning with Theodore Roosevelt's accession to the presidency in 1901 and ending with American entrance into World War I, or, at least, with Wilson's congressional losses in 1918. The period from 1918 until Franklin D. Roosevelt's election in 1932, or perhaps until the stock-market crash in 1929, was a period of war-inspired patriotism, postwar reaction (the "Red Scare"), return to "normalcy" under Harding and Coolidge, and complacent prosperity. The decline in the momentum of the New Deal is often dated from Democratic losses in the midterm elections of 1938, but World War II prolonged and partially revived the ideological climate of the thirties. (Someone has remarked that 1948 was the last year of the thirties.) The cold war, Korea, Republican victories, and the years of McCarthyism to which these events contributed gave a conservative cast to the fifties. The Left began to recapture some political initiative with the civil rights movement in the South in the late fifties, shortly followed by the rhetoric of the New Frontier and the resounding electoral repudiation of a militant right-wing presidential candidate in 1964. A few years later the "radicalization" of large segments of college youth and intellectuals in response to the Vietnam War created a mood of left-wing insurgency on a variety of fronts. Since 1968, however, reaction or "backlash" against the black, student, and peace movements has been a salient theme of our politics, exploited by George Wallace's candidacy in the 1968 and 1972 election campaigns, and very closely identified with the vice-president and the attorney-general who were the most publicized figures of the first Nixon administration. The mentality that led to Watergate fed off the mood of backlash.

Wars often appear to mark the beginning, the end, or the intensification of particular phases of the cycle. Schlesinger denied that there was "a correlation between foreign wars and the mass drift of sentiments," maintaining that "these conflicts have taken place about equally in conservative and liberal periods, sometimes coming at the start, sometimes at the end and sometimes midway." [5] But surely foreign wars differ in the ideological significance they possess for domestic currents of opinion. Also, their significance has certainly increased since the 1930s. Moreover, as Robert Nisbet has cogently argued, neither nations, continents, nor even units as large as civilizations can be treated as isolated, self-contained "systems" obeying their own internal laws.[6] They are parts of an international or supra-civilizational environment that interpenetrates them. Wars, international crises, and the issues of foreign policy to which these give rise can therefore neither be ignored as shaping agents of the domestic political process nor invoked as dei ex machina to account for internal political shifts. Theories of American exceptionalism and some Marxist analyses have minimized this fact.

In general, the ideological coloration of the perceived national enemy has complicated the impact of wars on the Left/Right dialectic. World War I divided the American Left; the Russian Revolution not only further divided it but gave impetus to the period of postwar reaction and repression that ended the Progressive era. World War II, on the other hand, was fought against nations seen as the incarnation of the values most bitterly opposed by the Left, and therefore did not displace New Deal liberalism and its radical allies. The cold war and Korea, fought against an enemy laying total claim to the ideological heritage of the Left, delegitimated the American Left almost completely obliterated its radical wing. In the sixties, however, the failure and unpopularity of the Vietnam War revived American radicalism and discredited the cold war. But the fact that responsibility for the Vietnam disaster rested on a liberal Democratic administration created a split in the Left that permitted Nixon's victory in 1968.

The Left, of course, is itself invariably divided into reformist and radical wings, and the shifting balance of unity and conflict achieved by its factions constitutes another dialectic within the larger dialectic of Left and Right. Obviously, the Right is also usually divided between militants and moderates, reactionaries and conservatives, although such divisions have not, I think, played as important a role in the United States as in some European countries.

Metaphors of pendular or tidal movements are misleading when applied to the cyclical rhythm of politics. For the pattern has not been one of a mere repetitive oscillation between fixed points. In Schlesinger's words, "a more appropriate figure than the pendulum is the spiral, in which the alternation proceeds at successively higher levels." [7] The classic Marxist conception of the movement of history has also been described as a spiral, combining a cyclical with a developmental or unilinear motion. But to disclose such a pattern in historical events is not to explain *why* it prevails, or *how* transitions from one stage to the next come about. No one who has read Robert Nisbet's brilliant book *Social Change and History* can retain any illusions on this score. [8] One must always ask, What makes the wheels go around? in the case of a cyclical motion; or What propels mankind upward and onward?—or at least forward in a given direction—if a unilinear trend is exhibited. Neither recurrent cycles, unilinear evolution, nor a spiral course combining them amount to self-sufficient, self-explaining "laws" of change. Schlesinger recognized this in his cyclical account of American politics, but his own explanations of the cycle were brief and vague, scarcely going beyond the assertion of inevitable "changes in mass psychology" resulting from boredom or disappointment with the prevailing phase of the cycle. In trying to account for the cyclical rhythm, Schlesinger also referred to alleged peculiarities of the American people, such as their preference for "empiricism" rather than "preconceived theory," and their belief in the virtues of competition—although he also acknowledged the existence of a similar rhythm in the Western European democracies.

In his autobiography, published in 1963, just two years before his death, Schlesinger reported that Franklin D. Roosevelt's adviser, David Niles, once told him that FDR was influenced in his decision to run for reelection in 1944 by Schlesinger's calculation that liberalism would remain dominant until 1948 (based on his figure of a 16.5 years' average duration of each phase of the cycle). [9] Schlesinger also mentioned a preelection column by James Reston in 1960 maintaining that John F. Kennedy "based his campaign on the assumption," derived from Schlesinger's "theory," that a turn to the Left was in the offing within a year or two. [10]

If these stories are true, Roosevelt and Kennedy seem to have understood the cyclical pattern in what Nisbet would regard as far too mechanical a fashion. Such efforts to predict the exact duration of periods of the cyclical rhythm, while they possess a dangerous fascination, do not increase our understanding of it. For a description of the rhythm, however accurate, *explains* nothing whatsoever; in the language of logicians, the rhythm is an "explanandum" rather than an "explanans"—an effect of underlying causes rather than a causal agency itself. Moreover, it is highly likely that in recent decades the rhythm has accelerated as a result of the increasing saturation of modern populations by the mass media. Nowadays a "new" generation seems to come along every five years or so.

An explanation of the rhythm of democratic politics must necessarily be historically specific, because party politics under conditions of mass suffrage are less than a century old even in most of the stable, "advanced" constitutional democracies of the West. Yet it may be possible to formulate explanatory generalizations that transcend the historical uniqueness of particular nations. Furthermore, it is at least worth observing in passing that there is some evidence of a similar periodicity in nondemocratic states. Despotic rulers of absolutist monarchies have often been followed by rulers more responsive to pressures from below. Totalitarian dictatorships undertake "great leaps forward" that are succeeded by periods of relaxed discipline in which "a hundred flowers" are encouraged to bloom. An analyst of Stalin's rule has written of the "artificial dialectic" imposed by the dictator on Soviet society, where rigorous demands for total ideological conformity and the use of terror to deter even the mildest dissent abruptly alternated with periods of greater permissiveness or "thaw." [11]

But an explanation of the rhythm of democratic politics must necessarily be specific to constitutional mass democracies. I shall try to summarize schematically the elements of such an explanation.

The political mobilization of the previously disenfranchised lower classes is a long and slow process, still incomplete in many of the major Western democracies, as indicated by higher, middle, and upper-class as against working-class rates of voting, higher working- and lower-class support for parties of the Right than of upper- and middle-class support for parties of the Left, and the occasional survival of formal and informal barriers to voting imposed on some low-status groups, such as blacks in the American South. Thus even after the winning of full citizenship rights, including the right to vote, by groups previously subject to legal discrimination, "conservative government," in Woodrow Wilson's words, "is in the saddle most of the time."

But Left parties and movements succeed in mobilizing a large enough proportion of their potential constituency to become leading opposition parties. Sometimes they displace older parties, as in the rise of Labour at the expense of the Liberals in Britain. Sometimes they emerge as the first and largest organized mass parties confronting electoral or governmental coalitions of smaller parties of the Right, as on the European continent. Sometimes they partially transform an older, heterogeneous, and factionalized party into a vehicle for the demands of newly mobilized lower-class groups, as in the United States. Sooner or later the Left party wins office, often, as I said earlier, as a result of a severe economic crisis or the impact of a war (especially a lost one) that discredits an existing government.

It has often been the fate of the Left parties to come to power at a time of such acute crisis for the entire society that they are forced to concentrate on improvised short-run policies to restore or maintain internal peace, with the result that their long-range goals of social reconstruction have to be shelved or severely modified, inspiring accusations of "class betrayal" from their more militant followers. The Social Democracy in the first and last years of the Weimar Republic is the classic case. Nevertheless, by coming to office the Left party wins a kind of legitimacy in the eyes of the electorate that it previously lacked, and it is usually able to carry out at least a part of its minimum program. But failure to resolve the crisis that brought the party to office, or the passing of the crisis whether or not the government's measures are given credit for this; splits between the party's or government's radical and moderate reformist wings once the minimum program has been passed; the retrenchment of the Right during a period in opposition; and a constant factor, what George Bernard Shaw called "the damned wantlessness of the poor"—all result in electoral defeat or the "co-optation" of prominent leaders before the Left party has done more than institute "incremental," or "token," reforms.

The return of the Right, however, is conditional on its persuading the electorate that it will not "turn the clock back" on the reforms achieved by the Left. Old issues bitterly contested in the past by the parties suddenly become obsolescent and periods of "Butskellism," or even Grand Coalitions between the rivals, become the order of the day, isolating and infuriating the more militant partisans on each side, who may break away and create splinter or "ginger" groups within legislatures or "extraparliamentary opposition" movements outside. The Right party, in an effort to enhance or consolidate its appeal to the constituency of the Left, may adopt hybrid, apparently contradictory names or slogans designed to suggest that it has outgrown past hostility to Left policies now in effect, such as "Tory Socialism," "Progressive Conservatism," "Christian Democracy," or "Moderate Republicanism"—this last a label favored by President Eisenhower shortly after his first election.

This recurrent sequence of events is the rhythm, or the "dialectic," of politically directed change in a democracy. It falls far short of realizing either the far-reaching hopes of the advocates or the apocalyptic fears of the opponents of universal suffrage in the nineteenth century. Why do parties of the Left become so pallidly reformist and achieve so little in the way of fundamental "structural change" in the direction of their egalitarian ideals? Machiavelli gave the most general answer long before the establishment of democratic institutions:

It must be considered that there is nothing more difficult to carry out, nor more doubtful of success nor more dangerous to handle, than to initiate a new order of things. For the reformer has enemies in all those who profit by the old order, and only lukewarm defenders in all those who would profit by the new order, this lukewarmness arising partly from fear of their adversaries, who have the laws in their favor; and partly from the incredulity of mankind, who do not truly believe in anything new until they have actual experience of it. Thus it arises that on every opportunity for attacking the reformer, his opponents do so with the zeal of partisans, the others only defend him half-heartedly so that between them he runs great danger.[12]

The contemporary social scientist would doubtless put it in different and far less elegant language, but his conclusion would be much the same as Machiavelli's.

Yet the potential electoral constituency of the Left in modern democracies is larger than that of the Right—"God must love the poor people for he made so many of them," Lincoln once remarked. Popular elections based on universal suffrage give decisive weight to the one political resource with which the lower classes are amply endowed—numbers. How does the Right counter this demographic superiority of their opponents? In the first place, the Right possesses a massive advantage with respect to other political resources—wealth, education, social status, traditional legitimacy—and is able to throw these into the balance in election campaigns as well as employing them on an enormous scale to influence government policy between elections. In confronting the electorate, however, the most regular and reliable strategy of the Right is to appeal to nationalist sentiment. Modern nationalism is itself, of course, a product of democratic ideology, born in the wake of the French and American revolutions. But this very fact has served to enhance its appeal in opposition to the class and antielitist populist appeals of the Left, which has so repeatedly and tragically underestimated the strength of national loyalties in this century.

The Right lays claim to the symbols of legitimacy identified with the past of the nation, indeed with its very existence in a world of competing nation-states, an existence usually achieved by wars of conquest or revolts against foreign domination that usually, though not in the United States, antedated the creation of democratic institutions and the extension of the franchise. Thus parties of the Right tend to wave the flag, to nominate generals who stand "above politics" as candidates for office, and to invoke the need for national unity, in contrast to the divisive appeals of the Left. National leaders of the Right have sometimes engaged in foreign adventurism and even embarked upon limited expansionist wars in order to overcome internal tensions generated by the domestic class struggle. War has often in this sense been "the health of the state," in Randolph Bourne's famous dictum. Parties of the Left, on the other hand, have traditionally been isolationist in the United States, internationalist and anti-imperialist on the European continent, and Little Englanders in Britain.

If events insure that sooner or later reformist parties of the Left will come to office, and if the return to office of conservative parties is partly conditional on their leaving untouched the popular reforms carried out by Left administrations, then there is *an unmistakable "leftward drift" inherent in the functioning over time of democratic politics.* The existence of such a drift alarms and enrages militants of the Right; its slowness and the many counterpressures to which it is subject disillusions and radicalizes utopians of the Left, who then dismiss parliament as a "talking-shop," the major parties as "Tweedledum and Tweedledee," and "the system" itself as a fraud in professing to offer opportunities for change. Militants of both Right and Left are disposed to conclude, with Machiavelli:

Thus it comes about that all armed prophets have conquered and unarmed ones failed; for . . . the character of peoples varies, and it is easy to persuade them of a thing, but difficult to keep them in that persuasion. And so it is necessary to order things so that when they no longer believe, they can be made to believe by force. [13]

Segments of both Right and Left, in short, are attracted by violent revolutionary or counterrevolutionary shortcuts: in the case of the Right, to arrest and even reverse the leftward drift; in the case of the Left, to accelerate and complete it. The Right calls for a government of "national unity" that will not hesitate to suspend constitutional liberties and suppress the opposition parties, while the Left succumbs to a mood of revolutionary impatience, or "utopian greed." In periods of acute national crisis and distress, a "dialectic of the extremes," to use a phrase of Raymond Aron's,[14] in which each side violently confronts the other, often enough in the streets, may take center stage and threaten the survival of democratic institutions. The last years of the Weimar Republic are, of course, the classic example of such a confrontation.

But even in less critical situations, this dialectic is visible at the periphery rather than at the center of the political arena and often seems to be gaining through the enlistment of growing numbers of partisans on each side. The tactic of Left militants is to attack the entire political system as part of a repressive "Establishment" moving toward "fascism," and the most plausible evidence for this is to be found in the efforts of militants on the Right to brand their customary political opponents as Communist sympathizers, or dangerous radicals encouraging disrespect for law, insurrectionary violence, treason, or all three. The Left calls for a "popular front" against "repression" and incipient "fascism." The Right reaffirms traditional values and calls for a closing of ranks against the fomenters of public disorder. At the level of rhetoric and public demonstrations, this kind of ultimatist ideological politics was fairly visible in the United States during the late 1960s. That it may become at least a permanent sideshow of American politics is one implication of the notion of the Europeanization of American politics to which I previously referred. The dialectic of the extremes reflects an effort, conscious or unconscious, to short-circuit the "normal" pattern of alternating periods of protest and stabilization with its built-in tendency toward a glacially slow "leftward drift."

Democratic conservatives, or "moderates," frequently reject "ideological politics" in favor of a "pragmatic politics" based on bargaining, compromise, and consensus on the rules of political competition. Their suspicion of those on both the Left and the Right who out of impatience with the stately rhythm of democratic politics wish to fracture it by making a forward "leap to socialism" or a restoration of an idealized status quo ante is surely well-founded. But the "ideological" demands of idealists, visionaries, "extremists," prophets, and seers are also part of the democratic political process—sources of "input," as some political scientists would gracelessly say. Without them, the professional politicians would have little to bargain about and strike compromises over. The major political philosopher of democracy, John Stuart Mill, recognized this when he wrote of his brief period of service in the House of Commons:

If . . . there were any intermediate course which had a claim to a trial, I well knew that to propose something which would be called extreme was the true way not to impede but to facilitate a more moderate experiment. . . . It is the character of the British people, or at least of the higher and middle classes who pass muster for the British people, that to induce them to approve any change, it is necessary that they should look upon it as a middle course; they think every proposal extreme and violent unless they hear of some other proposal going still further, upon which their antipathy to extreme views may discharge itself.[15]

Mill's tone reflects the relatively serene and civil politics of Britain in the Victorian age when the franchise was still restricted. Out of the experience of the disorder and violence of European mass politics in this century, Albert Camus observed: "Heads must roll, and blood must flow like rivers in the streets, merely to bring about a minor amendment to the Constitution." This is easily read as a despairing or cynical rejection of political effort. But recall that Camus's heroic exemplar of the human condition was Sisyphus. The task of the Left is always Sisyphean. Movement toward its goals is at best asymptotic. Disappointment is inevitable over the "wantlessness" and fickleness—often sourly labeled "false consciousness"—of the suffering and oppressed the Left seeks to serve. Committed neither in principle nor pragmatically to the world as it is, defined rather by its "project" in the Sartrean sense, the Left is inherently prone to bitter internal struggles over which ends, means, and agencies advance or hinder that project.

The left is often proclaimed to be obsolete as a result of the establishment of political democracy itself, since the voice of the people at any given time so rarely fully affirms the aspirations of the Left. The actual role of the Left is usually the undramatic one, as Barrington Moore, Jr., has recently defined it, of keeping "radical fire" under liberal reforms.[16] The Left might well attribute to political democracy as an ironic motto Galileo's famous aside when forced to recant his belief in the Copernican theory: *eppur si muove*—"and yet it still moves." But unlike the earth, kept moving by the purely mechanical force of the sun's gravity, the system of democratic politics is kept in motion by the effort and will of men and women on the Left.

FIFTEEN
Max Weber: The Scholar as Hero

IN RECENT YEARS the name of Max Weber has steadily inched closer to those of Marx and Freud as he has come to be considered an interpreter of man and society of almost canonical stature. One cannot quite yet say of him what Auden said of Freud: "To us he is no more a person/ Now but a whole climate of opinion/ Under whom we conduct our differing lives." But he is getting there. At least a superficial acquaintance with the leading ideas of this German sociologist and historian has become de rigeur for the knowledgeable intellectual, as more frequent references to him in journals of opinion attest. Contemporary protest against rigid bureaucracies in the advanced industrial countries, recently embodied in the New Left, owes a good deal to Weber's fatalistic and despairing analysis of bureaucratization as an irreversible social trend. Weber rather than Marx often seems to be the prophet who drew the clearest picture of the contemporary enemy, even though Weber was no revolutionary, described himself as a "class-conscious bourgeois," and from one perspective appears as much an apologist for bureaucracy as its critic.

Unlike Marx and Freud, Weber founded no movement with practical aims, political or therapeutic. Born in Berlin in 1864, the son of a National Liberal member of the Reichstag, after a brief legal career he became a professor at the comparatively early age of thirty, first at Freiburg and then at Heidelberg, where he lived for most of the rest of his life. However, he resigned his chair at Heidelberg in 1889, as the result of a mental illness from which he never fully recovered, and thereafter became primarily a private scholar. Later he would edit the most famous social-science journal in Germany, correspond with leading scholars and artists in a dozen or more fields, and preside over a cultural and intellectual circle that included such luminous figures as Ernst Troeltsch, Georg Lukács, Karl Jaspers, and Georg Simmel. Yet, during these years of his greatest creativity, he never resumed a regular academic post. His tortured, restless compulsion to synthesize a mass of historical knowledge could not be confined within the boundaries of a regular teaching routine.

Perhaps this failure accounts for the fact that he did not leave behind him an established academic school. Nor does one exist today. The Nazi era ended, of course, all serious scholarship in the social and historical disciplines in Germany itself. Yet the dispersion of German scholars and intellectuals after Hitler's coming to power has led to an extraordinary "Germanization" of Western cultural and intellectual life, nowhere more pronounced than in the United States, where the greatest number of them settled. As a result, since World War II Weber's influence has been greater in this country than in his native Germany. However, in contrast not only to Marxism and psychoanalysis, but also to phenomenology, existentialism, and neo-Hegelianism, there has not emerged a coherent school of thought, with acknowledged adepts and disciples, tracing its origins to Weber's teachings—not even within contemporary sociology, the discipline on which Weber has had the greatest impact, though he did not define himself as a sociologist until fairly late in his career.

The absence of a distinctive Weberian school is in part to be explained by the fact that Weber was not a system-building philosopher in the Germanic tradition, setting forth a total world view replete with an ontology and a metaphysics, the implications of which for more limited areas of inquiry could then be elaborated by followers and disciples. The presently fashionable work in sociology and psychology inspired by phenomenology represents just such a belated extension of the concepts and language of Edmund Husserl and his earliest disciples to concrete fields of social science investigation. Weber never aspired to be a Grand Master in the tradition of Kant, Hegel, Schelling, Husserl, or Heidegger. His influence has been more like that of Nietzsche, who also left no academic school but has remained a pervasive, brooding presence in the work of a multitude of philosophers and social commentators, including Weber himself.

Nietzsche, however, was a subjective and aphoristic thinker, a master of the piercing insight, a poet, even a confessional writer of sorts. Weber, on the other hand, was preeminently a scholar and an uncommonly rigorous one. His work expresses what two of his most perceptive critics, Hans Gerth and C. Wright Mills, have called the "pathos of objectivity" [1] in its combination of intellectual discipline with intense but restrained passion. Weber's starting point was always a concrete historical problem—the origins of Western capitalism, the growth of the medieval city, the agrarian problems of classical Rome—rather than a general doctrine. His work thus resists translation into a set of facile generalizations, let alone reduction to an ideology. Moreover, the scope of his learning was so immense, ranging across jurisprudence, economics, sociology, philosophy, aesthetics, comparative religion, and the histories of several nations and half a dozen civilizations both ancient and modern, that he is properly regarded as the Aristotle of the social sciences, the last thinker able to attain at least some acquaintance with the total body of knowledge available in his time. Since the same specialization of knowledge that centuries ago eliminated the possibility of another Aristotle has taken place in the social sciences since Weber's death, he sets an impossible example for contemporary scholars. His influence has therefore been a diffuse rather than a focused one, spreading unevenly across many diverse areas of study rather than stemming from the proselytizing energies of an identifiable school.

Many would regard as Weber's most enduring contribution his analysis of the methodological foundations of the social sciences. A recent interpreter remarks that "Weber is so nearly right about the logic of explanation in history and sociology that much subsequent discussion of it, whether by social scientists or philosophers, marks a regression rather than an advance." [2] Weber, as this quotation indicates, did not sharply separate problems of historical from sociological explanation in the manner of thinkers who try to assimilate the social to the natural sciences by treating historical situations as mere data from which to derive general "laws." Recent writers have more fully acknowledged and accepted Weber's "historicism," as well as his insistence on the need to understand human conduct in relation to

the subjective meanings and intentions of the human actors themselves.

In recent years, however, younger scholars have challenged one of
Weber's best-known methodological convictions: his advocacy of a
"value-free" social science requiring the sharp separation of the
scholar's moral and political values from his scholarly and scientific
work. Their argument is that, first, claims of objectivity are fraudu-
lent because works of social science are inevitably impregnated with
the values and ideological commitments of their authors; and second,
that the norm of value neutrality itself serves the narrow professional
interests of social scientists as a group in permitting them to disavow
the social and political implications and consequences of their research. Yet at the time Weber advanced his plea for a value-free
social science, it scarcely served, as it often has since, to protect an
entrenched professional group from involvement with controversial
topics, let alone to justify the researcher's disassociating himself from
the uses to which his findings might be put. For, as Alvin Gouldner
and Ralf Dahrendorf, among contemporary sociologists, have recently reminded us, Weber's value-free social science was intended as
an alternative to the reigning assumption in Wilhelminian Germany
that social science must serve the interests of the state, and that it
should even affirm the right-wing nationalist sentiments of most occupants of academic chairs. Weber's position, therefore, can hardly
be equated with that of the type of contemporary social scientist for
whom "thou shalt not commit a value judgement" has become the
first commandment of his calling.

Nor did Weber regard value freedom as a strictly methodological
norm dictated by the logical disjunction between factual statements
and evaluations, "existential" and "normative" propositions, or the
"is" and the "ought," as the distinction has been variously phrased.
True, he was influenced by the neo-Kantian philosophy of his day,
which accepted as basic Kant's differentiation between theoretical and
practical reason. But to Weber value freedom was no mere scholastic
tenet: it was itself a moral demand requiring of us the painful and
hard-won recognition that the world does not conform to the image
of our desires, that "for every party opinion there are facts that are ex-

tremely inconvenient, for my own no less than for others." To school oneself to look into the abyss without flinching or seeking consolation and yet to hold fast to one's own deepest values despite the world's inhospitality to them was, to Weber, itself a "moral achievement." The Kantians separated facts and values in order to preserve a realm of autonomy for the latter in face of the claims and achievements of natural science. Later social scientists insisted on the separation because they were anxious to overcome suspicions that social science was no more than a form of concealed ideological advocacy, so as to win the prestige for their disciplines already attained by the natural sciences. Weber's demand for objectivity strikes a different note from both of these attitudes: the striving for objectivity imposes a self-discipline that is both moral and intellectual. Objectivity is the only way of doing justice to the "irreconcilable conflict" between the values of "the various life-spheres in which we are placed, each of which is governed by different laws." Such a view, reflecting a concrete vision of the world as a world of "warring gods," is closer to modern existential philosophy than to a methodological formalism borrowed from what are taken to be the procedures of the natural sciences.

Science—or scholarship, as the term *Wissenschaft* is more accurately translated in Weber's usage—cannot, Weber argued, tell us which of the warring gods we should serve; it cannot answer Tolstoy's question "What shall we do, and how shall we arrange our lives?" But this limitation does not mean that the search for objective knowledge is indifferent to and detached from ethical and political issues. Only the discipline of objectivity can help us to achieve "the trained relentlessness in viewing the realities of life, and the ability to face such realities and to measure up to them inwardly" that is a prerequisite for effective service to a cause. Even in the case of those ultimate value choices on which science must remain mute, it can at least promote clarity in understanding the nature of a choice. Weber observed: "I am tempted to say of a teacher who succeeds in this: he stands in the service of 'moral' forces; he fulfils the duty of bringing about self-clarification and a sense of responsibility. And I believe he will be the more able to accomplish this, the more conscientiously he avoids the desire personally to impose upon or suggest to his audience his own stand." [3] The term "value freedom," which is a literal translation of Weber's *Wertfreiheit*, carries the unfortunate connotation of an inquiry that is uncontaminated by any contact with values. Clearly, Weber had nothing of the sort in mind.

Yet Weber drew an untenably rigid distinction between the "value relevance" that leads to the choice of a particular problem for study and the value-free methods that are required to investigate it. Nor did he keep them apart in his own work. His individualistic values pervade even his discussion of the methodological problems of the social sciences. A scholar's moral sentiments and religious or political beliefs cannot help but shape his style of thinking, his vision of the world, at a deeper level that that of the concepts and categories he explicitly deploys in his research. One may still, nevertheless, distinguish between this inescapable interpenetration of values and knowledge present in all worthwhile intellectual work and the open proclamation and advocacy of an ideological position. To be influenced by one's values in the basic perspective one adopts toward a problem, even to assert them openly, is still not to *preach* them with the primary intent of converting others. "The professor," Weber argued, "should not demand the right as a professor to carry the marshal's baton of the statesman or reformer in his knapsack." [4] For the politician, on the other hand, it is precisely his "damned duty" to take a forthright stand on the issues of the day.

Weber's conception of what he called "rationalization" as the master trend of modern history is both the unifying theme of much of his work and the source of its extraordinary resonance today. Weber meant by rationalization the process by which explicit, abstract, intellectually calculable rules and procedures are increasingly substituted for sentiment, tradition, and rule of thumb in all spheres of human activity. Science and technology are the most obvious forms of rationalization. In human relations, rationalization is exemplified by the spread of bureaucratic forms of organization which mobilize and utilize men ("personnel") as well as material resources in order to achieve with maximum efficiency limited functional goals: the mass production of a standardized product, the waging of mechanized war, the collection of taxes or of information ("data") from tens of millions of people. Rationalization instrumentalizes and demystifies large areas of life. It creates a utilitarian world dominated by what the late

Paul Tillich called "the dance of ends and means." In Weber's words,

It means that . . . there are no mysterious incalculable forces that come into play, but rather that one can, in principle, master all things by calculation. This means that the world is disenchanted. One need no longer have recourse to magical means in order to master or improve the spirits, as did the savage, for whom such mysterious powers existed. Technical means and calculations perform the service.[5]

But the dethronement of the gods and the dispelling of magic and myth do not, in Weber's view, result in increased understanding and mastery by the individual of the conditions under which he lives. Weber is far removed from the optimistic faith of the eighteenth-century philosophers that the progress of reason and the discrediting of religious and magical beliefs will promote greater enlightenment, happiness, and freedom. Machines, systematic techniques of all kinds, formalized laws and operational codes, and planned social organizations all embody the rationality that went into their design. But in "programming" the actions of men, they become self-maintaining, no longer dependent on the rationality and will to mastery of their creators but actually stunting and constricting the intelligence and self-determination of the men they dominate.

A lifeless machine is the materialization of mind. This fact alone gives it the power to force men into its service and to determine so coercively their everyday life in the factory. . . . That living machine which bureaucratic organization represents is also a materialization of mind, with its trained, specialized labor, its delimitation of areas of competence, its regulations, and its hierarchically stratified relations of obedience. In union with the dead machine, it is laboring to produce the cage of that bondage of the future to which one day powerless men will be forced to submit like the fellaheen of ancient Egypt.[6]

"The cage of that bondage of the future"—today the currently popular jeremiads against technology, bureaucracy, science, and even rationality itself seem to assume that the future Weber foresaw has now arrived. And with it has come what Weber called "the disenchantment of the world," a phrase borrowed from the poet Schiller which has obvious affinities with "alienation," that concept so recently debased by widespread circulation. Rationalization drains the world of all nonutilitarian and nonmaterial significance in a manner analogous to the reduction of physical energy to dead level postulated by the second law of thermodynamics. In identifying "progress" with the increasing methodical conquest of the world, stretching forward into a receding future, rationalization denudes the life cycle of the individual of intrinsic meaning and robs death of dignity and fulfillment. Men lose their sense of vital relatedness to nature, the past, and their fellows, a feeling formerly rooted in stable convictions with religious underpinnings enabling them to experience ultimate values as forces inhering in and emanating from the world rather than as human projections upon it. In his most devastatingly pessimistic indictment of the "iron cage" modern man was engaged in constructing for himself, Weber wrote in 1905: "For of the last stage of this cultural development, it might well be truly said: 'specialists without spirit, sensualists without heart; this nullity imagines that it has attained a level of civilization never before achieved.' " [7]

This gloomy prophecy is today widely taken as a factual description of the condition of advanced industrial societies, especially the United States. Rhetorical denunciations of the technocratic and bureaucratic "system" allegedly enslaving us all became in the late 1960s the stock in trade of New Left radicals, spokesmen for the "youth culture," and their middle-aged professorial gurus. No wonder Weber's star continues to rise! Yet as recently as 1964 a young scholar of European background, Ferdinand Kolegar, could still write that "the idea of rationalization, so central to Weber's sociology, has been curiously neglected by nearly all American students of Max Weber." [8]

Complaints against what Matthew Arnold called "this strange disease of modern life" date back, of course, to the early Romantic movement, and from the beginning attributed the spiritual malaise and emptiness experienced by sensitive men and women in modern society to the "life-destroying" rationalism of science, the corruptions of material progress, and the tyranny of the machine. By the end of the nineteenth century such complaints had become a swelling chorus and nowhere more so than in Germany, where neoromanticism and cultural pessimism were the dominant outlook of

bourgeois intellectuals in a nation in which the spirit of the Enlightenment had never prevailed. This outlook, while by no means leading necessarily to political engagement, frequently gave rise to a reactionary "politics of cultural despair," as Fritz Stern has characterized
it,[9] of which National Socialism became the crudest, most demonic
incarnation, as alien in spirit to the essentially aristocratic yearnings
of neoromanticism as it was to the Enlightenment rationalism repudiated by both. In America, which lacks a romantic reactionary or
even a nonbourgeois conservative ideological tradition, neoromantic
protests against the contemporary techno-bureaucratic order have recently come largely from the political Left and the youthful protest
movement.

But Max Weber was not simply another of the many gifted writers
and thinkers in fin-de-siècle Europe who were attracted to irratio-
nalist philosophies and dark yet wishful prophecies of the decline of
the West. He retained a stoical commitment to the Enlightenment
ideals of reason and freedom. His major achievement was the specifically sociological one of relating the spiritual costs of scientific and
economic progress to the enlargement in scale of modern social organization and the resultant depersonalization of its functioning—the
consequence of unprecedented population growth and expanded territorial administrations. Weber did not, like Oswald Spengler and
others, consider the cultural decline he feared the inevitable outcome
of a cyclical pattern of growth and decay to which all civilizations
were subject, nor, like the idealist philosophers, did he see it as the
result of the final exhaustion of a unique, self-moving *Geist*, or
ethos. While rationalization indeed reflected a distinctive ethos peculiar to the West, its dynamism inhered in institutional trends and
changes in social structure rather than in an autonomous spiritual
rhythm. Weber's relation to Marxism becomes, accordingly, a major
consideration in understanding his work.

Those aspects of Weber's thought which possess the greatest contemporary significance also tend to highlight its similarities to rather
than its differences from Marxism. With technology and bureaucracy
increasingly supplanting capitalism as the primary targets of radical
protest, Weber's theory of rationalization provides a more generalized
account of the evolution of industrial society than Marx's older

model based on mid-nineteenth-century capitalism. Weber's account has the advantage of treating capitalism as only one, if the first and for a long time the most powerful, of the rationalizing agencies in the modern world. The process he described can therefore be extended to include not only late welfare-state, or "postindustrial," capitalism, but also the Communist societies of Russia and Eastern Europe. Rationalization plays a similar role in Weber's thought to the process of capital accumulation in Marx's, and, as I have previously noted, there is a kinship between the disenchantment of the world and the Hegelian-Marxist idea of alienation seen, respectively, as the effects of each process. Like Marx, Weber also treats social conflict as the moving force of historical change, although, while not neglecting economic class struggles, he laid greater stress than Marx on conflicts between nation-states, between religious and ethnic communities, and, in general, between groups differing in values and moral outlook rather than primarily in economic interests. (The current cliché term "life-style" is of Weberian origin—perhaps it is the ultimate tribute to a thinker that his concepts pass into daily speech without anyone recalling their origin.)

Yet Weber first became known to the English-speaking world as a formidable critic of Marxism. One of his earliest writings to be translated was his famous essay *The Protestant Ethic and the Spirit of Capitalism*, which was in part an effort to show both that it was not possible "to deduce the Reformation, as a historically necessary result, from certain economic changes," and that the religious doctrines of Calvinist theology had actually played a crucial role in creating at least the "capitalist spirit," if not capitalism itself. A library of books has been published by scholars of many nationalities and political and religious persuasions, including a future premier of Italy, with the aim of refuting, confirming, qualifying, or enlarging upon Weber's thesis. Certainly, the thesis has not emerged unscathed from this examination, although today there would be close to general agreement that Weber at least succeeded in showing that there was a subtle and by no means self-evident "elective affinity" between Calvinist ethics and early capitalist motivations, however questionable some of his detailed historical evidence and interpretations now appear.

Before World War II, Max Weber was chiefly known, outside of a small circle of German or German-reading scholars, as an economic historian who had thrown down the gauntlet to Marxism on the crucial issue of the origins of modern capitalism. In the United States, Weber's work was introduced by Talcott Parsons, who edited and translated *The Protestant Ethic* and founded a school of sociological thought that stressed the primacy of common values and moral consensus in society, as opposed to the Marxist emphasis on material interests and class conflict. Weber was thus perceived primarily as an opponent of Marxism, and Albert Salomon's remark that his sociology is "a long and intense dialogue with the Ghost of Karl Marx" was frequently cited. This view, however, is a selective and distorted one, both because Weber was deeply influenced by intellectual traditions other than Marxism and because it minimizes his debts to Marx. If *The Protestant Ethic* was partly intended as a polemical thrust against historical materialism, Weber's later studies in the sociology of religion, which were not fully translated into English until the 1960s, share with Marxist thought a marked tendency to conceive of ideas and values as predominantly shaped by the class position of those groups upholding them. As Carlo Antoni, an Italian student of German historical thought, has observed of Weber's comparative studies of the great religions: "Even the most profound difference between East and West is, below all differences of faith, primarily a question of classes. . . . In spite of Weber's protestations, the various ethical systems appear only as projections of class interest—they are indelibly stamped with designations such as 'bureaucratic,' 'warlike,' 'bourgeois,' and 'petty bourgois.' " [10]

Actually, Weber's earlier criticisms of Marxism did not adequately distinguish between the thought of Karl Marx himself and the official orthodoxy of the theorists of pre–World War I German Social Democracy—including Friedrich Engels—which constituted "Marxism" at the time Weber undertook his studies. Weber rejected the passive economic determinism and historical inevitabilism of this German orthodox tradition, which have caused so many difficulties for later Marxists trying to square the doctrine with the victory of small Marxist-inspired revolutionary movements in backward countries such as Russia and China rather than in the mature capitalist nations. Denying that history conformed to laws of motion that could be discerned in advance, Weber wrote of industrial society: "No one knows who will live in this cage in the future, or whether at the end of this tremendous development entirely new prophets will arise, or there will be a great rebirth of old ideas and ideals, or, if neither, mechanized petrifaction, embellished with a sort of convulsive self-importance." [11]

Yet Weber clearly thought "mechanized petrifaction" the most likely outcome. If Marxist determinism is grounded in economic relations—the unfolding of the internal contradictions of capitalism—Weber's determinism was essentially political, based on the indispensability of bureaucratic organization that concentrates power in the hands of the few who control the apparatus. To Weber the facts of power rather than economic interest are fateful, and it is his insistence on "the primacy of politics," his refusal to reduce the political to a mere reflection of the underlying group structure of society, or of the reigning spirit of a culture (*Volksgeist*), that makes him today seem more of a contemporary than any other classical social theorist in a world of increasingly close connections between private and public power, of combined social and national revolutions, of totalitarian regimes restructuring ancient social orders, and of welfare and warfare bureaucracies penetrating the daily affairs of more and more citizens. Weber's bleak anticipation of universal bureaucratization encompassed socialism as well as capitalism. Socialism in modern mass societies, far from ushering in a stateless and classless utopia, could only accelerate bureaucratization by merging political and economic power and replacing competition among private capitalists with the domination of public officials and planning boards.

Here we arrive at the fundamental difference between Weber and Marx. Marx has truly been called the last great thinker of the Enlightenment; for Weber, "the rosy blush of the Enlightenment seems to be irretrievably fading." [12] Weber wrote at the beginning of this century, when Marxist hopes were still radiant, and before his death he witnessed their renewal with the Russian Revolution. But he saw no agency of deliverance or transcendence within the historical process itself, no potentiality for a revolutionary reversal of direction that would set man free by at last abolishing the gap between the Kingdom of Necessity and the Kingdom of Freedom. "The materialist interpretation of history is no cab to be taken at will," he remarked, "it does not stop short of the makers of revolutions." [13] Older Marxists, as Raymond Aron has observed, "cannot forgive Max Weber for having denounced in advance as a utopia something that up to now has indeed turned out to be utopian: the idea of a liberation of man by the modification of the system of ownership and a planned economy." [14] As a case in point Aron mentions Herbert Marcuse, who, at a 1964 conference in Heidelberg honoring the centenary of Weber's birth, delivered an address that "seemed motivated by a kind of fury against Max Weber, as if he were still alive and indomitable," [15] only to concede at the end that "today it looks as if he [Weber] was right." [16]

In opposition to bureaucratic domination stood only the forces of what Weber called "charisma." Charisma, a word of religious origin that literally means "gift of grace," signified to Weber the creative, vital, assertive powers of human nature, the source of freedom and of man's autonomy. Charisma comes close in meaning to the Eros of Freud's later writings; indeed, freeing himself from the asceticism of his Puritan background, Weber came to see in eroticism one locus of the revitalizing energies of charisma.

Weber's best-known use of the concept of charisma was to refer to the quality of belief and devotion inspired by a religious prophet or political leader who has convinced his followers of his sacred mission, his heroic deeds, and his extraordinary endowments setting him apart from other men. This usage has passed into contemporary journals in thoroughly banal form. Any politician who possesses some personal charm, or even a good television image, is said to have charisma, especially if teen-age girls scream with excitement at his approach. Thus the Kennedys, John Lindsay, and Pierre Trudeau all have charisma, while Johnson, Nixon, and Humphrey are unfortunate enough to lack it. But Weber meant a good deal more than this by charismatic leadership: he had in mind the impassioned prophet who proclaims "It is written, but I say unto you," and moves his entranced followers to pit themselves against the authority of tradition, legality, or bureaucratic routine. Few modern leaders arouse this kind of devotion, even fewer in the party politics of democracies.

Gandhi was perhaps the purest example of a charismatic leader in the present century, and it is no accident that he was successful in a religious rather than a secular culture. Castro, Hitler, and possibly Mao might also qualify, but all three to some extent, and especially the last two, raise doubts in view of the enormous machinery of publicity that a dictator can mobilize to impute charismatic qualities to himself. Stalin tried this and it is clear that he failed, but it nevertheless remains difficult to distinguish between true charismatic leadership and manufactured pseudo-charisma.

Charisma itself meant still more to Weber. Such conservative interpreters of Weber as Robert Nisbet and Edward Shils have recognized as much and have equated charisma with the sense of awe and reverence evoked by all long-established institutions and authorities. The trouble with this is that it virtually makes charisma identical with the sanctity of tradition, whereas Weber distinguished charisma not only from rational bureaucratic authority but from traditionalism, the authority of "eternal yesterday," as well. To Weber, charisma stood for all passionate attachments to life, the world, and other men that are intense enough to break the grip of everyday custom and routine. "Today it is only within the smallest and intimate circles, in personal human situations, in *pianissimo*, that something is pulsating that corresponds to the prophetic *pneuma*, which in former times swept through great communities like a firebrand, welding them together." [17] The influence of Nietzsche and his heroic individualism is most apparent in Weber's concept of charisma. The vision of a totally rationalized future society was his equivalent of Zarathustra's foreboding that "alas, the time is coming when man will no longer shoot the arrow of his longing beyond man." Recent Weber scholarship by Wolfgang Mommsen in Germany, Eugene Fleischmann in France, and Arthur Mitzman in the United States has amply documented the influence of Nietzsche, previously neglected in the attention given to Weber's relation to Marx.

Most interpreters of Weber have regarded charisma as inherently revolutionary or innovative, but others, such as Parsons, Shils, and Nisbet, have treated it as an essential attribute of the legitimacy of established institutions and therefore a conservative and stabilizing force. Charisma has most frequently been identified with the appeal

of extraordinary personalities, but some have stressed its diffusion
from personalities to offices, institutions, and even to the social order
as a whole. Karl Loewenstein has insisted on the primarily religious
nature of charisma and has questioned its relevance to secular political leaders in modern Western states.[18] Yet Loewenstein is aware of
writing at a time when the term is applied altogether indiscriminately
in popular journalistic usage.

All of these interpretations of charisma find at least *some* warrant in
Weber's writings. The Parsons-Shils-Nisbet view ends up virtually
equating charisma with Durkheim's "sacred" and, as I have previously argued, destroying the difference between the traditional and
the charismatic types of legitimation in Weber's thought. Yet human
beings undeniably tend to personalize general beliefs and collective
entities. A person—real or mythical—comes to symbolize an abstract
value, an established institution, or an entire society, thus reflecting
and contributing to their legitimacy in the eyes of multitudes.

But the innovative and even revolutionary nature of charisma was
central to Weber: he, after all, cited Christ's "It is written, but I say
unto you" as the prototype of a claim to charismatic legitimacy. New
religious and social movements seeking to transform men and the
world are the primary settings for the emergence of charismatic
leaders. The modern political figures most commonly mentioned as
examples of charismatic leaders are Lenin, Hitler, Gandhi, Mao, and
Castro—all of them leaders of revolutionary or national independence movements. Revolutions and revolutionary movements, however, are not always created by charismatic leaders. The French Revolution began when Robespierre was still an unknown. Revolutionary
leaders often resemble the man who, when asked why he was frantically pursuing a mob through the streets, answered "I must follow
them, for I am their leader." Recent revolutionary movements have
made a doctrinal point of denying their need for any coherent leadership at all, and their supporters have complained that the mass media
erroneously identify as leaders colorful individuals who in reality
have no such status.[19]

All political leadership, whether revolutionary, reformist, or conservative in aim, is to some degree innovative. The leader does not
merely register the collective will of his followers, nor is he a rubber

stamp carrying out a set of preformulated laws. Governments are governments of men and not merely of laws even in constitutional democracies. In his political writings toward the end of his life, Max Weber advocated parliamentary government and defined the democratic politician as a "charismatic demagogue" with a plebiscitary mandate to direct the bureaucracies of the modern state and economy. This view represents a tempering of his earlier despair over the ineluctable trend toward total rationalization in modern society, but it in no way implies the stark opposition between such charismatic politicians and the norms of constitutional democracy suggested by those who have accused Weber of providing a justification before the fact of Hitler's rule. These later writings of Weber's imply that "bureaucracy and charisma are not necessarily exclusive of each other and that, in fact, bureaucracies can be superior instruments for charismatic leaders." [20] Such a view qualifies the conception of charisma as necessarily standing in opposition to existing laws and institutions, without, however, depersonalizing it by ascribing it to norms and institutions in the manner of Parsons, Shils, and Nisbet.

Reinhard Bendix has mentioned the difficulty of distinguishing "between charismatic leadership and leadership *sans phrase*," a difficulty created by the presence of personal and innovative elements in all leadership (quite apart from the current promiscuous abuse of the term "charismatic"). Bendix argues that "charisma makes its appearance when leaders and led are convinced that . . . easy accommodations are no longer enough, when consummate belief, on one side, and the promptings of enthusiasm, despair, or hope, on the other, imperatively call for unconditional authority and discipline." [21] The identification of a truly charismatic leader is, as Bendix concedes, "difficult to make in practice, though not in theory."

Yet one ultimate touchstone suggests itself: if a leader is able to reverse sharply his past aims and policies without suffering total abandonment by his followers, then personal loyalty and devotion rather than self-interest or belief in an ideological cause presumably play a major role in sustaining the bond between leader and led. Unfortunately, the historical evidence in any given case is rarely unambiguous, and the careers of many leaders do not provide a definitive test, but several reasonably clear-cut examples come to mind. Lenin persuaded his party comrades to reject a half-century of Marxist doctrine and aim at a Bolshevik seizure of power in 1917. Hitler rejected the socialist content of the Nazi program upheld by the powerful Strasser brothers, and won over several of their leading lieutenants, notably Joseph Goebbels, before he came to power; afterwards he ordered the leaders of the Nazi Left killed in the Rohm purge. Gandhi was originally a disciple of Gokhale, the most moderate and pro-British of the early leaders of All-Indian nationalism. He reversed himself on cooperation with the British, imposed nonviolence, a concept of Jain rather than Hindu origin, on the Congress Party, fought Brahman orthodoxy on caste and on cooperation with the Muslims, and yet became India's first indisputably national leader. Castro merged his July 26th Movement with the Cuban Communist Party, which had opposed his anti-Batista strategy, led his nation into identification with and dependence on the Soviet Union, and still later downgraded the Cuban Communists in his own party and government.

It is hard to think of any national politicians in the Western democracies who could pass the test for charismatic leadership that I have suggested. Roosevelt and DeGaulle are the only two worthy of serious consideration. Churchill promised the British people nothing but "blood, sweat, and tears," but there was no strong pro-Nazi, collaborationist, or defeatist current of opinion in Britain at the time, and no sooner had the war ended than the British electorate voted him out of office. In recent American politics the only plausible candidates for charismatic status are such black leaders as Elijah Muhammed, Malcolm X, and Martin Luther King. Malcolm X, in particular, clearly passes the proposed test: he broke with the Black Muslims and reversed himself on the issue of political cooperation with whites without losing a large and passionate following—indeed, that was why he was assassinated. Significantly, all three of these men were religious as well as political leaders. The survival and continuing influence of the Black Muslims, as much or more a religious sect as a political movement, into the 1970s contrasts sharply with the decline of more secular and primarily political groups like SNCC, CORE, and the Black Panthers. For that matter, Adam Clayton Powell, like King a Christian minister, retained an impressive following in Harlem until his death, in spite of the troubles with Congress and the law which for some years prevented him from visiting his district. (A comparison with Juan Peron on a larger scale is instructive.) Perhaps the last white politician in America who was a genuine charismatic leader was William Jennings Bryan, and his support was centered in the "Bible Belt." * These examples lend credence to Loewenstein's argument that secular mass democracies are inimical to charismatic *political* leaders, who are far more likely to flourish in traditional religious cultures.

While recognizing the irrational, emotional roots of charisma and seeing it as an ever-renewable fount of creative energy at odds with the imposed routines of a rationalized society, Weber did not emulate Nietzsche in embracing romantic irrationalism, turning away in aristocratic aloofness from the social world and investing his hopes solely in a handful of superior individuals. For despite his dread of "the cage of bondage of the future," Weber regarded rationalization as the inescapable destiny of the West, the ultimate, if paradoxical, realization of its very highest values most fully embodied in the rational asceticism of the Protestant reformers, values which Weber himself still upheld even when they stood in opposition to their own objectification in bureaucracy and the machine. In affirming personal freedom and reason, Weber affirmed them not as ideals capable of being fulfilled in a utopia at the end of history, but precisely in their unavoidable tension with the rationalized world of the present and future. As Karl Loewith put it: "To act in the midst of this specialized and indoctrinated world of 'specialists without spirit, sensualists without heart' with the passionate force of negativity, piercing now here and now there through some structure of 'bondage'—this [to Weber] was the meaning of 'freedom.' " [22]

Not only the irrationalism of charisma but also the free rationality of the resolute individual are, then, at odds with the "frozen" rationality of modern culture and society. Weber's world is a world of

---

* An example from the Canadian side of the border is William Aberhart, the founder of the Social Credit Party of Canada, who was an evangelical Christian minister and who, like Bryan, won his greatest following from commercial farmers threatened by Eastern financial interests. See John A. Irving, *The Social Credit Movement in Alberta* (Toronto: University of Toronto Press, 1959).

fundamental values in "irreconcilable conflict": charisma and rationalization, individual freedom and efficient social organization, mystical withdrawal from and ascetic conquest of the world, politics with
its commitment to violence as the ultimate means and the ethics of
brotherhood. It is almost impossible to write about Weber without at
some point using the word "ambivalent" to characterize his attitude.
Yet it is his determination to acknowledge both the claims of rival
values and the inescapability of tension between them that accounts
for the searing honesty, the moral intensity, and the lack of bombast
or self-pity which his writing succeeds in communicating. An acquaintance wrote of Weber that for him "the test of moral behavior
rested in never choosing what corresponded to his own nature and
could be accomplished without inner resistance." [23] A masochistic
attitude, without doubt, certainly one rooted in the ascetic Calvinism
that was part of Weber's own family heritage as well as a major subject of his scholarship. But how magnificently he succeeded in objec-
tifying and universalizing his own sense of conflict in his vision of
history as ceaseless strife between institutions, group interests, and the
inexhaustible fertility of man's value-creating powers!

For most of his life Max Weber was torn between the rival claims
of politics and scholarship as vocations. His two well-known essays,
"Science as a Vocation" and "Politics as a Vocation," first delivered
as addresses to student audiences toward the end of his life, together
constitute an implicit *apologia pro vita sua* in addition to summarizing superbly the major themes of his scholarship. Weber was never
able to commit himself to a full political career, although throughout
his life he was politically active and at the time of his sudden death in
1920 there was a general expectation that he would play a leading
role in the Weimar Republic, the constitution of which he had
helped to frame.

Weber started out in the 1880s and 1890s as a critical supporter of
Bismarckian *Realpolitik*, an advocate of the modernization of the
German political and economic structure that would eliminate the
power of the Junkers and consolidate Germany's great-power status in
the world. He was, in essence, a liberal imperialist. Not until after
his breakdown, as Arthur Mitzman has shown in *The Iron Cage* (the
only detailed study relating Weber's ideas to his personal biography),

did Weber adopt his pessimistic outlook on the future of Western culture. In the years just before World War I, he was influenced by the prevailing revolt against the rigidities of Victorian morality and bourgeois repressiveness. His attraction at this time to the gods of charisma deepened his disaffection from bureaucratic rationalism. Like many others, he was affected by the euphoria attending the outbreak of World War I, but during the war he became a bitter critic of the Kaiser's policies, winning national attention. By the end of the war he was an ardent constitutional democrat, wishing to subordinate the irresponsible power of the Kaiser and the imperial bureaucracy to elected parliamentary politicians. The polarity between charisma and rationalization is reflected in the detailed contrast he drew in his political essays at this time between the politician and the bureaucrat. His belief that popular charismatic leaders might creatively direct the bureaucratic apparatus of modern society strikes a more positive note than his earlier despair over the consequences of rationalization. But he had little hope regarding Germany's future: "Not summer's bloom lies ahead of us, but rather a polar night of icy darkness and hardness, no matter which group may triumph now," he told a student audience in 1918 in Munich, the same city where just a few months later a thirty-year-old veteran of the war, whose highest military rank had been that of lance-corporal, received his first political job from the local army headquarters as a propagandist against left-wing and democratic ideas.

Weber died the following year, but the relation between his political ideas and the ideology of the dictatorial regime established by the ex-corporal remains a debated issue in Germany. Weber was, after all, an ardent German nationalist who came to favor democracy not as an ultimate value but because he thought it the system of government most likely to produce responsible political leaders. "For me constitutions are techniques just like other machines," he wrote in 1917; "I would be just as ready to fight against parliament and for the monarch if he were a politician or he gave promise of becoming one." [24] Was not Hitler the very prototype of the charismatic elected leader Weber favored? Such queries are probably unavoidable, but to examine in the garish light of the Nazi catastrophe the ideas of men who antedated it and could have no inkling of its horrors is to do

them a considerable injustice. Max Weber was, to be sure, not the
bland liberal democrat that his American admirers have often taken
him to be. "He who lets himself in for politics, that is, for power and
force as means, contracts with diabolical forces," [25] Weber asserted,
but he himself was quite prepared to give the devil his due, admired
Machiavelli, and accepted fully the power politics of conflict among
states and among social groups within a state. However, Weber's es-
pousal of a strong state headed by a plebiscitary leader comes far
closer to Gaullist conceptions of government than to the reality of
Hitler's rule. Occasionally, Weber even sounds like those American
advocates of a strengthened presidency, such as James McGregor
Burns or Richard Neustadt, who are presently on the defensive as a
result of the Vietnam debacle (not to speak of Watergate).

Whatever the merits or demerits of Weber's specific political proposals, today he is quoted approvingly by representatives of widely
differing political and intellectual viewpoints. Besides the obviously
appealing assaults on bureaucracy, contemporary radicals often employ the Weberian term "demystification" to describe their purpose
in denouncing existing institutions. A few years ago a middle-aged
sympathizer with "engaged youth" justified the blaring noise of a rock
band installed in the lobby of a campus building on the grounds that
it demystified the institution. A bit confusing, because for Weber it
was bureaucratic institutions themselves, such as the modern university, that progressively demystify our lives. Even more confusing, the
same writer went on to praise the "tribal" consciousness of student
activists, although primitive tribesmen clearly lived in a more en-
chanted world than ours, one full of mysterious powers and spirits.
As a matter of fact, those participants in the so-called counterculture
who have taken up astrology, tarot cards, and the exotica of Eastern
religions seem to be engaged in an effort to *remystify* the world and
overcome its disenchanted state. Weber remarked in 1918 on "the
need of some modern intellectuals to furnish their souls with, so to
speak, guaranteed genuine antiques," and observed that "they play at
decorating a sort of domestic chapel with small sacred images from
all over the world, or they produce surrogates through all sorts of
psychic experiences to which they ascribe the dignity of mystic holi-
ness, which they peddle in the book market." [26]

Sounds somewhat familiar, doesn't it? Weber dismissed this sort of thing as "plain humbug or self-deception," but he went on to add: "It is, however, no humbug but rather something very sincere and genuine if some of the youth groups who during recent years have quietly grown together give their human community the interpretation of a religious, cosmic, or mystical relation, although occasionally perhaps such interpretation rests on a misunderstanding of self." [27] Just before 1914 Weber visited on several occasions Bohemian colonies of young artists and utopians—ancestors of today's hippie communes—in the vicinity of the North Italian lakes. [28] While he did not think that the experience of these rebels provided an option for any but a tiny few, he was impressed with their sacrifices on behalf of their convictions. There are therefore grounds for believing that Weber would have shown considerable sympathetic understanding of today's young rebels, at least of those who have actually chosen to live by the ethic they profess. Weber's indictment of a world of "specialists without vision, sensualists without heart" has sometimes been quoted in support of the "counterculture's" values. Yet Mr. Sammler in Saul Bellow's great novel *Mr. Sammler's Planet* cites with approval the same passage and finds it suggestive of his own grim anticipation of a future America in which "an oligarchy of technicians, engineers, the men who ran the great machines . . . would come to govern vast slums filled with bohemian adolescents, narcotized, beflowered and 'whole.' " [29] After all, Max Weber never said that the specialists without vision and the sensualists without heart were necessarily conscious allies: the latter might assail the former with slogans culled from Marx, Marcuse, and even Weber himself and still be, as that other fellow said, part of the problem not part of the solution.

It is surely vain to speculate on what a dead thinker might have thought about Nazism or contemporary cultural and political protest, although the impulse to do so testifies to his surviving presence in our consciousness. Among American social scientists—omitting those of German origin—Weber has been a major influence on scholars as various as the late C. Wright Mills, a founding father of the New Left; Talcott Parsons, whose social theory and its political implications were one of Mills's major targets; Robert Nisbet, an articulate Tocquevillian conservative; and H. Stuart Hughes, a democratic socialist and former peace candidate for the Senate in Massachusetts. In sociology, Weber's conceptions of bureaucracy and of social stratification underlie most current theory and research in these areas. The search for a "functional equivalent" of the Protestant ethic in underdeveloped countries has inspired an enormous amount of research by students of economic development. In historical scholarship, Weber's studies of the Hebrew prophets, the religions of India and China, and state-building in medieval and early modern Europe continue to be a source of ideas and hypotheses, although much of his work has inevitably been outdated in detail. His essays on the philosophy and methodology of the social sciences remain unequaled in profundity and scope.

But Max Weber's most valuable heritage is, I believe, the personal example he gave of a man who persisted in grappling with the most difficult moral and intellectual issues, who did not hesitate to give painful answers, who never allowed himself to become intoxicated by his political passions, yet whose scholarly objectives, even when apparently remote, were always intimately related to the crisis of his, and our, time. Even his most bitter critics have recognized an aura of personal heroism surrounding him.

SIXTEEN
Ends and Means in Politics

MAX WEBER has been best known to American political scientists and sociologists for his three types of legitimacy—of publicly accepted belief systems enjoining obedience to the established order. Yet Weber also recognized that the political man, the man with a true calling for politics, does not accept the present order in its entirety: he espouses ideal values or identifies himself with collective goals which are not fully realized in existing institutions. What general principles guide him in attempting to advance his cause in a refractory world in which other men are committed to rival causes?

Weber discerned two polar moralities that provide answers to this question: an ethic of responsibility (*Verantwortungsethink*) and an ethic of absolute ends (*Gesinnungsethik*). Although he discussed these two ethics chiefly in relation to politics, they represent general attitudes toward the world, just as the three types of legitimacy also apply to institutions other than the political. Essentially they are religious in origin and represent different responses to "the age-old problem of theodicy . . . the experience of the irrationality of the world which has been the driving force of all religious evolution." [1]

Weber, in fact, argues that the ethic of absolute ends is specifically inappropriate to politics. Because "politics operates with very special means, namely power backed up by *violence*," there is an irreducible tension between the requirements of political action and absolute ethical values. "He who seeks the salvation of the soul, of his own and of others, should not seek it along the avenue of politics, for the quite different task of politics can only be solved by violence. . . . Everything that is striven for through political action operating with violent means and following an ethic of responsibility endangers the 'salvation of the soul.' " [2]

The proponent of an ethic of absolute ends strives in his conduct to live by principles and values, whether religiously inspired or secular, that are for him the *summum bonum*. He does not take into account the possible or probable consequences of strictly abiding by his principles in an imperfect world in which other men do not honor or live by them; it is enough that he has acted in conformity with a moral standard that for him is absolute. Weber quotes in illustration the maxim "the Christian does rightly and leaves the results with the Lord." In effect, the believer in an ethic of absolute ends acts as if he were already living in the kingdom of heaven, the good society, or in a utopia beyond the terror of history. Although he knows that evil has not yet been vanquished, he "feels 'responsible' only for seeing to it that the flame of pure intentions is not quelched." He avoids the moral dilemma posed by "the fact that in numerous instances the attainment of 'good' ends is bound to the fact that one must be willing to pay the price of using morally dubious means or at least dangerous ones—and facing the possibility or even the probability of evil ramifications." [3] The believer in an ethic of absolute ends chooses, as it were, to "live his end"; he thus denies any possible tension between means and ends by refusing to distinguish between them, collapsing his means into his ends. Since politics makes use of the "morally dubious means" of violence, he must either renounce the world of politics altogether or confine himself to recommending exemplary action.

Whereas all or most men engage on occasion in the type of action Weber called value rational, or *wertrationale*, the believer in an ethic of absolute ends elevates this mode of conduct into a standard for all conduct. The follower of an ethic of responsibility, on the other hand, is concerned with the ultimate historical fate of his cause and recognizes the necessity of acting instrumentally, or in a *zweckrationale* manner, in order to promote it. Thus he cannot escape confronting the antinomies of means and ends. He holds himself responsible for the actual consequences of his decisions rather than feeling responsible only to God, to an ideal, or to the inner dictates of his conscience. He does not hesitate to dirty his hands by engaging in

politics: "he lets himself in for the diabolic forces lurking in all violence." Weber's insistence on the violence of politics follows, of
course, from his definition of the state as "a human community that
successfully claims the *monopoly of the legitimate use of violence*
within a given territory" and of politics as the "striving to share power
or striving to influence the distribution of power, either among states
or among groups within a state." [4] Apart from implicating himself in
the violence that is the ultimate means, the court of last resort, in all
politics, the responsible participant in even the peaceful, routine politics of democracy cannot avoid compromising other values he may
cherish, as ideals or in personal relations: he indulges in "campaign
oratory," making promises he knows he cannot completely fulfill; he
conceals unpleasant truths from his supporters; pretends to a moral
superiority over his opponents that he may not truly feel; and, in general, resorts to a demagoguery that is both potentially corrupting and
unavoidable if he is to win and to hold the support of the masses. [5]

The two ethics are ideal types. Few men—at least today, with the
waning of religious faith—have the courage, or, if you like, the fanat-
icism, to hold genuinely and consistently to an ethic of absolute
ends. Most men are not even failed saints, for, as George Orwell
pointed out in his essay on Gandhi, the average human being does
not truly aspire to sainthood. Weber recognized that many men affected to follow an ethic of absolute ends, but he dismissed most of
them as "windbags who do not fully realize what they take upon
themselves but who intoxicate themselves with romantic sensations."
This is surely no less true today. One recalls those professed apostles
of Gandhi, Albert Camus, and Martin Luther King who within the
space of a few years renounced the nonviolence to which they had
previously been committed and began to advocate guerrilla warfare in
the urban ghettos and on the campuses, hailing Che Guevara, Frantz
Fanon, and Ho Chi Minh as their heroes.

Saints, "the great *virtuosi* of acosmic love of humanity and good-
ness," are the most complete exemplars of the ethic of absolute ends.
Here Weber has sometimes been misinterpreted. Daniel Bell, for example, regards the political extremist for whom "all sacrifices, all
means are acceptable for the achievement of one's beliefs" as a follower of the ethic of absolute ends, whereas "for those who take on

responsibility . . . one's role can be only to reject all absolutes and accept pragmatic compromise." [6] Bell reserves rational, expedient, "responsible" conduct for the politics of compromise and moderation he favors, so he assigns the extremist, the revolutionary, the totalitarian to Weber's other type, the believer in an ethic of absolute ends. But the political fanatic who believes that his end justifies *any* means stands at the opposite pole from the man of boundless faith who refuses to separate means from ends at all. The former is in truth an extreme or ultimate proponent of Weber's ethic of responsibility, justifying whatever course of action promises to be successful in advancing his cause. Arthur Koestler's polarity of the yogi and the commissar refers to the extreme versions of each ethic.[7] True, in a psychological sense it is often the case that *les extrèmes se touchent*, as Weber acutely perceived, noting that: "In the world of realities, as a rule, we encounter the ever-renewed experience that the adherent of an ethic of ultimate ends suddenly turns into a chiliastic prophet. Those, for example, who have just preached 'love against violence' now call for the use of force for the *last* violent deed, which would then lead to a state of affairs in which *all* violence is annihilated." [8] Thus peace-making statesmen become ardent leaders of a "war to end all wars," anarchist-pacifists suddenly turn into bomb-throwing terrorists, and the "flower-child" preaching love and peace becomes a mini-revolutionary adopting "up against the wall!" as his slogan.

But if few men are courageous or otherworldly enough to be true practitioners of the ethic of absolute ends, it is also the case that few men are ruthless enough to act *only* with regard to the immediate consequences of their acts which bear on the fortunes of their cause. The extreme adherent to an ethic of responsibility is also an ideal type infrequently encountered in reality. If all politics—indeed all life among men—involves acting in accordance with the maxim "the end justifies the means," this does not mean that any and all efficacious means are equally acceptable. Actually, the phrase "the end justifies the means," far from expressing an amoral Machiavellianism, is a simple tautology, for "means" *are* nothing but acts that are chosen because it is believed they will achieve given ends. Only the ends they are thought to serve *can* justify particular means. The Machiavellian in the popular sense, or the follower of Koestler's "Commissar

Ethics," is not he who justifies his means by the ends they serve, but he who is prepared to act without restraint and with total opportunism to advance his ends. He is no less a follower of the ethic of responsibility than a moderate, compromising politician: "responsibility" was not to Weber a "halo word" but a purely descriptive term connoting the taking into account of the consequences of one's actions rather than merely the intentions motivating them.

Since most politicians are neither saints nor Machiavellians, they combine at some level the two ethics. They act responsibly up to a point where they find themselves inwardly compelled to announce in Luther's words "here I stand; I can do no other." At some point a principle becomes absolute for them even though the consequences of complying with it may be temporarily or permanently unfavorable. They will fight an election campaign fiercely but acquiesce in a negative verdict of the voters even if they could stay in office by force; they will wage a war but refrain from the wanton killing of civilian populations (unhappily, this century has seen few such national leaders!); they will strive to persuade their constituents to support a policy they approve, but if unsuccessful will vote their principles rather than their interest in reelection. Some of these examples suggest rare political courage. For men who display it, Weber observed, "an ethic of ultimate ends and an ethic of responsibility are not absolute contrasts but rather supplements, which only in unison constitute a genuine man—a man who *can* have the 'calling for politics.' " [9] Men who live *off* rather than *for* politics, making a living from political office as other men do from the pursuit of other occupations, are, Weber thought, far more common. And many of those who "profess the *ethos* of politics as a cause" are romantics or braggarts who lack "the trained relentlessness in viewing the realities of life and the ability to face such realities and to measure up to them inwardly" that a true calling for politics requires. Weber's admiration for the exceptional man, the hero, the charismatic leader of his people, is evident in these passages. But the average politician is neither a hero, a scoundrel, nor a totally self-interested time-server: he too at some level combines an ethic of responsibility with an ethic of absolute ends.

Weber died in 1920 before the disorder, violence, and horrors of twentieth-century politics had reached their zenith—before Stalin and Hitler, the interwar triumphs of fascism, nuclear weapons, and the rise of revolutionary nationalism in the Third World. It is illuminating to extend his analysis of the two political ethics by examining the strains they have undergone and the new forms and combinations they have assumed in the experience of recent ideological movements.

Weber regarded anarcho-syndicalism as a contemporary, secularized example of adherence to an ethic of absolute ends. But, as we have seen, he remarked on the tendency of believers in universal love and altruism to become by dialectical reversal "chiliastic prophets," advocating a last great explosion of violence that would for once and for all achieve the leap from history to utopia. Karl Mannheim has provided a fuller analysis of the chiliastic mentality from the Anabaptists to modern anarchism. "Chiliasm," he maintained, "sees the revolution as a value in itself, not as an unavoidable means to a rationally set end." [10] He cites in support Bakunin's famous statement, "the will to destroy is a creative will," and his avowal, "I do not believe in constitutions or laws. . . . We need something different. Storm and vitality and a new lawless and consequently free world." Collective solidarity and the ecstasy of brotherly communion forged by revolutionary struggle are the ultimate values affirmed by this outlook rather than destruction and revolution as such. The chiliastic revolutionary sees the purifying, ennobling experience of collective revolt as redeeming men, transvaluing all values, and burning away the husks of their old corrupt selves—this is what moves him to action rather than a coherent vision of a new, more just social order which can only be attained after the painful but necessary surgery of the violent overthrow of existing institutions. Fanon's Sorelian belief in the psychologically liberating role of violence in achieving manhood for the victims of colonial exploitation is a contemporary version of this outlook. [11] Some observers have detected such thoroughly un-Marxist chiliastic aspirations in Mao's effort to revive a revolutionary élan in China nearly two decades after his successful conquest of power.

Chiliastic movements, however, have not succeeded in transforming the world by storming its gates. Sometimes their failure has been followed by a reversal of the transition from saint to revolutionary that Weber described in which the movement turns inward and "no longer dares to venture forth into the world, and loses its contact with worldly happenings." [12] But when the chiliastic spirit "ebbs and deserts these movements, there remains behind in the world a naked mass-frenzy and a de-spiritualized fury." [13] Chiliasts, therefore, may take the alternative direction of a nihilism that regards violence and banditry to be of exemplary value in constantly "rekindling the flame of protest against the injustice of the social order." [14] That wing of anarchism represented by Nechayev and the Black International, with its extolling of the "propaganda of the deed" and the total commitment of the revolutionary to acts of terrorism, embodies a nihilism in which violence and heroic conflict are seen as their own justification apart from consequences.

Mannheim noted the similarity between the "absolute presentness" of chiliastic faith and the ahistorical "apotheosis of the deed" he saw as characteristic of fascism. The writings of Georges Sorel were an ideological link between fascism and the revolutionism of the Left in the early part of this century. Today many observers have discerned similarities to nihilism and fascism in the crude *soi-disant* guerrilla Marxism of New Left student movements. The German sociologist, Jürgen Habermas, an erstwhile sympathizer, has described the German student movement as a species of "left fascism." Lewis Coser has noted the resemblances between Nechayevism, Mannheim's characterization of the fascist outlook, and the ideology of guerrilla warfare in the influential writings of the young French philosopher-revolutionary, Régis Debray. [15] Many others have commented on the extent to which the tactics of confrontation, disruption, and the presentation of "nonnegotiable demands" have seemed to become ends in themselves for student radicals lacking any systematic ideology but full of militant determination to make a "revolution for the hell of it," as one of them has only half-facetiously put it.

Mannheim's analysis of fascism drew largely on the somewhat more structured ideology of Italian fascism rather than on Nazism. But, as all of Hitler's biographers have noted, the experience of front-line combat in World War I fundamentally shaped his outlook and that of most of the other early Nazis, who were aptly described by Konrad Heiden as "armed bohemians to whom war is home and civil war fatherland." At its crudest level, Nazism worshipped war, violence, physical brutality, and marching men as absolute values, rationalizing these sentiments with clichés and vulgarizations drawn from Neitzschean, Darwinian, and racist theories. To Weber, the Christian who truly lives by the teachings of the Sermon on the Mount, turning the other cheek and eschewing all violence, was the true apostle of the ethic of absolute ends. He failed to see that the total inversion of these teachings can also lead to a kind of ethic—or antiethic—of absolute ends, exalting violence, war, and the slaughter of one's enemies rather than peace, love, and the service of others.* But then he died before Hitler.

Nihilism and violence worship still represent individualized credos, attracting Heiden's "armed bohemians," Arendt's "leaders of the mob," and Stern's "apostles of cultural despair" in a world that seems hostile or indifferent to their aspirations.[16] The leaders of a totalitarian party in power, however, are compelled to develop at least exoteric legitimations to win the allegiance of their ordinary, conservative subjects. Weber did not foresee the peculiar blend of charismatic and bureaucratic elements in totalitarian appeals for legitimacy. The totalitarian rulers' personal resolution of the ends-means dilemmas posed by political action—the elite's esoteric legitimation of its role, as it were—suggests another route away from an ethic of responsibility toward an ethic of absolute ends.

Its nature is best revealed in the famous speech of Orwell's prosecutor, O'Brien, in 1984:

> The Party seeks power entirely for its own sake. We are not interested in the good of others; we are interested solely in power. Not wealth or luxury or long life or happiness; only power, pure power. . . . We are different from all the oligarchies of the past in that we know what we are doing. All the others, even those who resembled ourselves, were cowards and hypocrites. The German Nazis and the Russian Communists came very close to us in

---

* "The point . . . is not the use of violence *per se*, not even on an unprecedented scale, but that 'totalitarian indifference' to moral considerations is actually based upon a reversal of all our legal and moral concepts, which ultimately rest on the commandment, 'Thou shalt not kill.' Against this, totalitarian 'morals' preaches almost openly the precept: Thou shalt kill!" Hannah Arendt, "Discussion," in Carl J. Friedrich, ed., *Totalitarianism* (New York: Grosset and Dunlap, 1964), p. 78.

their methods, but they never had the courage to recognize their own motives. They pretended, perhaps they even believed, that they had seized power unwillingly and for a limited time, and that just around the corner there lay a paradise where human beings would be free and equal. We are not like that. We know that no one ever seizes power with the intention of relinquishing it. Power is not a means; it is an end. One does not establish a dictatorship in order to safeguard a revolution; one makes the revolution in order to establish the dictatorship. The object of persecution is persecution. The object of torture is torture. The object of power is power. [17]

Orwell, as Philip Rahv has noted, intended this speech both to recall and to refute the ideas of Dostoyevsky's Grand Inquisitor, whose famous argument for the despotism of a "dedicated sect doing evil that good may come" deeply influenced Weber's formulation of the inevitable tension between ethics and politics. Orwell meant in O'Brien's speech to lay bare the fundamental praxis of totalitarian movements according to which the exalted utopian goals they profess to serve become mere ritual incantations imposing no limits on their freedom to maneuver with a maximum of opportunism and flexibility, to reverse the "party line" overnight, if necessary. Totalitarian movements are, as Raymond Aron has brilliantly put it, "orthodoxies without doctrines." Their real aims are those expressed by O'Brien and their ultimate object of worship is the "organizational weapon" of the party cadres. As Irving Howe and Lewis Coser, writing of the Stalinists, observe, it was not "ideology as such which bound the members . . . in reality it was *the organization as the faith made visible* which was the primary object of loyalty." [18] The totalitarian activist collapses his professed ends into his means, reversing the procedure by which the saintly adherent to an ethic of absolute ends abolishes the ends-means distinction and the painful choices it involves. In Weberian terms, the organizational instrument for attaining power, the party, becomes itself a charismatic object even as it continues to be a disciplined, purposeful, rationally organized association. Thus bureaucracy is invested with charisma to a degree seldom achieved by most bureaucratic structures, which in their functional rationality spread disenchantment and alienation rather than passionate dedication. [19] Or, in another Weberian dichotomy, the totalitarian party commands the total allegiance of its members that is characteristic of the religious sect while retaining at the same time the hierarchical and differentiated structure of an established church.

The power worship of the totalitarian *apparatchik* is not accounted for by the familiar argument that ruthless means corrupt those who use them and thus defeat noble ends, although this occurs often enough in reality. The follower's loyalty to the movement is a form of belief with *sui generis* psychological sources rather than the eventual outcome of a process of socialization, or rather desocialization. It is a belief differing markedly from that of the committed revolutionary who is convinced that "Alas, we who wished to lay the foundations of kindness could not ourselves be kind" (Brecht), or who, like Sartre's Hoederer in *Les Mains Sales*, argues that humanity can only be saved by those who are prepared to "plunge their hands up to the elbows in blood and shit." Such men are extreme representatives of an ethic of responsibility, acutely aware of the tragic tension between means and ends; they are usually the founders and earliest followers of revolutionary movements long before the acquisition of power. After the movement has triumphed, they are likely to be the victims of purges carried out by new men who are thralls to the fetishism of the organization.

But the totalitarian conversion of an organizational instrument into an ultimate value is only an extreme instance of a more general process that has been noted by many students of bureaucracy. Michels' "iron law of oligarchy," for example, involves the substitution by the leaders of a mass organization of organizational survival and their own continued incumbency in office for the ideological goals and the interests of the rank-and-file members which are the organization's ostensible *raison d'être*. Eduard Bernstein, who was neither a totalitarian nor even a revolutionary but a convinced democrat, said "the goal is nothing, the movement is all," a slogan that appealed to Sorel, who influenced both anarcho-syndicalist and fascist ideology.[20] Merton's "bureaucratic personality type" and Whyte's "organization man" also attribute intrinsic value to functional, special-purpose organizations and their operating rules, and are pictured as flourishing today in all such organizations.

What Merton refers to as the "process of sanctification" of bureaucratic methods and structures,[21] however, does not imply that those subject to it are fully conscious of and able to articulate the values that are revealed in their behavior. Merton and other analysts of the pathologies of bureaucracy are describing rather an objective tendency implicit in the daily routines of the bureaucratic functionary. The junior business executive is likely to be somewhat shamefaced if he becomes aware of the degree to which he has permitted the corporation to dominate his mind and spirit—at least the alleged success of Whyte's book among executives suggests as much. Even in the case of the totalitarian partisan, Orwell's O'Brien maintains that the Nazis and Communists, unlike himself, were unable to face up to what they were really doing and deceived themselves with rationalizations. Since O'Brien is a fictional character, one may readily agree with Philip Rahv that:

Orwell fails to distinguish, in the behavior of O'Brien, between psychological and objective truth. Undoubtedly it is O'Brien, rather than Dostoievski's Grand Inquisitor, who reveals the real nature of total power; yet that does not settle the question of O'Brien's personal psychology, the question, that is, of his ability to live with this naked truth as his sole support; nor is it conceivable that the party-elite to which he belongs could live with this truth for very long. Evil, far more than good, is in need of the pseudoreligious justifications so readily provided by the ideologies of world happiness and compulsory salvation, ideologies generated by both the Left and the Right.[22]

I have moved some distance from Weber's discussion of different orientations toward politics, for he was primarily concerned with manifest judgments and values and the degree of "inner poise" with which they were held. Yet, as his account of the evolution of ascetic Calvinism into a shallow, worldly acquisitiveness indicates, he was highly sensitive to the tortuous dialectic of ideas in history that so often produces caricatures and travesties of what their original adherents intended. Weber anticipated the obsolescence of the leading political ideologies of his time and was to that extent a herald of what later came to be called with considerable overstatement the "end of ideology." Yet he died before the grip of ideologies on men, including the nationalism to which he himself was committed, helped bring about a European civil war that reduced not only Germany but Europe itself to the status of a second-rate power in world politics.

Weber's political sociology remained incomplete. He developed an exhaustive typology of religious attitudes and beliefs in his sociology of religion, and the starting point of his analysis of different political outlooks was the recognition of inescapable conflict between religious ethics and the "demon of politics." He was aware of the continuing dependence of political ideals on religious world views. One has the impression that today political ideologies have become more autonomous, that religious ideas have become parasitic upon secular belief systems rather than the reverse. Divorced from their religious origins, political ideologies become more menacing in their remorseless worldliness, their failure to provide experiences of transcendence while unavoidably frustrating the millenarian hopes and expectations they arouse. We need urgently to understand the modalities of political faith and apostasy; Weber provides a valuable beginning.

SEVENTEEN

On Thinking about the Future

A SUBJECT like "The Future of America" is an invitation to utopian dreams or Doomsday nightmares. I have nothing against such mental constructions: visions and fantasies are indispensable in setting outer limits to our efforts to imagine the future. But there is scarcely a dearth of them in America today—they have become entirely fashionable. Even supposedly sober social scientists have recently created yet another specialty in "futurology," the study of the future. The social scientists, of course, do not see themselves as indulging in untrammeled imaginative speculation but rather as predicting the future by analyzing present realities and tendencies, an undertaking which restricts them to forecasts of what America will be like a generation or two from now at most—say, by the year 2000.

The most certain thing that can be said about America twenty-five or thirty years from now is that it will resemble America as it is today in a far greater number of particulars than otherwise. This is obvious to the point of banality, but often manages to be overlooked, or at least underplayed, by those who are addicted to the melodramatic prophetic mode that pervades contemporary culture and has by no means left the social sciences untouched.

Yet social scientists have not been very successful in the past at making even limited, short-run predictions, though they have not done any worse than others. In recent decades, three major approaches to forecasting the future, all of them questionable, have prevailed.

1. No magical technique for avoiding the ancient fallacy of Eternalizing the Present has been discovered. Even those who most

loudly affirm the priority of social change over stability and continuity are guilty of this fallacy. The charge that sociologists of the recent past, in particular structural-functionalists and the "end of ideology" writers, imputed an unwarranted stability to the status quo became a cliché in the 1960s and continues to be tiresomely reiterated by self-styled sociological "radicals" who seem to believe that sheer insistence on the undeniable fact that change and conflict actually take place—the two are often erroneously equated—in itself amounts to a weighty theoretical position. The partisans of change, however, are prone to assume that tendencies and movements of protest visible at the moment will spread and accelerate rather than turning out to be, as so often happens, ephemeral and limited in their consequences. I shall discuss this particular error in greater detail below, but it is clearly a variant of the fallacy of eternalizing the present.

2. Much predicting of social change, particularly in areas where refined statistical measures and complex computer-based technology are applicable, takes the form of extrapolating forward existing trends. However complicated the methodology, much of this reminds one, as Robert Nisbet has said, "of a mad physiologist predicting giants at age twenty on the basis of growth rates at age ten." [1] Apart from the sheer measurement and plotting of trends, sociologists have often arrived at a comprehensive explanation of a major trend just at the moment when it unexpectedly began to reverse itself, recalling Hegel's famous dictum that "the Owl of Minerva spreads her wings only when the shades of night are falling." Some well-known examples: Demography is one of the most precise and "hard data" based fields of sociology. Sociological demographers had finally decided in the late thirties that the declining fertility of the past half-century reflected the fact that the modern family was inherently inimical to reproduction when the wartime and postwar "baby boom" burst upon them. No sooner had it been determined that the relatively high fertility of the forties and fifties was the result of an emerging "suburban" family-size norm of three or four children than all the fertility rates turned downward in the late fifties, declining through the sixties to their present all-time low levels. After Truman's 1948 victory, political scientists and political sociologists described the rise and crystallization of the New Deal coalition that had made

the Democrats the nation's majority party, only to be confronted with six successive presidential elections—seven if we also count 1948—in which the Democrats only once won a majority of the popular vote for president, while the Republicans did so three times and would have added a fourth in 1968 had Wallace not run as a regional candidate.

3. In the past decade, the breathless proclamation of the new, the revolutionary, the unprecedented, of momentous transitions utterly discontinuous with the past, requiring conceptual innovations and the discarding of all traditional categories of interpretation to comprehend them, has been the mode. This style, however, is itself hardly discontinuous with the past, for it at least perpetuates the inveterate futurism, to use Toynbee's phrase, of the traditional American ethos. Dedication to "the tradition of the new," as Harold Rosenberg has called it, is an old American custom.

There have been, first of all, the *post* boys, defining our age as postindustrial, or postbourgeois, or postcapitalist, or postmodern, or posteconomic, or post-Christian, or post-Marxist, or posttraditional, or even postcivilized. Daniel Bell has exhaustively catalogued the variations on the *post* theme.[2] There are enough posts in contemporary social thought to build a picket fence!

Favoring a rather more apocalyptic rhetoric, there are the Thanatologists, announcing the Death of God, or of Man, or of the Family, or the end of liberalism or of ideology, or of culture, or of literature, or, more bathetically, of the novel. That the entities consigned to the past obviously continue to clutter up the landscape is clearly a source of annoyance to these prophets, who, like the revolting Columbia students of 1968 addressing an elderly couple on the campus, are disposed to shout, "Why don't you just go home and die?"

Within the more restricted sphere of academic sociology, there have been calls for a New Sociology, a Critical Sociology, a Radical Sociology, and even a Transcendental Sociology, all of which define themselves by a rhetorical rejection of the bad old sociologies of the past and present. A few have even proclaimed the end of sociology on the assumption that our Nixon-voting Everyman is now equipped to be his own sociologist, as he presumably wasn't in the nineteenth century, or even as recently as the 1950s.[3]

Now, none of these approaches to the future—and the exponents of each and every one of them know it—bases its anticipation of things to come on any established scientific laws of group behavior or historical development. When it comes to *explanation* as opposed to mere *extrapolation*, even the determinedly scientific measurers and projecters of trends are disposed of by Karl Popper's argument that *a trend is not a law*.[4] That there are no established laws in social science is conceded by one of the very few sociologists to have written a book in recent years upholding a positivist, natural-science-based conception of social science, a book which is also unusual in that it is refreshingly free of the usual desiccated prose (and spirit) of positivists, adopting a mordant, debunking tone toward the follies of intellectuals reminiscent of Pareto. I refer to Gwynn Nettler's *Explanations*. At one point, Nettler claims as the only verified law of social psychology the proposition that "He who does you dirt a first time will do so again, if you stick around long enough." [5]

But this is a law of social psychology applicable to individual conduct and not necessarily to the actions of groups. Where the latter are concerned, I am tempted to enunciate what I shall call with predictable vanity "Wrong's Law of Twice but not Thrice." Some examples of predictions—purely negative ones—I am prepared to make based on this law: Twice in this century Germany tried to conquer Europe and failed. There will be no third attempt. Twice within twenty years the United States became involved in land wars in Asia that were unpopular at home. Korea and Vietnam will have no sequels. Two Soviet satellite nations in Eastern Europe attempted far-reaching democratizations and liberalizations of the totalitarian regimes that had been imposed upon them by Moscow. The Red Army terminated both efforts and a third such attempt will not be made. Twice in a decade the major American political parties nominated candidates from their ideologically extreme wings. Both candidates lost by landslides to not particularly popular opponents and similar nominations will not be made again for a long time.

Summarizing current developments in European social and philosophical thought, my friend Norman Birnbaum remarked of Raymond Aron that he has "set himself the task of persuading his contemporaries that the world being what it is, it is not likely to change very much." [6] Not a bad rule of thumb, though no more than that, for foreseeing the near future, I think, although it infuriates the promoters of more heady visions. But Aron was the man who first used the phrase the "end of ideology" back in the fifties; and here I shall repeat a story against myself that I have been telling my classes in a self-mocking and deprecatory spirit for several years now.

In the summer of 1962 I taught summer session on the Berkeley campus of the University of California. I shortly became aware of an extraordinary amount of activity on the campus by left-wing political groups, activity the like of which I hadn't seen since my own graduate student days at Columbia in the forties. The groups were, as a matter of fact, largely the same groups that were around then, though now 3,000 miles to the West, and, in fact, some of the same, now graying individuals were serving as nonstudent mentors and advisers to them. There was talk about socialism, about the possibilities of a third party in American politics, of the mobilization of the working class, and even of the prospects of revolution in America—painfully familiar talk to me that I had, however, scarcely heard for over a decade. One of the larger groups invited me to give a public lecture. Possessing a rooted inclination to try to tell audiences what I think they don't want to hear, I proceeded to argue that the working class had clearly failed to fulfill its Marxist mission as a revolutionary or even a socialist force and was likely, if anything, to become more conservative in the future; that the main hope for social reform in America was to build a coalition of different groups uniting on limited objectives within the Democratic Party; and that talk of revolution in advanced industrial countries with democratic governments was altogether vain and self-indulgent. To cap my argument, I asked, in tones of withering contempt, a rhetorical question: "Just *who* is going to make this revolution—the graduate students?" As we poured out of the hall into Sproul Plaza, I did not imagine that I would get a kind of an answer right on that very spot only two years later: "Yes, the graduate students—why not?"

I said that I used to tell this story on myself, for I obviously had no idea at the time that students right there in Berkeley would be so quixotic as to try to make a revolution whatever the odds against success, or that their example would spread like wildfire in the late sixties to other campuses, including some in the East, or even that the sixties would witness a striking revival of radicalism in which "revolution" would once again become a "god-term." However, telling this story in 1974 rather than in 1969, I'm not so sure it is so unmistakably "on" me. For, after all, I was right in most of what I said about the prospects for change by political action in America. This is clear for all to see now that we are well into the 1970s, with the reelection by a landslide of Richard Nixon marking an appropriate symbolic divide from the fevered hopes and dreams of the sixties.

Only a few years ago it was the routine practice of radical and some not-so-radical sociologists to jeer at the "end of ideology" writers for having failed to foresee the turmoil and social conflicts of the sixties. The ritual slaying of Seymour Martin Lipset or Daniel Bell was a ubiquitous ceremony at conclaves of *engagé* sociologists. Now, I happen to have been one of the first people to criticize in print—in 1960 no less—the end-of-ideology argument,[7] and I certainly do not feel it necessary to shed any tears today over those who propounded it for the obloquy to which they were subjected. Several of them are, after all, tenured professors at Harvard, and all of them have been considerably more productive and individually eminent than most of their detractors, even if Seymour Martin Lipset has failed to be elected president of the American Sociological Association. But it is at least worth pointing out that the end-of-ideology sociologists were in large measure right about politics in contemporary America, a vindication by subsequent events that their erstwhile critics are unlikely to grant them.

On the other hand, one doubts that those who foresaw just a few years ago the "greening of America," or the triumph of the "psychedelic culture," or the imminence of a new "irrepressible conflict" between the "slave" mentality of the "old culture" and the "freedom" of the new "counterculture," will have *their* statements held up to ridicule as Bell's and Lipset's were in the sixties, now that it is evident that the revolution has been called off on account of lack of support, even from the constituencies that were supposed to spearhead it. Few of those committed to an activist sociology are likely to be as candid as one of our very best sociologists, Barrington Moore, Jr., a neo-Marxist of sorts and an early sympathizer with student radicals on his own campus, who recently observed: "The men of action and conviction have failed enough of late to warrant reversing a famous apothegm of Marx: philosophers have tried to change the world; now it is time to try to understand it." [8]

The conservative is undoubtedly prone to eternalize the present because he likes it, but the radical is guilty of a variant of the same fallacy. He projects present tendencies he favors forward to a grand apocalyptic climax: revolution leading to the emergence of an unspecified "better society," or, in a catastrophist version, the triumph of reaction—"fascism"—as a prelude to the eventual revolt of vastly expanded numbers of the oppressed and victimized. That revolutions are rare events and most attempts to make them fail ignominiously; that protest movements wane as well as wax, especially when their minimal demands are granted and appease their followers; that the fate of most new emancipating ideas or cultural creations is what Harold Lasswell once called "acceptance by partial incorporation"; that ideological movements, especially when they undergo an internal shift to greater militance and extremism, frequently evoke a countering response that strengthens and solidifies their opponents— all of these not-altogether-novel sociological truths were overlooked by those who thought they saw the wave of the future in the New Left, or the counterculture, or the student rebellion, or even the New Politics. [9]

In sociology, a highly sophisticated theoretical perspective that bridges the gap between understanding social reality and political engagement has recently become popular. Let us examine its bearing on forecasting the future. The future, this view holds, is determined by no laws comparable to the laws discovered by the natural sciences because human affairs are not reducible to the models of explanation and prediction that have proved so successful in the natural sciences. There is therefore no warrant for historial inevitabilism: the future is yet to be created, or "socially constructed," by the consciousness and action of men in the present. The views we now take of the future will themselves shape what it will be. They may very well turn out to be gloriously self-fulfilling if we have sufficient faith that we can forge a new world closer to our heart's desire, or they may be happily self-defeating if our forebodings of Doomsday are widely heeded. To say, therefore, that the future will resemble the past is to help guarantee that it will, and amounts to a defeatist, or pessimistic, or plain de facto conservative attitude from the standpoint of utopian possibility. This outlook grounds itself in "social construction of reality" theories and in the more voluntaristic brands of neo-Marxism in contemporary sociology. An extreme conclusion to be drawn from it is that *all* statements about the future—indeed all statements about social reality—are inescapably political, since the impact of such statements will either create a new future or reproduce existing social realities. There is therefore no nonpolitical sociology, and we might as well try to persuade people to create a future that will "realize" our own values and make this our primary aim as sociologists. Some call this the "unity of theory and practice" (or praxis).

I think this view is dangerously mistaken, although I agree that there are not now and never will be known laws from which we can deduce the future, and that the statements of sociologists are part of and will affect the situations they are observing and trying to understand. It is a wrong view because it ignores the inescapable tension between truth, or rather truth-telling, and the requirements of action, or of politics. As that very great lady, Hannah Arendt, has pointed out, there is an affinity between the liar and the political actor: "the liar . . . is a man of action . . . he says what is not so because he wants things to be different from what they are—that is, he wants to change the world. . . . That we can change the circumstances under which we live at all is because we are relatively free from them, and it is this freedom that is abused and perverted through mendacity." [10]

We know that futures—every past and present was once someone's future—rarely if ever correspond to the intended or desired outcomes sought by those who made them. My words about the future, my expressed optimism or pessimism, the implicit support I may lend to conservative or radical political actors, are not likely to shape definitively the future in their image. Neither I, nor any sociologist, nor all sociologists together, have *that* much influence or power, though we have some. I choose therefore to be a truth-teller rather than a political actor; to quote Arendt again, "to look upon politics from the perspective of truth . . . means to take one's stand outside the political realm. This standpoint is the standpoint of the truthteller who forfeits his position—and, with it, the validity of what he has to say—if he tries to interfere directly in human affairs and to speak the language of persuasion or of violence": [11] if, in other words, he commits himself to making the truths he proclaims become flesh in the future in addition to performing his primary task of discovering and articulating truths about the world. I think it is the collective mission of the social sciences to try to tell the truth as such, even in full awareness that the truths they announce have political consequences that will help to shape the future.

Yet the commitment to truth-telling, to the telling of truths that are, in Max Weber's words, "inconvenient for . . . party opinions," [12] including one's own party opinion, plays a role itself in the political process. For, as Arendt recognizes, the most committed political actors have often acknowledged the need for institutions—she mentions the judiciary and the universities—that strive, however often they may fail, to stand "outside the power struggle." Note how eager partisans are to seize upon and make use of the statements of officially nonpartisan arbiters, whether garbed in the robes of justice or of science or scholarship, to fortify their own case, a tactic that would be unavailable to them if everyone became an open, acknowledged partisan. (The Watergate crisis provides ample reminders in this regard.) More important, however, "at least in constitutionally ruled countries, the political realm has recognized, even in the event of conflict, that it has a stake in the existence of men and institutions over which it has no power." [13] I believe sociologists should strive to be such an institution, especially when engaged in efforts to assess the future. That is why labels such as Radical Sociology, and even its weaker sisters Critical or Transcendental Sociology, impress me as amounting to contradictions in terms.

Notes

Prologue: On Skeptical Sociology

1. C. Wright Mills, *The Sociological Imagination* (New York: Oxford University Press, 1959), p. 19.

2. Anthony Giddens, ed., *Positivism and Sociology* (London: Heinemann, 1974), p. 2. Giddens defines positivism in sociology as consisting of three propositions: "1. That the *methodological* procedures of natural science may be directly adapted to sociology [since] . . . the phenomena of human subjectivity, of volition and will, do not offer any particular barriers to the treatment of social conduct as an 'object' on a par with objects in the natural world. 2. That the *outcome* or end-result of sociological investigations can be formulated in terms parallel to those of natural science: that is to say, that the goal of sociological analysis can and must be to formulate 'laws' or 'law-like' generalizations of the same kind as those which have been established in relation to natural reality. 3. That sociology has a *technical* character, providing knowledge which is purely 'instrumental' in form; in other words, that the findings of sociological research do not carry any logically given implications for practical policy or for the pursuit of values. Sociology, like natural science, is 'neutral' in respect of values." Ibid., pp. 3–4; italics in text.

3. Herbert Marcuse, *One-Dimensional Man* (Boston: Beacon Press, 1964), pp. 120, 123.

4. Alvin W. Gouldner, *For Sociology* (New York: Basic Books, 1974), p. 58.

5. Henry Pachter, "On Being an Exile," in Robert Boyers, ed., *The Legacy of the German Refugee Intellectuals*, special issue of *Salmagundi* (Fall 1969–Winter 1970), p. 36; Martin Jay, *The Dialectical Imagination* (Boston: Little, Brown, 1973), p. 44. Critics of critical theory have charged its major proponents with reverting to the pre-Marxist idealism of the Young Hegelians. See, for example, the unjustly neglected book by Neil McInnes, *The Western Marxists* (New York: Library Press, 1972); also, Alasdair MacIntyre, *Herbert Marcuse* (New York: The Viking Press, 1970), especially chapter 3.

6. Edward Shils, "The Calling of Sociology," in Talcott Parsons, Edward Shils, Kaspar D. Naegele, Jesse R. Pitts, eds., *Theories of Society*, 2 vols. (New York: The Free Press of Glencoe, 1961), vol. 2, p. 1425.

Prologue: On Skeptical Sociology (*cont.*)

7. Jay, *The Dialectical Imagination*, pp. 293–95; H. Stuart Hughes, *The Sea Change: The Migration of Social Thought, 1930–1965* (New York: Harper and Row, 1975), p. 187.

8. Jay, *The Dialectical Imagination*, p. 279.

9. I echo here something I wrote in 1964, just before the frenzied revival of utopianism a few years later, in "Re-Imagining Society," *Commentary* 37 (April 1964), 78. This was a long review of George Kateb, *Utopia and Its Enemies* (New York: The Free Press, 1963). Other things I wrote at roughly the same time suggesting the permanent need for utopian imagination were "The Perils of Political Moderation," *Commentary* 27 (January 1959), 1–8; "Reflections on the End of Ideology," *Dissent* 7 (Summer 1960), 286–91; "The Cold War and the West," *Partisan Review* 29 (Summer 1962), 89 (contribution to a symposium). George Kateb, incidentally, in a new preface to a paperback edition of *Utopia and Its Enemies* (New York: Schocken Books, 1972), expresses some second thoughts about utopianism in the wake of its revival in the 1960s, writing: "It may be that the world has grown so rich in actuality and near-actuality that any effort to legislate for a whole society, in the name of utopia, impoverishes the sense of life. The very wish to compose a utopia, to set forth in detail a utopian way of life, may in fact be repressive."

10. Norman O. Brown, *Life against Death* (Middletown, Conn.: Wesleyan University Press, 1959).

11. Saul Bellow, *Mr. Sammler's Planet* (New York: Fawcett World Library, 1970), p. 34.

12. See chapter 14 in this volume.

13. Walter Benjamin, "Theses on the Philosophy of History," in Benjamin, *Illuminations* (New York: Harcourt, Brace and World, 1968), pp. 259–60. I have used the translated version that appears on the title page of George Lichtheim, *Europe in the Twentieth Century* (New York: Praeger, 1972).

14. The *locus classicus* for discussion of the conservative pedigree of sociology has recently become Robert Nisbet, *The Sociological Tradition* (New York: Basic Books, 1966), although I am not alone in thinking that Nisbet overstates the impact of Counter-Enlightenment thought on classical sociology. For a short recent statement that stresses the dual heritage of sociology, see Alan Dawe, "The Two Sociologies," in Kenneth Thompson and Jeremy Tunstall, eds., *Sociological Perspectives* (Harmondsworth, Middlesex: Penguin Books, 1971), pp. 542–54. See also Anthony Giddens, "Classical Social Theory and the Origins of Modern Sociology," *American Journal of Sociology* 81 (January 1976), 710–14.

15. Jay, *The Dialectical Imagination*, pp. 56, 262. Herbert Marcuse, however, in contrast to Adorno and Horkheimer, has not observed their reticence about describing utopia in either *Eros and Civilization* (Boston: Beacon Press, 1955) or *An Essay on Liberation* (Boston: Beacon Press, 1969). See Jay's article, "The Metapolitics of Utopianism," *Dissent* 17 (July–August, 1970), 342–50.

16. "The Functional Theory of Stratification: Some Neglected Considerations," included in this volume as chapter 6, was a contribution—neither the first nor the last—to this debate. Although he wishes to dissociate himself from the functionalist arguments of several of the debaters on both sides, Ralf Dahrendorf's "On the Origin of Inequality among Men," in Dahrendorf, *Essays on the Theory of Society* (Stanford: Stanford University Press, 1968), pp. 151–78, is essentially a continuation of this debate.

17. James Joyce, *Ulysses* (New York: Random House, Modern Library ed., 1967), pp. 20–21.

18. Raymond Aron, *Main Currents in Sociological Thought* (New York: Basic Books, 1967), vol. 2, p. 245.

19. Leo Strauss, *Natural Right and History* (Chicago: University of Chicago Press, 1953), p. 48.

20. Sigmund Freud, *Civilization and Its Discontents* (New York: W. W. Norton, 1961), p. 92.

21. Max Weber, "Science as a Vocation," in H. H. Gerth and C. Wright Mills, eds., *From Max Weber: Essays in Sociology* (New York: Oxford University Press, 1946), pp. 155–56.

Part One: Introduction

1. A history of the entire debate, including my own contribution to it, may be found in Robert W. Friedrichs, *A Sociology of Sociology* (New York: The Free Press, 1970), chapter 2.

2. Talcott Parsons, "Individual Autonomy and Social Pressure: An Answer to Dennis Wrong," *Psychoanalysis and The Psychoanalytic Review* 4 (Summer 1962), 70–79.

3. Robert Nisbet's first book was entitled *The Quest for Community* (New York: Oxford University Press, 1953). Allen Wheelis wrote *The Quest for Identity* (New York: W. W. Norton, 1958). Both books were fairly widely discussed beyond the circle of professional social scientists.

4. William M. Dobriner, *Class and Suburbia* (Englewood Cliffs, N.J.: Prentice-Hall, 1963), p. 57.

5. Kenneth Keniston, *The Uncommitted: Alienated Youth in American Society* (New York: Dell, 1967).

One. C. Wright Mills and the Sociological Imagination

1. C. Wright Mills, *The Sociological Imagination* (New York: Oxford University Press, 1959).

2. Max Weber, "Science as a Vocation," in H. H. Gerth and C. Wright Mills, eds., *From Max Weber: Essays in Sociology* (New York: Oxford University Press, 1946), p. 135.

One. C. Wright Mills and the Sociological Imagination (*cont.*)

3. Mills, *The Sociological Imagination*, p. 105.
4. Talcott Parsons, "The Distribution of Power in American Society," in *Structure and Process in Modern Societies* (Glencoe, Ill.: The Free Press, 1960), p. 220. (Parsons's discussion was originally published in *World Politics*, October 1957).
5. Ibid., p. 222.
6. George Lichtheim, "Rethinking World Politics," *Commentary* 28 (September 1959), 255–57.
7. Hans Gerth and C. Wright Mills, *Character and Social Structure* (New York: Harcourt, Brace, 1953), pp. xiii–xiv.
8. Philip Selznick, review, *American Sociological Review* 19 (August 1954), 485–86.
9. Mills, *The Sociological Imagination*, p. 134.
10. Ibid., p. 215.
11. Nikolai Gogol, *Dead Souls* (2 vols in 1; New York: Random House, Modern Library, 1923), vol. 2, p. 171.

Two. The Oversocialized Conception of Man in Modern Society

1. Barrington Moore, Jr., *Political Power and Social Theory* (Cambridge: Harvard University Press, 1958); C. Wright Mills, *The Sociological Imagination* (New York: Oxford University Press, 1959).
2. Hannah Arendt, "Understanding and Politics," *Partisan Review* 20 (July–August 1953), 392. For a view of social theory close to the one adumbrated in the present paper, see Theodore Abel, "The Present Status of Social Theory," *American Sociological Review* 17 (April 1952), 156–64.
3. Reinhard Bendix and Bennett Berger, "Images of Society and Problems of Concept Formation in Sociology," in Llewellyn Gross, ed., *Symposium on Sociological Theory* (Evanston, Ill.: Row, Peterson, 1959), pp. 92–118; Lewis A. Coser, *The Functions of Social Conflict* (Glencoe, Ill.: The Free Press, 1956); Ralf Dahrendorf, "Out of Utopia: Towards a Re-Orientation of Sociological Analysis," *American Journal of Sociology* 64 (September 1958), 115–27; and *Class and Class Conflict in Industrial Society* (Stanford: Stanford University Press, 1959); David Lockwood, "Some Remarks on 'The Social System,' " *British Journal of Sociology* 7 (June 1956), 134–46.
4. Talcott Parsons, *The Structure of Social Action* (New York: McGraw-Hill, 1937), pp. 89–94.
5. Coser, *The Functions of Social Conflict*, p. 21; Mills, *The Sociological Imagination*, p. 44.
6. A recent critic of Parsons follows Hobbes in seeing the relation between the normative order in society and what he calls "the sub-stratum of social action" and

other sociologists have called the "factual order" as similar to the relation between the war of all against all and the authority of the state. David Lockwood writes: "The existence of the normative order . . . is in one very important sense inextricably bound up with potential conflicts of interest over scarce resources . . . ; the very existence of a normative order mirrors the continual potentiality of conflict." Lockwood, "Some Remarks on 'The Social System,' " p. 137.

7. R. G. Collingwood, *The New Leviathan* (Oxford: The Clarendon Press, 1942), p. 183.

8. Francis X. Sutton et al., *The American Business Creed* (Cambridge: Harvard University Press, 1956), p. 304. I have cited this study and, on several occasions, textbooks and fugitive articles rather than better-known and directly theoretical writings because I am just as concerned with what sociological concepts and theories are taken to mean when they are actually used in research, teaching, and introductory exposition as with their elaboration in more self-conscious and explicitly theoretical discourse. Since the model of human nature I am criticizing is partially implicit and "buried" in our concepts, cruder and less qualified illustrations are as relevant as the formulations of leading theorists. I am also aware that some older theorists, notably Cooley and MacIver, were shrewd and worldly-wise enough to reject the implication that man is ever fully socialized. Yet they failed to develop competing images of man which were concise and systematic enough to counter the appeal of the oversocialized models.

9. Collingwood, *The New Leviathan*, pp. 181–82.

10. Cf. Mills, *The Sociological Imagination*, pp. 32–33, 42. While Mills does not discuss the use of the concept of internalization by Parsonian theorists, I have argued elsewhere that his view of the relation between power and values is insufficiently dialectical. See "C. Wright Mills and the Sociological Imagination" in this volume.

11. Parsons, *The Structure of Social Action*, pp. 378–90.

12. Ibid., p. 382.

13. Harry M. Johnson, *Sociology: A Systematic Introduction* (New York: Harcourt, Brace, 1960), p. 22.

14. Sigmund Freud, *Civilization and Its Discontents* (New York: Doubleday, Anchor Books), 1958, pp. 80–81.

15. Paul Kecskemeti, *Meaning, Communication, and Value* (Chicago: University of Chicago Press, 1952), pp. 244–45.

16. Robert Dubin, "Deviant Behavior and Social Structure: Continuities in Social Theory," *American Sociological Review* 24 (April 1959), 147–64; Robert K. Merton, "Social Conformity, Deviation, and Opportunity Structures: A Comment on the Contributions of Dubin and Cloward," ibid., pp. 178–89.

17. Abram Kardiner, *The Individual and His Society* (New York: Columbia University Press, 1939), pp. 65, 72–75.

18. Mills, *The Sociological Imagination*, pp. 39–41; Dahrendorf, *Class and Class Conflict*, pp. 157–65.

19. Freud, *Civilization and Its Discontents*, pp. 78–79.

Two. The Oversocialized Conception of Man in
Modern Society (*cont.*)

20. Sutton, et al., *The American Business Creed*, p. 264.

21. Robert Cooley Angell, *Free Society and Moral Crisis* (Ann Arbor: University of Michigan Press, 1958), p. 34.

22. Ralph Linton, *The Cultural Background of Personality* (New York: Appleton-Century, 1945), p. 91.

23. On this point see Robert Gutman and Dennis H. Wrong, "Riesman's Typology of Character," in Seymour Martin Lipset and Leo Lowenthal, eds., *Culture and Social Character* (New York: The Free Press, 1961), pp. 302–11; and William H. Whyte, *The Organization Man* (New York: Simon and Schuster, 1956), chapters 3–5.

24. See David Riesman, Nathan Glazer, and Reuel Denny, *The Lonely Crowd* (New York: Doubleday, Anchor Books, 1953), pp. 17 ff.

25. Gutman and Wrong, "Riesman's Typology of Character," p. 298.

26. Hans L. Zetterberg, "Compliant Actions," *Acta Sociologia* 2 (1957), 189.

27. Ibid., p. 188.

28. Ibid., p. 189.

29. Dahrendorf, *Class and Class Conflict*, p. 158.

30. Thorstein Veblen, *The Theory of the Leisure Class* (New York: Mentor Books, 1953), p. 38.

31. Emile Durkheim, *The Rules of Sociological Method* (Chicago: University of Chicago Press, 1938), p. 71.

32. George C. Homans, *The Human Group* (New York: Harcourt, Brace, 1950), pp. 317–19.

33. Robert K. Merton, *Social Theory and Social Structure* (rev. ed.; Glencoe, Ill.: The Free Press, 1957), p. 131. Merton's view is representative of that of most contemporary sociologists. See also Hans Gerth and C. Wright Mills, *Character and Social Structure* (New York: Harcourt, Brace, 1953), pp. 112–13. For a similar view by a "neo-Freudian," see Erich Fromm, *The Sane Society* (New York: Rinehart, 1955), pp. 74–77.

34. John Dollard, *Criteria for the Life History* (New Haven: Yale University Press, 1935), p. 120. This valuable book has been neglected, presumably because it appears to be a purely methodological effort to set up standards for judging the adequacy of biographical and autobiographical data. Actually, the standards serve as well to evaluate the adequacy of general theories of personality or human nature and even to prescribe in part what a sound theory ought to include.

35. One of the few attempts by a social scientist to relate systematically man's anatomical structure and biological history to his social nature and his unique cultural creativity is Weston La Barre's *The Human Animal* (Chicago: University of Chicago Press, 1954). See especially chapters 4–6, but the entire book is relevant. It is an exception to Paul Goodman's observation that anthropologists nowadays "commence

with a chapter on Physical Anthropology and then forget the whole topic and go on to Culture." See his "Growing up Absurd," *Dissent* 7 (Spring 1960), 121.

36. Paul Goodman has developed a similar distinction. "Growing up Absurd," pp. 123–25.

37. Whether it might be possible to create a society that does not repress the bodily drives is a separate question. See Herbert Marcuse, *Eros and Civilization* (Boston: Beacon Press, 1955); and Norman O. Brown, *Life against Death* (Middletown, Conn.: Wesleyan University Press, 1959). Nether Marcuse nor Brown are guilty in their brilliant, provocative, and visionary books of assuming a "natural man" who awaits liberation from social bonds. They differ from such sociological utopians as Fromm, in *The Sane Society*, in their lack of sympathy for the desexualized man of the neo-Freudians. For the more traditional Freudian view, see Walter A. Weisskopf, "The 'Socialization' of Psychoanalysis in Contemporary America," in Benjamin Nelson, ed., *Psychoanalysis and the Future* (New York: National Psychological Association for Psychoanalysis, 1957), pp. 51–56; Hans Meyerhoff, "Freud and the Ambiguity of Culture," *Partisan Review* 24 (Winter 1957), 117–30.

38. Norman O. Brown, *Life against Death*, pp. 3–19.

Postscript 1975

1. "Human Nature and the Perspective of Sociology," included in this volume.

2. Ralf Dahrendorf, "Out of Utopia: Towards a Reorientation of Sociological Analysis," *American Journal of Sociology* 64 (September 1958), 115–27.

3. Herminio Martins, "Time and Theory in Sociology," in John Rex, ed., *Approaches to Sociology* (London and Boston: Routledge and Kegan Paul, 1974), p. 247. His observation applies to the United States as well as to Britain.

4. Peter L. Berger and Thomas Luckmann, *The Social Construction of Reality* (Garden City, N.Y.: Doubleday, 1966).

5. Aaron Cicourel, *Cognitive Sociology* (New York: The Free Press, 1974).

6. George Herbert Mead, *Mind, Self and Society* (Chicago: University of Chicago Press, 1934), p. 173.

Three. Human Nature and the Perspective of Sociology

1. See, for example, Robert Redfield, *Human Nature and the Study of Society* (Chicago: University of Chicago Press, 1962), p. 444.

2. Talcott Parsons, "Individual Autonomy and Social Pressure: An Answer to Dennis Wrong," *Psychoanalysis and The Psychoanalytic Review* 49 (Summer 1962), p. 78. My original article, "The Oversocialized Conception of Man in Modern Sociology" (included in this volume), was reprinted in the same issue of *Psychoanalysis and The Psychoanalytic Review*.

3. Barrington Moore, Jr., *Political Power and Social Theory* (Cambridge, Mass.:

Three. Human Nature and the Perspective of Sociology (*cont.*)

Harvard University Press, 1958), p. 203; Alexander Gershenkron, *Economic Back-wardness in Historical Perspective* (Cambridge, Mass.: Harvard University Press, Belknap Press, 1962), pp. 59–60.

4. William J. Goode, *After Divorce* (Glencoe, Ill.: The Free Press, 1956), p. 43.

5. See, for example, Philip M. Hauser and Otis Dudley Duncan in Hauser and Duncan, eds., *The Study of Population: An Inventory and Appraisal* (Chicago: University of Chicago Press, 1959), pp. 96–102. Hauser and Duncan maintain that efforts to investigate the motives underlying fertility behavior and migration constitute a form of "psychological reductionism . . . based on the premise that the only meaningful explanation [of demographic phenomena] is one couched in psychological terms." See my discussion of their position in a review of the book in *Social Forces* 38 (October 1959), 72–74.

6. Similar criteria are suggested by Alex Inkeles, "Psychoanalysis and Sociology," in Sidney Hook, ed., *Psychoanalysis, Scientific Method, and Philosophy* (New York: Grove Press, 1959), pp. 126–27.

7. John Dollard, *Criteria for the Life History* (New Haven: Yale University Press, 1935), p. 277.

8. Alfred Baldwin, "The Parsonian Theory of Personality," in Max Black, ed., *The Social Theories of Talcott Parsons* (Englewood Cliffs, N.J.: Prentice-Hall, 1961), pp. 153–54.

9. Hans Gerth and C. Wright Mills, *Character and Social Structure* (New York: Harcourt, Brace, 1953). Philip Selznick noted in an acute review of this book that, in spite of the claims of distinctiveness the authors make for their point of view, they actually differ little from other sociologists in their basic conceptions; *American Sociological Review* 19 (August 1954), pp. 485–86.

10. W. H. Walsh notes that historians take for granted certain propositions, certain "basic beliefs," which play a leading role in their interpretations. ". . . There is the problem of how the historian comes by these basic beliefs. The obvious answer would be 'from the recognized authorities on the subject,' i.e., from those who make it their business to study human nature in the modern sciences of psychology and sociology. But the puzzle is that there are plenty of competent historians, men whose judgments of particular historical situations can be trusted, who are largely ignorant of those sciences, their methods and results. They apparently know a great deal about human nature and can make good use of their knowledge, though they have never made a formal study of the human mind or of the general characteristics of human society." *An Introduction to the Philosophy of History* (London: Hutchinson University Library, 1951), p. 66.

11. Dollard, *Criteria for the Life History*, pp. 17–18.

12. Gresham M. Sykes and David Matza, "Techniques of Neutralization," *American Sociological Review* 22 (December 1957), 664–70; David Matza and Gresham M. Sykes, "Juvenile Delinquency and Subterranean Values," *American Sociological Review* 26 (October 1961), 712–19.

13. The best analysis I know of the difference between the perspective of the sociologist and that of the psychiatrist is Reinhard Bendix, "Compliant Behavior and Individual Personality," *American Journal of Sociology* 58 (November 1952), 292–95.

14. Robert S. Lynd, *Knowledge for What?* (Princeton, N.J.: Princeton University Press, 1939), p. 41.

15. Tamotsu Shibutani, *Society and Personality* (Englewood Cliffs, N.J.: Prentice-Hall, 1961), especially pp. 139–75; Ralph H. Turner, "Role-Taking: Process Versus Conformity," in Arnold M. Rose, ed., *Human Behavior and Social Processes* (Boston: Houghton Mifflin, 1962), pp. 20–38; Herbert Blumer, "Society as Symbolic Interaction," in ibid., pp. 186–92.

16. George Herbert Mead, *Mind, Self and Society* (Chicago: University of Chicago Press, 1934), p. 173.

17. Blumer, "Society as Symbolic Interaction." See also Blumer, "The Psychological Import of the Human Group," in Muzafer Sherif, ed., *Group Relations at the Crossroads* (New York: Harper and Brothers, 1953), pp. 185–202; and Blumer, "Attitudes and the Social Act," *Social Problems* 3 (October 1955), 59–65.

18. The term is Erving Goffman's; *Encounters* (Indianapolis: Bobbs-Merrill, 1961), p. 96.

19. Parsons, "Individual Autonomy and Social Pressure," p. 77.

20. Max Weber, *The Methodology of the Social Sciences* (Glencoe, Ill.: The Free Press, 1949), 159–60. Talcott Parsons has ably summarized this argument of Weber's, though, not surprisingly, he expresses disagreement with it, in *The Structure of Social Action* (New York: McGraw-Hill, 1937), pp. 591–601. See also Barrington Moore, Jr.'s sympathetic restatement of Weber's position in *Political Power and Social Theory*, pp. 145–46. Weber's argument, of course, derives from that of H. Rickert.

21. The phrase is Moore's, ibid., p. 113.

Four. The Idea of Community: A Critique

1. See, for example, Robert Nisbet, *The Quest for Community* (New York: Oxford University Press, 1953); Maurice R. Stein, *The Eclipse of Community* (Princeton, N.J.: Princeton University Press, 1960).

2. Hannah Arendt, *Between Past and Future* (New York: The Viking Press), 1961, p. 140.

3. Daniel Bell, *The End of Ideology* (Glencoe, Ill.: The Free Press, 1960), p. 35.

4. See, for example, Everett K. Wilson, "Conformity Revisited," *Trans-Action* 2 (November–December 1964), 28–32, and the rebuttals to Wilson by Dennis H. Wrong and Ernest van den Haag in the same issue, pp. 33–36.

5. William J. Newman, *The Futilitarian Society* (New York: George Braziller, 1960), p. 355.

6. Stein, *The Eclipse of Community*, p. 248.

Four. The Idea of Community: A Critique (*cont.*)

7. An account of sociology's conservative intellectual pedigree is Robert Nisbet, *The Sociological Tradition* (New York: Basic Books, 1966).

8. Raymond Williams, *Culture and Society* (Garden City, N.Y.: Doubleday, Anchor Books, 1960), p. 277.

9. Quoted by Williams, ibid., p. 279.

10. Stein, *The Eclipse of Community*, p. 248.

11. Erich Kahler, *The Tower and the Abyss* (New York: George Braziller, 1957), p. 87.

Five. Identity: Problem and Catchword

1. Erik H. Erikson, *Identity, Youth and Crisis* (New York: W. W. Norton, 1968).

2. Ibid., pp. 28–29.

3. E. V. Walter, "Mass Society: The Late Stages of an Idea," *Social Research* 31 (Winter 1964), 409–410.

4. Erikson, *Identity, Youth and Crisis*, p. 228.

5. Ibid., p. 230.

6. Erving Goffman uses the term "situated roles" in *Encounters* (Indianapolis: Bobbs-Merrill, 1961), p. 96.

7. Thomas Luckmann and Peter Berger, "Social Mobility and Personal Identity," *European Journal of Sociology* 5 (1964), 331–44.

8. Erikson, *Identity, Youth and Crisis*, pp. 158–59.

9. Ibid., p. 159.

10. Ibid.

11. Ibid., p. 209.

12. Ibid., p. 208.

13. Ibid., p. 314.

14. Jean-Paul Sartre, *Being and Nothingness* (New York: Philosophical Library, 1956), p. 59.

15. Ibid.

16. John H. Schaar, *Escape from Authority* (New York: Harper Torchbooks, 1964), p. 225.

17. Maurice R. Stein, *The Eclipse of Community* (Princeton: Princeton University Press, 1960), p. 248.

18. Erikson, *Identity, Youth and Crisis*, p. 295.

19. Ibid., p. 304.

20. See Ellison's intense discussion of this issue in *Shadow and Act* (New York: Random House, 1964), especially in the essay "The World and the Jug," pp. 107–43.

21. Luckmann and Berger, "Social Mobility and Personal Identity," pp. 338–39. The concept of "anticipatory socialization" was first introduced by Robert K. Merton and Alice S. Rossi. See Merton, *Social Theory and Social Structure* (rev. ed.; New York: The Free Press, 1957), pp. 265–68.

22. Phillipe Aries, *Centuries of Childhood* (New York: Alfred A. Knopf, 1962), pp. 207, 411–15; Philip Mason, *Prospero's Magic: Some Thoughts on Class and Race* (New York and Toronto: Oxford University Press, 1962).

23. Robert K. Merton, *Mass Persuasion* (New York: Harper and Brothers, 1946), p. 142.

24. Hannah Arendt, *The Human Condition* (Chicago: University of Chicago Press, 1958), p. 322.

25. Herbert Marcuse, *One-Dimensional Man* (Boston: Beacon Press, 1964), pp. 252–53.

26. Max Weber, "Science as a Vocation," in H. H. Gerth and C. Wright Mills, eds., *From Max Weber: Essays in Sociology* (New York: Oxford University Press, 1946), p. 139.

27. George Orwell, *The Road to Wigan Pier* (New York: Berkeley Medallion Books, 1961), p. 167.

28. Goffman, *Encounters*, pp. 85–152.

Part Two: Introduction

1. Celia S. Heller, ed., *Structured Social Inequality* (New York: Macmillan 1969), p. 482.

2. Ibid., p. 4 (italics in text).

3. Kingsley Davis, "The Myth of Functional Analysis in Sociology and Anthropology," *American Sociological Review* 24 (December 1959), 757–72.

4. Dennis H. Wrong, "All Men Are Equal but Some . . ." *Dissent* 7 (Spring 1960), 207–10.

5. Dennis H. Wrong, "Ontario's Jews in the Larger Community," in Albert Rose, ed., *A People and Its Faith: Essays on Jews and Reform Judaism in a Changing Canada* (Toronto: University of Toronto Press, 1959), pp. 45–59; and "The Psychology of Prejudice and the Future of Anti-Semitism in America," *European Journal of Sociology* 6 (1965), 311–28. A slightly different version of this last article was also printed in Charles Herbert Stember et al., *Jews in the Mind of America* (New York: Basic Books, 1966), pp. 323–40.

6. Irving Howe, ed., *The World of the Blue Collar Worker* (New York: Quadrangle Books, 1972).

Six. The Functional Theory of Stratification: Some Neglected Considerations

1. Walter Buckley, "Social Stratification and the Functional Theory of Social Differentiation," *American Sociological Review* 23 (August 1958), 369–75.

2. Kingsley Davis, "The Abominable Heresy: A Reply to Dr. Buckley," *American Sociological Review* 24 (February 1959), 82–83.

3. Richard L. Simpson, "A Modification of the Functional Theory of Social Stratification," *Social Forces* 35 (December 1956), 132.

4. Melvin M. Tumin, "Some Principles of Stratification: A Critical Analysis,"

Six. The Functional Theory of Stratification:
Some Neglected Considerations (cont.)

American Sociological Review 18 (August 1953), 390. Davis replies that Tumin ignores the "onerous necessity of studying," but no such defense is required to uphold his theory. Davis, "Reply," *American Sociological Review* 18 (August 1953), 396.

5. G. L. Arnold (George Lichtheim), "Collectivism Reconsidered," *British Journal of Sociology* 6 (March 1955), 9.

6. Barrington Moore, Jr., *Political Power and Social Theory* (Cambridge: Harvard University Press, 1958), p. 137.

7. E. Digby Baltzell, *Philadelphia Gentlemen: The Making of a National Upper Class* (Glencoe, Ill.: The Free Press, 1958), pp. 1, 396.

8. Marx's view is stated most succinctly in *The Critique of the Gotha Programme*, part I, point 3, any edition.

9. See, e.g., Talcott Parsons, "A Revised Analytical Approach to the Theory of Social Stratification," in R. Bendix and S. M. Lipset, eds., *Class, Status, and Power* (Glencoe, Ill.: The Free Press, 1953), pp. 92–128; Bernard Barber, *Social Stratification* (New York: Harcourt, Brace, 1957), pp. 1–16.

10. Tumin, "Some Principles of Stratification: A Critical Analysis," p. 391.

11. Melvin M. Tumin, "Reply to Kingsley Davis," *American Sociological Review*, 18 (December 1953), 672.

12. Melvin M. Tumin, "Rewards and Task-Orientations," *American Sociological Review* 20 (August 1955), 419–23.

13. Kingsley Davis, *Human Society*, (New York: Macmillan, 1949), pp. 369–70.

14. Ibid., pp. 382–85.

15. Ibid., p. 370. See also Davis, "Reply," p. 395.

16. Joseph A. Schumpeter, *Imperialism and Social Classes* (New York: Meridian Books, 1955), p. 111. Schumpeter's brilliant essay on social classes, first published in German in 1926, encompasses nearly all of the issues raised by the participants in the debate over the functionalist theory of stratification, including those raised here.

17. Paul Kecskemeti, "The Psychological Theory of Prejudice," *Commentary* 18 (October 1954), 359–66; also Bruno Bettelheim, "Discrimination and Science," *Commentary* 21 (April 1956), pp. 384–86; and Dennis H. Wrong, "Political Bias and the Social Sciences," *Columbia University Forum* 2 (Fall 1959), 28–32.

18. For the concept of *shape* or *profile* of stratification, see Pitirim A. Sorokin, *Social Mobility* (New York: Harper and Brothers, 1927), pp. 36 ff. For the concept of *pure mobility*, see Natalie Rogoff, *Recent Trends in Occupational Mobility* (Glencoe, Ill.: The Free Press, 1953), pp. 30–31; also Ralph Ross and Ernest van den Haag, *The Fabric of Society* (New York: Harcourt, Brace, 1957), chapter 10, which contains an excellent general theoretical discussion of the different factors affecting mobility.

19. I am indebted for this (I hope) fanciful example to Russell Kirk, *Academic Freedom: An Essay in Definition* (Chicago: Regnery, 1955), pp. 170–71.

20. Kingsley Davis and Wilbert E. Moore, "Some Principles of Stratification," *American Sociological Review* 10 (April 1945), 247.

21. Baltzell, *Philadelphia Gentlemen*, pp. 4–5.

22. C. Wright Mills, "Introduction to the Mentor Edition," Thorstein Veblen, *The Theory of the Leisure Class* (New York: Mentor Books, 1953), p. xiv.

23. Representative are Karen Horney, *The Neurotic Personality of Our Time* (New York: Norton, 1937); Robert S. Lynd, *Knowledge for What?* (Princeton: Princeton University Press, 1939), esp. chapter 3; Robert K. Merton, "Social Structure and Anomie," *American Sociological Review* 3 (October 1938), 672–82. Treatments of American society in the books of Margaret Mead, Ruth Benedict, Lawrence Frank, Abram Kardiner, Elton Mayo, and others also stress this theme.

24. The only examples I have found of American sociologists who have made the general point that rapid mobility may be "dysfunctional," as distinct from noting particular unpleasant consequences of recent mobility in analyses of ethnic prejudice or of "McCarthyism," are Baltzell, *Philadelphia Gentlemen*, pp. 4–5, and Seymour Martin Lipset and Reinhard Bendix, *Social Mobility in Industrial Society* (Berkeley: University of California Press, 1959), pp. 260–65, 285–87. Lipset and Bendix mention the neglect of this topic by American sociologists and refer to an article by Melvin M. Tumin, "Some Unapplauded Consequences of Social Mobility in a Mass Society," *Social Forces* 36 (October 1957), 32–37. This article, however, is chiefly concerned with the "unapplauded" consequences of status discrepancies between high occupational position and low ethnic or kinship status, and of mobility defined in terms of consumption gains alone.

25. See Paul Kecskemeti, *Meaning, Communication and Value* (Chicago: University of Chicago Press, 1952), pp. 268–74; David Potter, *People of Plenty* (Chicago: University of Chicago Press, 1954), pp. 103–10; Peregrine Worsthorne, "The New Inequality," *Encounter* 7 (November 1956), 24–34; C. A. R. Crosland, *The Future of Socialism* (New York: Macmillan, 1957), chapter 10; Ross and van den Haag, *The Fabric of Society*, pp. 126–27, 132–34; Michael Young, *The Rise of the Meritocracy* (London: Thames and Hudson, 1958), passim; Raymond Williams, *Culture and Society, 1780–1950* (London: Chatto and Windus, 1958), pp. 331–32. Of these writers only Young is a professional sociologist by background and his entire book argues the undesirability of a society in which full equality of opportunity is institutionalized; see the review by Charles Curran in *Encounter* 12 (February 1959), 68–72, which makes precisely the Davis-Moore point that such a society is impossible because of man's "philo-progenitive" impulses.

26. All these doubts have been expressed by two or more of the writers cited in notes 24 and 25.

27. George Orwell, *1984* (New York: Harcourt, Brace, 1949), pp. 210–11.

28. Buckley, "Social Stratification," pp. 370–71.

29. See Tumin, "Some Unapplauded Consequences of Social Mobility." I have ignored in this paper the different types of mobility: occupational, status, consumption, etc. For a discussion of these, see Lipset and Bendix, *Social Mobility in Industrial Society*, pp. 269–277; also Lipset and Hans L. Zetterberg, "A Comparative Study of Social Mobility, Its Causes and Consequences," *Prod* 2 (September 1958), 7–11. The fact that England has traditionally possessed a steeper status hierarchy than the United States and one in which status distinctions are much more sharply

Six. The Functional Theory of Stratification:
Some Neglected Considerations (*cont.*)

drawn probably accounts for the greater misgivings of English social analysts about the advantages of equality of opportunity per se.

30. Inequalities of power are probably increasing as modern society becomes more bureaucratized at the same time that "consumer equality" is becoming more marked. For perceptive discussions of this trend, see Worsthorne, "The New Inequality," and Arnold, "Collectivism Reconsidered"; also G. L. Arnold, *The Pattern of World Conflict* (New York: Dial, 1955), pp. 130–31. (G. L. Arnold was a pseudonym used by George Lichtheim.)

Seven. Social Inequality without Social Stratification

1. Herbert Blumer, "What is Wrong with Social Theory?" *American Sociological Review* 19 (February 1954), 3–10.

2. Melvin M. Tumin, "Reply to Kingsley Davis," *American Sociological Review* 18 (December 1953), 372.

3. Arnold M. Rose, "The Concept of Class and American Sociology," *Social Research* 25 (Spring 1958), 53–69; Robert A. Nisbet, "The Decline and Fall of Social Class," *Pacific Sociological Review* 2 (Spring 1959), 11–17; Wilbert E. Moore, "But Some Are More Equal than Others," *American Sociological Review* 28 (February 1963), 14–15.

4. T. H. Marshall, "General Survey of Changes in Social Stratification in the Twentieth Century," in *Transactions of the Third World Congress of Sociology*, vol. 3 (International Sociological Association, 1956), pp. 1–17, included in Marshall, *Class, Citizenship, and Social Development* (Garden City, N.Y.: Doubleday, 1964), pp. 123–43; George Lichtheim, *The New Europe: Today and Tomorrow* (New York: Praeger, 1963), pp. 198–215.

5. Marshall, "General Survey of Changes," p. 15.

6. Joseph A. Schumpeter, *Imperialism and Social Classes* (New York: Meridian Books, 1955), p. 107.

7. Marshall, "General Survey of Changes," pp. 5–6; Rose, "The Concept of Class," pp. 65–69.

8. See, for example, Bernard Barber, *Social Stratification* (New York: Harcourt, Brace and World, 1957), pp. 76–77; Nelson N. Foote, et al., "Alternative Assumptions in Stratification Research," in *Transactions of the Second World Congress of Sociology*, vol. 2 (International Sociological Association, 1953), pp. 386–87.

9. As Andreas Miller has written: "A social class is a real group, set aside from its social environment by natural boundaries. . . . In a classless society one can speak of differences in social status. It would, however, be of no value to look for a class-system without differences in social status. . . . An adequate conception of the class-system can only be reached by answering the question whether the community investigated is divided into strata by clear boundaries, what is their number, location, and strength." "The Problem of Class Boundaries and Its Significance for Research

into Class Structure," in *Transactions of the Second World Congress of Sociology*, vol. 2, pp. 343, 348–49.

10. Stanislaw Ossowski, "Old Notions and New Problems: Interpretations of Social Structure in Modern Society," *Transactions of the Third World Congress of Sociology*, pp. 18–25.

11. Stanislaw Ossowski, *Class Structure in the Social Consciousness* (New York: The Free Press of Glencoe, 1963), pp. 100–18.

12. Nathan Glazer, "Ethnic Groups in America: From National Culture to Ideology," in Morroe Berger, Theodore Abel, and Charles H. Page, eds., *Freedom and Control in Modern Society* (New York: Van Nostrand, 1954), pp. 172–73.

13. Seymour Martin Lipset and Reinhard Bendix, *Social Mobility in Industrial Society* (Berkeley: University of California Press, 1959), pp. 11–75.

14. Alex Inkeles and Peter H. Rossi, "National Comparisons of Occupational Prestige," *American Journal of Sociology* 61 (January 1956), 329–39.

15. Rudolph Heberle, "Recovery of Class Theory," *Pacific Sociological Review* 2 (Spring 1959), 18–28.

16. Seymour Martin Lipset, *Political Man* (Garden City, N.Y.: Doubleday, 1960), especially chapters 9 and 13.

17. Marshall, "General Survey of Changes," p. 13.

18. Ralf Dahrendorf, *Class and Class Conflict in Industrial Society* (Stanford: Stanford University Press, 1959), especially Part Two.

19. Both Kurt B. Mayer and Lewis A. Coser have similarly criticized Dahrendorf's thesis in reviews of his book. See Mayer's review of the German edition, *American Sociological Review* 23 (October 1958), 592–93, and of the English edition, *American Sociological Review* 25 (April 1960), 288; and Coser, *American Journal of Sociology* 55 (March 1960), 520–21.

20. A study of poverty in the United States by Oscar Ornati indicates that the following were "poverty-linked characteristics" in 1960: nonwhite, female head of household, age 65 and over, age 14–24 head of household, rural farm, residence in South, non–wage earner, part-time wage earner, more than 6 children under 18, education less than 8 years. None of the groups defined by these characteristics, with the possible exception of rural farm, represents a socioeconomic class. See Oscar A. Ornati, *Poverty and Affluence: A Report on a Research Project Carried Out at the New School for Social Research* (New York: Twentieth Century Fund, 1966), chapter 5. For a discussion of the nonclass nature of contemporary American poverty, see Henry Pachter, "The Income Revolution," *Dissent* 4 (Summer 1957), 315–18.

21. Rose, "The Concept of Class," p. 64.

22. See, for example, Barber, *Social Stratification*, pp. 1–16; also by the same author, "Discussion of Papers by Professor Nisbet and Professor Heberle," *Pacific Sociological Review* 2 (Spring 1959), 25–27. In answering Nisbet's argument that social classes are disappearing, Barber observes that " 'status,' or social class, is a subject that is peculiarly sociological" (my italics), although the entire point of Nisbet's paper was to distinguish between social classes and status gradations without in any way denying the prevalence or importance of the latter in American society.

23. Thus Talcott Parsons, although a close student of Max Weber's work, charges

Seven. Social Inequality without Social Stratification (*cont.*)

C. Wright Mills with employing the term "class" in a way that is "contrary to most sociological usage," despite the fact that Mills's use of the term and his formal definition of it were strictly Weberian in emphasizing the economic essence of class. See *Structure and Process in Modern Societies* (Glencoe, Ill.: The Free Press, 1960), p. 202.

24. Moore, "But Some Are More Equal than Others," pp. 14–15.

25. I am indebted to Oscar Ornati for showing me, in advance of publication, the data from a section of his *Poverty and Affluence* that indicate this to be unmistakably the case.

26. See especially Walter Buckley, "Social Stratification and the Functional Theory of Social Differentiation," *American Sociological Review* 23 (August 1958), 369–75; and Kurt B. Mayer, "The Changing Shape of the American Class Structure," *Social Research* 30 (Winter 1963), 458–68.

27. Robert E. Lane, *Political Ideology: Why the American Common Man Believes What He Does* (New York: The Free Press of Glencoe, 1962), pp. 57–81.

28. Michael Young, *The Rise of the Meritocracy: 1870–2033* (London: Thames and Hudson, 1958), passim.

29. See, however, Dennis H. Wrong, "The Functional Theory of Stratification: Some Neglected Considerations," included in this volume; and "All Men Are Equal but Some . . . ," *Dissent* 7 (Spring 1960), 207–10.

30. Several writers have recently argued that the maintenance of high rates of economic growth sets severe limits to the achievement of greater equality of condition as distinct from equality of opportunity. See Lichtheim, *The New Europe*, pp. 188–89; also, C. A. R. Crosland, *The Conservative Enemy* (New York: Schocken Books, 1962), pp. 29–34.

31. Stimson Bullitt, *To Be a Politician* (Garden City, N.Y.: Doubleday, Anchor Books, 1961), pp. 162–93.

32. Ibid., pp. 177–78.

Eight. Jews, Gentiles, and the New Establishment

1. E. Digby Baltzell, *The Protestant Establishment: Aristocracy and Caste in America* (New York: Random House, 1964).

2. Ibid., pp. 332–33.

3. Ibid., p. 333.

4. Ibid., p. 301.

5. Ibid., p. 337.

Nine. How Important Is Social Class?

1. Gerhard Lenski, "The Religious Factor in Detroit: Revisited," *American Sociological Review* 36 (February 1971), p. 50.

2. For a summary of this debate, see Dennis H. Wrong, "Suburbs and Myths of Suburbia," in Wrong and Harry L. Gracey, eds., *Readings in Introductory Sociology* (2d ed.; New York: Macmillan, 1972), pp. 305–311.

3. Nathan Glazer and Daniel Patrick Moynihan, "Introduction to the Second Edition: New York City in 1970," *Beyond the Melting Pot* (Cambridge, Mass.: MIT Press, 1970), pp. vii–viii.

4. Herbert Gans, *The Urban Villagers* (New York: Macmillan–Free Press, 1962).

5. From Peter Rossi's review of *The Urban Villagers* in the *American Journal of Sociology*, November 1964, pp. 381–82.

6. Herbert Gans, *The Levittowners* (New York: Pantheon Books, 1967).

7. Bennett Berger, *Working-Class Suburb* (Berkeley and Los Angeles: University of California Press, 1960), p. 95.

8. From Harold Wilensky's review of *Working-Class Suburb* in the *American Sociological Review* 26 (April 1961), 310–12.

9. Harold Wilensky, "Class, Class Consciousness and American Workers," in William Haber, ed., *Labor in a Changing America* (New York: Basic Books, 1966), pp. 12–28.

10. See Guenther Roth, *The Social Democrats in Imperial Germany* (Totowa, N.J.: Bedminster Press, 1963).

11. Stanislaw Ossowski, *Class Structure in the Social Consciousness* (New York: Macmillan–Free Press, 1963).

12. Frank Tannenbaum, *A Philosophy of Labor* (New York: Alfred A. Knopf, 1951).

13. Milton Gordon, *Assimilation in American Life* (New York: Oxford University Press, 1964).

14. Andrew M. Greeley, *Why Can't They Be Like Us?* (New York: E. P. Dutton, 1971), p. 40.

15. Ibid., p. 86.

16. Glazer and Moynihan, *Beyond the Melting Pot*, pp. xxxiv–xxxv.

17. Christopher Lasch, *The Agony of the American Left* (New York: Alfred A. Knopf, 1969), p. 133. For a critique, see Dennis H. Wrong, "Radical Agonies," *Commentary* 48 (July 1969), 59–62.

18. For a brief summary of the evidence, see Seymour Martin Lipset and Earl Raab, "The Non-Generation Gap," *Commentary* 50 (August 1970), 35–39.

19. Greeley, *Why Can't They Be Like Us?*, pp. 98–99; Warren Bennis and Philip E. Slater, *The Temporary Society* (New York: Harper and Row, 1968); Robert Jay Lifton, *History and Human Survival* (New York: Random House, 1970), chapter 15; William Irwin Thompson, *At the Edge of History* (New York: Harper and Row, 1971), chapter 1.

20. Nathan Glazer, *The Social Basis of American Communism* (New York: Harcourt, Brace and World, 1961), chapter 2.

21. James Weinstein, *The Decline of Socialism in America, 1912–1925* (New York: Random House, 1967), p. 328.

Part Three: Introduction

1. Robert L. Heilbroner, "Counterrevolutionary America," *Commentary*, 43 (April 1967), 31–38.

2. The exchange from *Dissent* with the addition of Heilbroner's original *Commentary* article appeared, however, in Irving Howe, ed., *A Dissenter's Guide to Foreign Policy* (Garden City, N.Y.: Doubleday, 1968), pp. 241–82.

3. "Robert L. Heilbroner Replies," *Dissent* 14 (November–December 1967), 738.

4. Robert L. Heilbroner, *An Inquiry into the Human Prospect* (New York: W. W. Norton, 1974).

5. Kingsley Davis, "Population Policy: Will Current Programs Succeed?" *Science* 158 (November 10, 1967), 730–39.

6. Lewis A. Coser and Irving Howe, eds., *The New Conservatives: A Critique from the Left* (New York: Quadrangle Books, 1974).

7. Nathan Glazer, review of Coser and Howe, *The New Conservatives*, *Contemporary Sociology* 4 (July 1975), 447.

8. "Max Weber: the Scholar as Hero," *Columbia University Forum* 5 (Summer 1962), 30–37.

9. Martin Green, *The von Richthofen Sisters* (New York: Basic Books, 1974).

10. "Introduction," Dennis H. Wrong, ed., *Max Weber* (Englewood Cliffs, N.J.: Prentice-Hall, 1970), pp. 58–69.

Ten. Problems in Defining Power

1. Geoffrey Gorer quoted by Erich Fromm, *Escape from Freedom* (New York: Farrar and Rinehart, 1941), n. 6, p. 157.

2. Gilbert Ryle, *The Concept of Mind* (New York: Barnes and Noble, 1949), pp. 116–25.

3. Thomas Hobbes, *Leviathan*, Parts I and II (Indianapolis: Bobbs-Merrill, 1958), p. 78.

4. Bertrand Russell, *Power: A New Social Analysis* (London: George Allen and Unwin, 1938), p. 25.

5. Ryle, *The Concept of Mind*, p. 117.

6. See especially the passages in *Power: A New Social Analysis*, pp. 21–22, referring to and generalizing from Bruno Mussolini's account of his air-bombing of villages in the Abyssinian war.

7. For example, John McDermott, "Technology: The Opiate of the Intellectuals," *New York Review of Books*, July 31, 1969, pp. 25–35.

8. Lasswell and Kaplan also accept with modification Russell's definition; see Harold Lasswell and Abraham Kaplan, *Power and Society* (New Haven: Yale University Press, 1950), pp. 75–76.

9. See "The Oversocialized Conception of Man in Modern Sociology" in this volume.

10. R. G. Collingwood, *The New Leviathan* (Oxford: The Clarendon Press, 1942), p. 176.

11. Robert A. Dahl and Charles Lindblom, *Politics, Economics and Welfare* (New York: Harper and Brothers, 1953), pp. 99–104.

12. Robert K. Merton, *Social Theory and Social Structure* (rev. ed.; New York: The Free Press, 1957), p. 68. Several writers have defined power in such a way as to include explicitly *unintended* effects on others, such as Felix Oppenheim, *Dimensions of Freedom: An Analysis* (New York: St. Martin's Press, 1961), pp. 92–95 and J. A. A. Van Doorn, "Sociology and the Problem of Power," *Sociologia Neerlandica* 1 (Winter 1962–63), 12. The majority of the authors cited in this chapter, however, as well as many others, have implicitly or explicitly restricted the term power to *intentional* influence on others. See the discussion by P. H. Partridge, "Some Notes on the Concept of Power," *Political Studies* 11 (June 1963), 113–15.

13. Ryle, *The Concept of Mind*, p. 116.

14. See the full discussion of this distinction by Oppenheim, *Dimensions of Freedom*, pp. 100–2.

15. See the discussion of this distinction by Van Doorn, "Sociology and the Problem of Power," pp. 8–10.

16. Carl J. Friedrich, *Constitutional Government and Politics* (New York: Harper and Brothers, 1937), pp. 16–18; for a later and fuller discussion, see Friedrich's *Man and Government* (New York: McGraw-Hill, 1963), pp. 199–215.

17. Robert Bierstedt, "An Analysis of Social Power," *American Sociological Review* 15 (December 1950), 735.

18. Max Weber, *Economy and Society*, Guenther Roth and Claus Wittich, eds., 3 vols., (New York: Bedminster Press, 1968), vol. 1, p. 53.

19. Arnold M. Rose notes that many social scientists have in effect taken this position without consistently committing themselves to its implications. Rose, *The Power Structure: Political Process in American Society* (New York: Oxford University Press, 1967), pp. 44–50. See also Partridge, "Some Notes on the Concept of Power," pp. 115–17.

20. Van Doorn, "Sociology and the Problem of Power," p. 9.

21. An at least partial instance of this is the case of a small-town leader mentioned by Arthur Vidich and Joseph Bensman in *Small Town in Mass Society* (Princeton: Princeton University Press, 1958), pp. 276–77.

22. See Nelson W. Polsby, *Community Power and Political Theory* (New Haven: Yale University Press, 1963), pp. 47–53, and "Community Power Meets Air Pollution," *Contemporary Sociology* 1 (March 1972), 99–101; Robert A. Dahl in William V. D'Antonio and Howard I. Ehrlich, eds., *Power and Democracy in America* (Notre Dame, Ind.: University of Notre Dame Press, 1961), pp. 101–4; Raymond Wolfinger, "Reputation and Reality in the Study of Community Power," *American Sociological Review* 25 (October 1960), 636–44.

23. Raymond Aron, "*Macht*, Power, Puissance: prose démocratique ou poésie démoniaque?" *European Journal of Sociology* 5 (1964) 27–33.

Ten. Problems in Defining Power (*cont.*)

24. See Georg Simmel, *The Sociology of Georg Simmel*, Kurt H. Wolff, ed. and trans. (Glencoe, Ill.: The Free Press, 1950), pp. 181–82.

25. Hans Gerth and C. Wright Mills, *Character and Social Structure* (New York: Harcourt, Brace, 1953), p. 193.

26. Peter M. Blau, *Exchange and Power in Social Life* (New York: John Wiley and Sons, 1964), p. 118.

27. This distinction was formulated by Theodor Geiger. See the discussion, to which I am much indebted, by Van Doorn, "Sociology and the Problem of Power," pp. 16–18. Geiger's distinction resembles that of Edward W. Lehman between what he calls *systemic* and *inter-member* power in "Toward a Macrosociology of Power," *American Sociological Review* 34 (August 1969), 453–63. See also William Gamson, *Power and Discontent* (Homewood, Ill.: Dorsey Press, 1968), chapter 1.

28. David Riesman et al., *The Lonely Crowd* (New Haven: Yale University Press 1950), pp. 244–55.

29. Franz Neumann, *The Democratic and the Authoritarian State* (Glencoe, Ill.: The Free Press, 1957), p. 7.

30. Ibid., p. 17.

31. Ibid., pp. 257–69. Neumann points out that in foreign policy, integral power ("the political element") "prevails absolutely and without regard for Law"; p. 259.

32. See the discussion of this issue by Jack H. Nagel, "Some Questions about the Concept of Power," *Behavioral Science* 13 (March 1969), 133–34.

33. Peter Bachrach and Morton S. Baratz, "Decisions and Non-decisions: An Analytical Framework," *American Political Science Review* 57 (September 1963), 632–42.

34. Bertrand de Jouvenel, "Authority: The Efficient Imperative," in Carl J. Friedrich, ed., *Authority*, Nomos I (Cambridge, Mass.: Harvard University Press, 1958), p. 160. P. H. Partridge identifies independently the same three "dimensions" of power, calling the first *range*, the second *zone of acceptance*, and the third *intensity*; "Some Notes on the Concept of Power," p. 118.

35. Aristotle, *Politics and Poetics*, Benjamin Jowett and Thomas Twining, trans. (Cleveland: Fine Editions Press, 1952), "Politics," book 3, chapter 7, pp. 69–70.

36. This statement is, as T. B. Bottomore notes, less applicable to Mosca than to Pareto; Bottomore, *Elites and Society* (London: C. A. Watts, 1964), pp. 4–5.

37. Robert A. Dahl, *Modern Political Analysis* (Englewood Cliffs, N.J.: Prentice-Hall, 1963), pp. 45–46.

38. Erving Goffman, *Encounters* (Indianapolis: Bobbs-Merrill, 1961), p. 96.

39. Mark DeWolfe Howe, ed., *Holmes-Laski Letters* (Cambridge, Mass.: Harvard University Press, 1953), vol. I, p. 8. See also p. 762.

40. Philip E. Slater, "On Social Regression," *American Sociological Review* 28 (June 1963), 348–61.

41. Hannah Arendt, *The Origins of Totalitarianism* (New York: Harcourt, Brace,

1951), pp. 303–5; Michael Polanyi, *Personal Knowledge* (London: Routledge and Kegan Paul, 1958), pp. 224–25.

42. Arendt, *The Origins of Totalitarianism*, pp. 414–28.

Eleven. Force and the Threat of Force as Distinct Forms of Power

1. Georg Simmel, *The Sociology of Georg Simmel*, Kurt H. Wolff, ed. and trans. (Glencoe, Ill.: The Free Press, 1950), pp. 182–83.

2. Hannah Arendt, *On Violence* (New York: Harcourt, Brace, and World, 1970), p. 56.

3. David Easton, "The Perception of Authority and Political Change," in Carl J. Friedrich, ed., *Authority*, Nomos I (Cambridge, Mass.: Harvard University Press, 1958), p. 183.

4. E. V. Walter, "Power and Violence," *American Political Science Review* 58 (June 1964), 354; Harold Garfinkel, "Conditions of Successful Degradation Ceremonies," *American Journal of Sociology* 61 (March 1956), 420–24.

5. Talcott Parsons, "On the Concept of Political Power," in Roderick Bell, David V. Edwards, and R. Harrison Wagner, eds., *Political Power: A Reader in Theory and Research* (New York: The Free Press, 1969), pp. 263–64.

6. Harold Lasswell and Abraham Kaplan, *Power and Society* (New Haven: Yale University Press, 1950), p. 75; Robert Bierstedt, "An Analysis of Social Power," *American Sociological Review* 15 (December 1950), p. 750; Hans H. Gerth and C. Wright Mills, *Character and Social Structure* (New York: Harcourt, Brace, 1953), p. 193; Max Weber, *Economy and Society*, Guenther Roth and Claus Wittch, eds., 3 vols. (New York: Bedminster Press, 1968), vol. 1, p. 53.

7. Robert Bierstedt, *Power and Progress: Essays in Sociological Theory* (New York: McGraw-Hill, 1974), pp. 249–255; Peter M. Blau, *Exchange and Power in Social Life* (New York: John Wiley and Sons, 1964), pp. 205–13.

8. Easton, "The Perception of Authority," p. 182.

9. Arendt, *On Violence*, p. 53.

10. Ralf Dahrendorf, *Essays in the Theory of Society* (Stanford: Stanford University Press, 1968), pp. 129–50.

11. William J. Goode, "The Place of Force in Human Society," *American Sociological Review* 37 (October 1972), 507–19.

12. Ibid., p. 507.

13. Kenneth Boulding, "Toward a Pure Theory of Threat Systems," in Bell, Edwards, and Wagner, *Political Power*, p. 288.

14. Ibid.

15. For a recent version of this argument, see Arendt, *On Violence*, p. 50.

16. Michael Polanyi, *Personal Knowledge* (London: Routledge and Kegan Paul, 1958), pp. 224–25.

Twelve. Competent Authority: Reality and Legitimating Model

1. Hannah Arendt, *Between Past and Future* (New York: The Viking Press, 1961), p. 111.

2. Aristotle, *Politics and Poetics*, Benjamin Jowett and Thomas Twining, trans. (Cleveland: Fine Editions Press, 1952), "Politics," book 3, chapter 6, p. 68.

3. Plato, *The Republic*, Benjamin Jowett, trans. (Garden City, N.Y.: Doubleday Anchor Books, 1973), book 1, p. 26.

4. Aristotle, *Politics*, p. 68.

5. Talcott Parsons, "Introduction" to Max Weber, *The Theory of Social and Economic Organization* (New York: Oxford University Press, 1947), pp. 58–59.

6. Carl J. Friedrich, "Authority, Reason, and Discretion," in Friedrich, ed., *Authority*, Nomos I (Cambridge, Mass.: Harvard University Press, 1958), p. 35.

7. Eliot Freidson, "The Impurity of Professional Authority," in Howard S. Becker, Blanche Geer, David Riesman, and Robert S. Weiss, eds., *Institutions and the Person* (Chicago: Aldine, 1968), p. 30.

8. Ibid., p. 34.

9. Eliot Freidson, *Profession of Medicine* (New York: Dodd, Mead, 1972), p. 337.

10. I have actually combined *two* famous statements in the quotation. The first sentence is from Weber, *The Theory of Social and Economic Organization*, p. 339; the second is from Hans Gerth and C. Wright Mills, eds., *From Max Weber: Essays in Sociology* (New York: Oxford University Press, 1946), p. 214.

11. Charles Perrow, *Complex Organizations: A Critical Essay* (Glenview, Ill.: Scott, Foresman, 1972), pp. 56–58.

12. Amitai Etzioni, *The Active Society* (New York: The Free Press, 1968), pp. 357–59.

13. Renford Bambrough, "Plato's Political Analogies," in Peter Laslett, ed., *Philosophy, Politics and Society* (New York: Macmillan, 1956), pp. 98–115. This is a valuable analytical critique of the cogency of Plato's analogies. See also T. D. Weldon, *The Vocabulary of Politics* (Harmondsworth, Middlesex: Penguin, 1953), pp. 138–43.

14. Bertrand Russell, *A History of Western Philosophy* (New York: Simon and Schuster, 1945), pp. 106–7.

15. Immanuel Kant, *Perpetual Peace* (New York: The Liberal Arts Press, 1957), p. 34.

16. Freidson, *Profession of Medicine*, p. 337.

17. Daniel Bell, "Veblen and the New Class," *The American Scholar* 32 (Autumn 1963), 628–29.

18. Everett C. Hughes, *Men and Their Work* (Glencoe, Ill.: The Free Press, 1958), p. 139.

19. The term is from Suzanne Keller, *Beyond the Ruling Class* (New York: Random House, 1963).

20. Giovanni Sartori, "Technological Forecasting and Politics," *Survey* 16

(Winter 1971), 66–68. For a valuable discussion, see also Anthony Giddens, *The Class Structure of the Advanced Societies* (London: Hutchinson, 1973), pp. 255–64.

21. Jürgen Habermas, *Toward a Rational Society* (Boston: Beacon Press, 1970), p. 111.

22. Daniel Bell, *The Coming of Post-Industrial Society* (New York: Basic Books, 1973), p. 263.

23. Lewis A. Coser, *Men of Ideas* (New York: The Free Press, 1965), p. 238.

24. See the discussion by Hannah Arendt, *Between Past and Future*, pp. 104–15.

25. See the chapter on scientists in Neal Wood, *Communism and British Intellectuals* (New York: Columbia University Press, 1959), pp. 121–51.

26. Hannah Arendt, *The Origins of Totalitarianism* (New York: Harcourt, Brace, 1951), pp. 336–40.

27. A valuable recent discussion is that of Shlomo Avineri, "Marx's Vision of Future Society," *Dissent* 20 (Summer 1973), 323–31.

28. George Lichtheim, *From Marx to Hegel* (New York: Herder and Herder, 1971), p. 199.

Thirteen. Economic Development and Democracy

1. Robert L. Heilbroner, "Counterrevolutionary America," *Commentary* 43 (April 1967), 31–38.

2. Robert L. Heilbroner, *The Great Ascent* (New York: Harper Torchbooks, 1963).

3. For a critique resembling in some respects the present one of prevalent assumptions about modernization in the Third World, see Charles C. Moskos, Jr., and Wendell Bell, "Emerging Nations and Ideologies of American Social Scientists," *The American Sociologist* 2 (May 1967), 67–72.

4. Heilbroner, *The Great Ascent*, p. 100.

5. See *Commentary* 44 (July 1967), 18–20.

6. Barrington Moore, Jr., *The Social Origins of Dictatorship and Democracy* (Boston: Beacon Press, 1966), p. 271.

7. Ibid., p. 104; Heilbroner, "Counterrevolutionary America," p. 34.

8. Heilbroner in *Commentary* 44 (July 1967), 20.

9. Heilbroner, "Counterrevolutionary America," p. 32.

10. Donald Bogue, "The End of the Population Explosion," *The Public Interest*, Spring 1967, pp. 11–20.

11. Including myself. See, for example, Dennis H. Wrong, "Population Myths," *Commentary* 38 (November 1964), 61–64.

12. J. Mayone Stycos, *Human Fertility in Latin America* (Ithaca, N.Y.: Cornell University Press, 1968).

13. See William McCord, "Armies and Politics: A Problem in the Third World," *Dissent* 14 (July–August 1967), 444–52.

14. Moskos and Bell, "Emerging Nations and Ideologies of American Social Scientists," p. 69.

Thirteen. Economic Development and Democracy (*cont.*)

15. Heilbroner in *Commentary* (July 1967), 20.
16. Donald Zagoria, "Communism in Asia," *Commentary* 39 (February 1965), 53–58.
17. Frank W. Notestein, "The Population Crisis: Reasons for Hope," *Foreign Affairs* 46 (October 1967), 167–80.

Fourteen. The Rhythm of Democratic Politics

1. For a useful critique, see Giovanni Sartori, "From the Sociology of Politics to Political Sociology," in Seymour Martin Lipset, ed., *Politics and the Social Sciences* (New York: Oxford University Press, 1969), pp. 77–80.
2. Karl Mannheim, *Ideology and Utopia* (New York: Harcourt, Brace, 1946), p. 207. See also Mannheim, *Essays on Sociology and Social Psychology* (New York: Oxford University Press, 1953), pp. 98–101.
3. Theodore Lowi, *The Politics of Disorder* (New York: Basic Books, 1971), pp. 3–61. Lowi mentions the civil rights movement of the early sixties as an example of such a social movement outside the established parties and interest organizations (p. 60). See also Lowi's earlier book, *The End of Liberalism* (New York: W. W. Norton, 1969).
4. Arthur Schlesinger, Sr., *Paths to the Present* (New York: Macmillan 1949), pp. 77–92.
5. Ibid., p. 88.
6. Robert Nisbet, *Social Change and History* (New York: Oxford University Press, 1969), pp. 240–62.
7. Schlesinger, *Paths to the Present*, p. 87.
8. Nisbet, *Social Change and History*, pp. 284–304.
9. Arthur Schlesinger, Sr., *In Retrospect: The History of a Historian* (New York: Harcourt, Brace and World, 1963), p. 108.
10. Ibid., pp. 190–91.
11. O. Utis, "Generalissimo Stalin and the Art of Government," *Foreign Affairs* 30 (January 1952), 197–214. The author writes: "This—the 'artificial dialectic'—is Generalissimo Stalin's most original invention, his major contribution to the art of government . . ." (p. 210). "O. Utis," which means "nobody" in classical Greek, was a pseudonym here adopted by Isaiah Berlin.
12. *The Prince*, chapter 6. See pp. 21–22 in the Modern Library edition (New York: Random House, 1940).
13. Ibid., p. 22.
14. Raymond Aron, *The Century of Total War* (Garden City, N.Y.: Doubleday, 1954), pp. 241–61. I am much indebted to Aron's brilliant discussion.
15. John Stuart Mill, *Autobiography* (London: Longmans, Green, 1908), p. 168.
16. Barrington Moore, Jr., *Reflections on the Causes of Human Misery and Upon Certain Proposals to Eliminate Them* (Boston: Beacon Press, 1972), pp. 156–68.

Fifteen. Max Weber: The Scholar as Hero

1. Hans Gerth and C. Wright Mills, eds., *From Max Weber: Essays in Sociology* (New York: Oxford University Press, 1946), p. 27.

2. W. G. Runciman, *A Critique of Max Weber's Philosophy of Social Science* (Cambridge: Cambridge University Press, 1972), p. 63.

3. Gerth and Mills, *From Max Weber*, p. 152. The several other direct quotations from Weber in this and the previous paragraph are also from the essays "Politics as a Vocation" or "Science as a Vocation" in the Gerth-Mills collection.

4. Max Weber, *The Methodology of the Social Sciences*, Edward A. Shils and Henry A. Finch, eds. and trans. (Glencoe, Ill.: The Free Press, 1949), p. 5.

5. Gerth and Mills, *From Max Weber*, p. 139.

6. Max Weber, *Economy and Society*, Guenther Roth and Claus Wittich, eds., 3 vols. (New York: Bedminster Press, 1968), vol. 3, p. 1402.

7. Max Weber, *The Protestant Ethic and the Spirit of Capitalism* (New York: Charles Scribner's Sons, 1930), p. 182.

8. Ferdinand Kolegar, "The Concept of 'Rationalization' and Cultural Pessimism in Max Weber's Sociology," *The Sociological Quarterly* 5 (Fall 1964), p. 355.

9. Fritz Stern, *The Politics of Cultural Despair* (Berkeley and Los Angeles: University of California Press, 1961).

10. Carlo Antoni, *From History to Sociology* (Detroit: Wayne State University Press, 1959), p. 167.

11. Weber, *The Protestant Ethic*, p. 182.

12. Ibid.

13. Gerth and Mills, *From Max Weber*, p. 125.

14. Raymond Aron, *Main Currents in Sociological Thought*, 2 vols. (New York: Basic Books, 1967), vol. 2, p. 250.

15. Ibid., p. 247.

16. Quoted in German by Aron, ibid., p. 250. See Herbert Marcuse, *Negations* (Boston: Beacon Press, 1968), p. 225.

17. Gerth and Mills, *From Max Weber*, p. 155.

18. Karl Loewenstein, *Max Weber's Political Ideas in the Perspective of Our Time* (Amherst, Mass.: University of Massachusetts Press, 1966), pp. 74–88.

19. Mostafa Rejai, *The Strategy of Political Revolution* (Garden City, N.Y.: Doubleday, Anchor Books, 1973), pp. 105–9. Rejai's discussion is confined to the French student revolutionaries of 1968, but student radicals in the United States and elsewhere during the 1960s also claimed to have dispensed with recognized leaders.

20. Guenther Roth, "Personal Rulership, Patrimonialism, and Empire-Building," in Reinhard Bendix and Guenther Roth, *Scholarship and Partisanship: Essays on Max Weber* (Berkeley, Los Angeles, and London: University of California Press, 1971), p. 162. For a balanced discussion of whether or not democracy is compatible with Weber's conception of charismatic leadership, see Wolfgang J. Mommsen, *The Age of Bureaucracy: Perspectives on the Political Sociology of Max Weber* (Oxford: Blackwell, 1974), pp. 86–94.

Fifteen. Max Weber: The Scholar as Hero (cont.)

21. Reinhard Bendix, "Reflections on Charismatic Leadership," in Bendix, ed., *The State and Society* (Boston: Little, Brown, 1969), p. 629.

22. Karl Loewith, "Weber's Interpretation of the Bourgeois-Capitalistic World in Terms of the Guiding Principle of 'Rationalization,'" in Dennis H. Wrong, ed., *Max Weber* (Englewood Cliffs, N.J.: Prentice-Hall, 1970), p. 121.

23. Quoted by Arthur Mitzman in *The Iron Cage: An Historical Interpretation of Max Weber* (New York: Alfred A. Knopf, 1970), p. 271.

24. Max Weber, "The Political Scene," in S. M. Miller, ed., *Max Weber: Selections from his Work* (New York: Thomas Y. Crowell, 1959), p. 86.

25. Gerth and Mills, *From Max Weber*, p. 123.

26. Ibid., p. 154.

27. Ibid., p. 155.

28. Mitzman, *The Iron Cage*, pp. 288–289.

29. Saul Bellow, *Mr. Sammler's Planet* (New York: Fawcett World Library, 1970), pp. 166–167.

Sixteen. Ends and Means in Politics

1. Hans Gerth and C. Wright Mills, eds. and trans., *From Max Weber: Essays in Sociology* (New York: Oxford University Press, 1946), p. 122, also pp. 274–86.

2. Ibid., p. 126.

3. Ibid., p. 121.

4. Ibid., p. 78 (my emphasis). I have substituted "violence" for Gerth and Mills's "physical force" in the translation.

5. That "demagoguery" is an inevitable consequence of democratic politics was recognized by Weber in his article "Parliament and Government in a Reconstructed Germany," which is included as Appendix II in Guenther Roth and Claus Wittich, eds., *Economy and Society*, 3 vols. (New York: Bedminster Press, 1968), vol. 3, pp. 1381–1469.

6. Daniel Bell, *The End of Ideology* (Glencoe, Ill.: The Free Press, 1960), pp. 288–89.

7. Arthur Koestler, *The Yogi and the Commissar* (New York: Macmillan, 1945), pp. 3–14.

8. Gerth and Mills, *From Max Weber*, p. 122.

9. Ibid., p. 127.

10. Karl Mannheim, *Ideology and Utopia* (New York: Harcourt, Brace, 1946), p. 196.

11. Frantz Fanon, *The Wretched of the Earth* (New York: Grove Press, 1963).

12. Mannheim, *Ideology and Utopia*, p. 213.

13. Ibid., p. 196.

14. Gerth and Mills, *From Max Weber*, p. 121.

15. Lewis A. Coser, "Nechayev in the Andes," *Dissent* 15 (January–February 1968), 41–44.

16. Konrad Heiden, *Der Fuehrer* (Boston: Houghton Mifflin, 1944), p. 100; Hannah Arendt, *The Origins of Totalitarianism* (New York: Harcourt, Brace, 1951), pp. 319–32; Fritz Stern, *The Politics of Cultural Despair* (Garden City, N.Y.: Doubleday, Anchor Books, 1965), pp. 350–61.

17. George Orwell, *1984* (New York: Harcourt, Brace, 1949), pp. 266–67.

18. Irving Howe and Lewis A. Coser, *The American Communist Party: A Critical History* (Boston: Beacon Press, 1957), p. 521 (italics in original). The best analysis of the totalitarian belief in "organizational omnipotence" is Hannah Arendt, *The Origins of Totalitarianism*, pp. 396–98.

19. Helen Constas, "Max Weber's Two Conceptions of Bureaucracy," *American Journal of Sociology* 53 (January 1958), 400–9.

20. E. H. Carr, *Studies in Revolution* (London: Macmillan, 1950), p. 158.

21. Robert K. Merton, *Social Theory and Social Structure* (Revised and Enlarged Edition, New York: The Free Press, 1957), p. 202.

22. Philip Rahv, "The Unfuture of Utopia," *Partisan Review* 16 (July 1949), 748.

Seventeen. On Thinking about the Future

1. Robert Nisbet, "The Year 2000 and all that," *Commentary* 45 (June 1968), 63.

2. Daniel Bell, *The Coming of Post-Industrial Society* (New York: Basic Books, 1973), pp. 51–54.

3. See, for example, Richard Quinney, "From Repression to Liberation: Social Theory in a Radical Age," in Robert A. Scott and Jack D. Douglas, eds., *Theoretical Perspectives in Deviance* (New York: Basic Books, 1972), pp. 317–41.

4. Karl Popper, *The Poverty of Historicism* (New York: Harper Torchbooks, 1964), pp. 105–30.

5. Gwynn Nettler, *Explanations* (New York: McGraw-Hill, 1970), p. 137.

6. Norman Birnbaum, "Foreword," in Robert W. Friedrichs, *A Sociology of Sociology* (New York: The Free Press, 1970), p. xv.

7. Dennis H. Wrong, "Reflections on the End of Ideology," *Dissent* 7 (Summer 1960), 286–91. Reprinted in Chaim I. Waxman, ed., *The End of Ideology Debate* (New York: Funk and Wagnalls, 1968), pp. 116–25.

8. Barrington Moore, Jr., *Reflections on the Causes of Human Misery and Upon Certain Proposals to Eliminate Them* (Boston: Beacon Press, 1972), p. 168.

9. For further discussion, see "The Rhythm of Democratic Politics," included in this volume.

10. Hannah Arendt, *Between Past and Future*, (rev. ed.; New York: The Viking Press, 1968), p. 250.

11. Ibid., p. 259.

12. H. H. Gerth and C. Wright Mills, eds., *From Max Weber: Essays in Sociology* (New York: Oxford University Press), 1946, p. 147.

13. Arendt, *Between Past and Future*, p. 261.

Index